# DIGGING UP BRITAIN

MIKE PITTS

# DIGGING UP BRITAIN

## TEN DISCOVERIES, A MILLION YEARS OF HISTORY

Thames & Hudson

*If it weren't for the strongly held belief that
'indigenous' Brits are a white race, with a pristine
culture stemming from time immemorial, then the
debate around immigration could conceivably be a
rational one....Instead what we have is an emotional,
and emotive, story of threat and invasion.*
Afua Hirsch, *Brit(ish)*
London: Jonathan Cape, 2018, p. 298

## For Mia

Frontispiece: The Weymouth mass-burial (detail, see p. 29)

*Digging up Britain* © 2019 Thames & Hudson Ltd, London
Text © 2019 Digging Deeper Ltd

Designed by Adam Hay Studio

First published in 2019 in the United States of America by
Thames & Hudson Inc., 500 Fifth Avenue, New York, New York 10110

www.thamesandhudsonusa.com

Library of Congress Control Number 2019932285

ISBN 978-0-500-05190-0

Printed and bound in India by Replika Press Pvt Ltd

# Contents

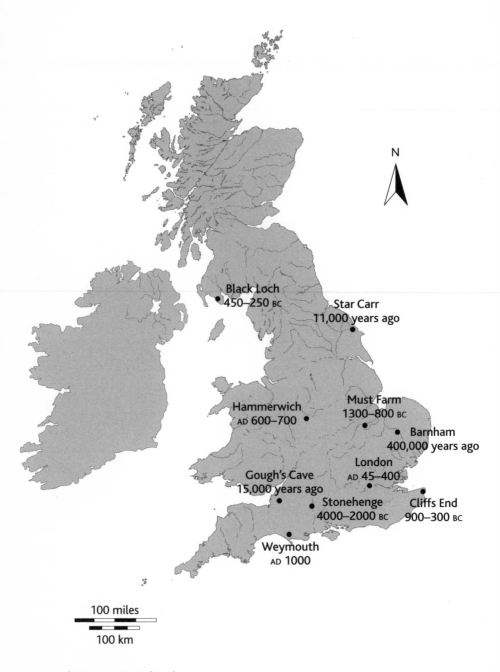

Black Loch
450–250 BC

Star Carr
11,000 years ago

Hammerwich
AD 600–700

Must Farm
1300–800 BC

Barnham
400,000 years ago

Gough's Cave
15,000 years ago

London
AD 45–400

Stonehenge
4000–2000 BC

Cliffs End
900–300 BC

Weymouth
AD 1000

N

100 miles

100 km

Map of sites mentioned in the text.

# Preface

When I began studying archaeology, humans were thought to have first reached Britain 200,000 years ago. We now know that people have been here for at least 850,000 years – and perhaps 950,000, depending on how we read the evidence. Few archaeologists would be greatly surprised if new discoveries were to show that people have been in Britain for over a million years.

This fivefold increase in the duration of human occupation is extraordinary. It affects not just how we think about early people and the worlds they inhabited, but also our understanding of ourselves, of the paths our ancestors took as they became who we are and our position in the great web of life. We have barely begun even to wonder at the implications.

In recent decades there has been a huge surge in the amount of excavation across the UK – so much so that even with an equally impressive growth in the number of archaeologists, there is a shortage of skilled diggers, and we struggle to keep up with new data. And it's not just that more stuff is being found.

What we can do with it has been transformed by a continuing revolution in archaeological sciences. New technologies offer previously unimagined ways of learning, with accelerating efficiency and cost-effectiveness, driven by a powerful competitive curiosity at the heart of our universities. In all of this the UK is one of the leading world laboratories for exploring human antiquity.

You might conclude that we can now tell the definitive story of ancient Britain. You would be wrong. If we know anything, it is that there is so much more we don't know. We open a door and see a new world: but all around are a hundred more doors, and we have no idea what lies behind them. We do, however, have the skills to explore further, and to confront more questions. If an outpouring of new data threatens continually to undermine the way we think about the past, this is without doubt the most exciting time to be an archaeologist.

You don't have to be one, however, to share in that excitement. In this book I describe ten different projects, most of which have been headlined around the world, where extraordinary new things are being learnt. Each of them combines a quest for knowledge with revelations that bring us close to individuals who lived long ago. Stories of excavations and discoveries – how they happen and the people involved, and what they tell us about the past – make compelling detective adventures.

There is also a greater perspective that speaks to us all. Who are we? Where do we come from? What is Britain, and what does it mean to be British? Such questions have acquired a new urgency in an atmosphere of heated debate about the nation's relationship with the rest of Europe and beyond, but they are not new. To a significant extent, answers have always come from how we think about our past. Though often perceived as something simple and fixed, it is neither of those things; instead, we see a deep antiquity that reaches back millennia and embraces once unimagined variety and change, in cultures, religions and landscapes, and even human species.

The more people discuss issues of national identity, the more the topic is simplified beyond credibility. That dishonours our story, and diminishes our view of the world. The history once taught at British schools, beyond excursions into ancient Egypt or other lost civilizations, typically began around the time of what is often seen as the last successful invasion, the Norman Conquest in AD 1066. The latest curriculum means children now learn more about what happened in earlier centuries: the youngest are taught about Britain in prehistoric, Roman and Anglo-Saxon times. But as they grow older, learning to 'use historical concepts in increasingly sophisticated ways', children drop the early stuff.[1] Now their concern is 'the modern nation' and the 20th century, and the longer view, it seems, is not considered an essential part of a modern citizen's knowledge.

Yet modern humans – people physically and, at least in their capacity for thought, mentally almost exactly like us – have lived continuously in the UK for over 10,000 years. Most Britons carry some of their genes, and every one of us carries genes of their distant ancestors. Their cumulative efforts shaped the landscapes we know. Their technological discoveries, and their ideas about beauty, good food and the afterlife, trickled down through the centuries, even as such things changed, which they often did. Their stories, I believe, are important to us today, to our identity and to our place in the world.

The English writer Bruce Chatwin believed that travel, especially on foot, was the essence of being human. Journeying was instinctive, and inhumanities – aggression, war, despotism – arose when the virtue and dignity of travel were suppressed. Deprived of travel in life, we'd aspire to an afterlife of voyaging (ancient Egyptians, he wrote, projected 'on to the next world the journeys they failed to make in this one').[2]

It's impossible to identify such motivations in antiquity objectively, and we might disagree with Chatwin's judgment (in Chapter 1 we will encounter a massacre involving some of the most well-journeyed people in world history). But it's hard to avoid the extent to which travel, from routine excursions to trading voyages, pilgrimages, migrations and invasions, seems to run through our islands' story. Charting and explaining such movements, and understanding their significance, has long been a challenging but essential part of what archaeologists do. In this quest we are now greatly benefiting from new scientific advances, especially in the analysis of isotopes and ancient DNA, which are revealing profound and unexpected stories.

Histories are usually written chronologically – by which we mean going forward, from past to present. I have not done that here. Instead, we begin with the most recent event and travel backwards, until we find ourselves on a beach, scrutinizing, literally, the first human footprints, as if we might be Crusoe, exceedingly surprised that the island was inhabited.

This reversal of the usual sequence came about for several reasons. Archaeologists are trained to work from the known to the unknown, an essential perspective when you are feeling your way through layers of earth and debris that reveal themselves only as you excavate. Those layers accumulated chronologically, from old at the bottom to young higher up, so that as you dig you work down from young to old. Archaeologists discover the past backwards, and as this is mostly a story of excavations, it seemed natural to me to write in that direction.

Secondly, I assume no familiarity with archaeology, which leaves me with rather a lot of explaining to do; the practice of archaeology is highly technical. As a rule, the further back into the past we go, the slighter is the evidence and the more dependent we are on sophisticated sciences and long-debated principles of interpretation. Starting with the most recent remains, where preservation is good and we have some contemporary literature to help us, allows me to introduce procedures at a measured pace throughout the book.

Finally, conventional chronological history can impose a way of seeing the past that, especially with the long spans of prehistory, is unhelpful. When we read about Anglo-Saxon England knowing the Norman Conquest is on the horizon, it's very difficult, even if unconsciously, not to think that the earlier world is doomed; without realizing it we can end up imagining that Anglo-Saxon people knew that too. We judge them against what came after they were gone.

This is especially dangerous with a timeline of millennia, the 'progression' (see?) of the ages of Stone, Bronze and Iron, and the almost inevitable sense of the dark mysteries of antiquity. We have to guard against wondering how people in the Bronze Age managed without writing, or in the Stone Age without metals. By thinking backwards, our perspective in a particular chapter is our subjects' present and a less clear idea of their past – which is exactly how they would have understood things, ignorant of what was to follow.

Little of what you will read here could have been written even five years ago. As a journalist and editor, I learn about excavations across the country as they take place. I meet people who are uncovering and analysing the stuff of future history books and exhibitions. As an archaeologist, I can critically evaluate what I see and read, and I engage in a little research and excavation myself. The stories are new, and if the discoveries are sometimes less immediately so – the Staffordshire Hoard, as we shall see in Chapter 2, was found in 2009 – their analysis and scientific publication are only now being completed. Study continues at several of the locations featured in this book.

So it is that we begin our excavation of Britain in Viking-age England. A thousand years ago (four seconds in the hour of the entire span of Britain's human occupation), a group of people from across Europe gathered on a Dorset hillside. Many of them never left.

Chapter 1

# A Viking Massacre

*Weymouth,* AD *1000*

The 2012 Summer Olympics were often called the London Olympics, but not everything happened in the capital. Sailing took place off the coast of Dorset. Among local development projects that the attention made possible was the long-awaited construction of a bypass, taking traffic out of the seaside resort of Weymouth and north to Dorchester.

Following standard practice, archaeologists were among those who worked on the road at an early stage, advising on routes less damaging to heritage. They found previously unknown prehistoric villages and graves, common fare. But at one point they came across something that none of them had ever experienced before.[1]

Above Weymouth is a protected landscape known as the Dorset Ridgeway, where green hills wander for miles more or less parallel to the coast. There was a narrow strip of ground where the new, deeper route, cutting through the ridge, was to merge with the old road. For health and safety reasons the archaeologists were unable to excavate there in advance, and instead, when works were in place that controlled the traffic, they stepped in to record anything of interest that could be seen as heavy-wheeled machinery removed the soil.

A thick hedge stood between the old road and the new works. As it was being dug out with a mechanical excavator, the alert operator noticed something in his great toothed yellow bucket: bone. He might have ignored it and got on with the job, and something extraordinary that had been unknown would also have become unknowable. But Skanska, the contractor, and the people at Oxford Archaeology had a good working relationship, and the driver did as instructed. He phoned for help.

The bone in the bucket was not alone. It would be six months before the archaeologists had finished. They exposed the top of a large filled pit, its soil showing dark against the white chalk into which it had been dug like a small pond. It was May. Conditions were good: dry and not so warm that the ground turned to dust before you could see what was there. The site was in a sag in the top of the ridge, a draw for a succession of old tracks and roads. The hollow restricts views along the ridge to either side. But to the north you can see the sprawling ramparts of Maiden Castle, one of the great wonders of ancient Britain, and to the south Weymouth, the small, cliff-edged Isle of Portland – a limestone outcrop that hangs like a drip of ice-cream from the Dorset coast – and the sea.

The mechanical excavator had scattered and crushed bones. But it became apparent that most of the remains were still in the ground. In one corner of the pit, which was squarish in shape, a tightly packed group of nearly fifty human skulls was revealed, looking like a nest of dinosaur eggs. Lower jaws were more or less in place, as if still attached: it was not bones that had been buried, but heads, with hair and flesh. Not skulls, but faces. Judging from the skulls that could be seen, they might all have been men. And deeper across the rest of the pit were the bodies.

Who were these people? It's common for graves to contain artefacts as well as human remains – sometimes objects are all that survive. Such things can be the best guide to identity, who the people were and when they died. The pit above Weymouth, however, was not a normal grave.

The archaeologists found only a few pieces of broken pottery to hint at when it might have been dug or who the men were. The sherds seemed to be Iron Age or Roman, from pots made between 100 BC and AD 100. But they were accidental rubbish rather than goods placed in the grave. The only certain thing that could be said was that the deaths had not occurred much before 3,000 years ago. There were deep, clean cutmarks on some of the bones

Excavating the Weymouth burials in 2009, with skulls piled on
the southern edge of the pit.

where heads had been removed, which could only have been made with metal blades. The first swords in Britain were cast in bronze around 1300 BC.

Nonetheless it was tempting to think the men were Roman. The road that was now being rebuilt followed a Roman road that connected a small port in what is now Weymouth with Dorchester. On the way it passed Maiden Castle, where excavation in the 1930s revealed a cluster of over fifty graves. The archaeologist, Mortimer Wheeler, dubbed the site a War Cemetery. Many of the people had died violently. In one famous case a man was buried with an iron bolt from a Roman spear embedded in his spine. Here, said Wheeler, was evidence for an assault by an invading Roman army on one of Britain's great tribal centres. This was no mass burial, however: mourners had had time to dig separate graves for each of the dead, and lay them down with pots and joints of meat. So perhaps the pit on Ridgeway Hill was witness to an even more brutal confrontation between Roman and native.[2]

Dorset County Council was thrilled, and in June it issued a press release describing the find. The burials dated from late Iron Age or early Roman times, said the statement, but how they got there was a mystery. 'It seems highly likely', said Oxford Archaeology, 'that some kind of catastrophic event such as war, disease or execution has occurred.' The council asked the public to keep away. The site was dangerous, and under 24-hour security. This was a wise precaution: shortly after the skulls had been surveyed, one went walkabout, never to be seen again.[3]

With the research tools available to Mortimer Wheeler, that would have been pretty much the end of it. But now we have a battery of forensic sciences. Oxford Archaeology sent a sample of bone to a radiocarbon dating lab in Glasgow.

The result came back in July. It showed the executed men not to be so ancient: they were alive in Anglo-Saxon times, when, as the council's new press release put it, there was 'considerable conflict between the resident Saxon population and invading Danes'. So were they residents or invaders? One's immediate reaction was to imagine a Viking massacre: here was the grave of men slaughtered as they defended their homes and families against marauders from across the sea. The shocking details revealed over the following two years of lab work, however, brought a further twist to the story.

Excavation continued. The bodies were entangled, their legs and arms overlapping. Ribs concealed feet. The hands of one man spread unfeeling fingers over the curved spine of another. There was such a confusion of bone, it was difficult to make sense of what was there. The archaeologists poked and scraped and brushed with little hand tools, to expose as much as they could without disturbing the remains. This way they could identify individual bodies and determine how one lay over another – the order in which they had been buried. Careful recording should allow each individual to be identified.

Louise Loe, head of burials at Oxford Archaeology (archaeological work can be as boring and bureaucratic as any other kind, but you get good job titles),[4] was at that very moment also overseeing an excavation on a First World War battlefield, at Fromelles in northern France. By September the archaeologists would have exhumed the remains and possessions of 250 men. They were Allied troops, buried by German soldiers in large communal pits holding a small proportion of the thousands who died there, one night in July 1916.

Louise ensured that the same recording techniques were used in Weymouth as at Fromelles. Every skull and skeleton was given a unique number, and drawn as it lay before being removed. Many photographs were taken. Osteologists noted down what could be seen, looking for indications of age and gender, missing bones and disease, and, especially, wounds. For every skeleton, the positions of forty-four points were precisely recorded with digital surveying equipment, so that the way the bodies lay could be recreated in the lab.

Then the archaeologists lifted and bagged the bones, one by one, to take to Oxford.

With the bones gone, the archaeologists could look more closely at the pit. It transpired that the burials had not lain on its base: 75–85 centimetres (2 or 3 feet) of silt had already accumulated before the bodies were thrown in. It was a wide pit, about 7 metres (23 feet) across and originally about the depth of a standing person. So when the executioners had looked for a place to dispose of their victims, they had chosen a grown-over hollow rather than face the effort of digging a mass grave; perhaps the pit itself had determined the precise location of the atrocity. The bones had not been disturbed by animals, so the bodies must have been covered over rapidly with a layer of shovelled chalk and earth.

# Chapter 1

For some years after, the grass would have grown thicker and greener. Then everything that ever happened there was forgotten.

*

In the clean stillness of the lab in Oxford, away from the noise of machinery and road traffic, the dirt of excavation and the interruptions of visiting film crews, the question had to be faced. Who on earth were these people?

It was the same question that had motivated the excavation at Fromelles. There, Oxford Archaeology had set up forensic labs beside the pits in which they had found the soldiers' remains. These were reburied in a military cemetery, and by 2014, when an identification committee met for the last time, an unexpected number of men had been named. Archaeologists and scientists built up a picture of each individual from their physical remains and possessions. The latter were often just scraps of boots and uniform, the insignia of soldiery, but some were more poignant. A leather heart contained a lock of hair; a second-class return train ticket from Freemantle to Perth had been secreted inside a gas mask, unused. With such information pointing to known casualties, DNA was collected from bones and from living descendants. Eventually 144 men were identified, all Australian, and their names were engraved on stones in the cemetery. Of the others, seventy-five had also served in the Australian Army, and two for Britain. Just twenty-nine remained, alone, 'known unto God'.[5]

None of the men in the Weymouth pit could be named, and any descendants would forever remain unidentified. They had died too long ago. But there was another problem, resulting from their manner of death.

Much bone had been damaged by the mechanical excavator, including most of the skulls. Many other pieces had been separated from the bodies, so that there was a substantial collection of disarticulated bone that could not be allocated to any one person. As a result, after months of study the archaeologists were unable to say exactly how many people had been buried. There are various ways of calculating from excavated remains what archaeologists call the 'minimum number of individuals'. Each method came up with a

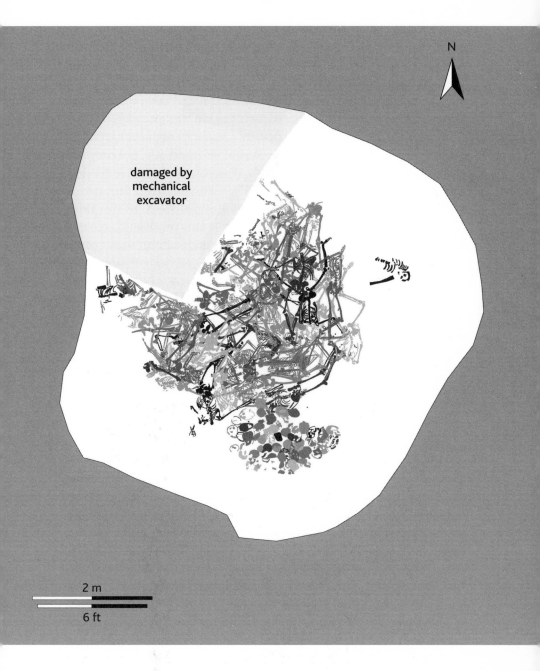

The pit above Weymouth as excavated, with all human remains plotted, showing bodies in the centre and heads to the south. All pit plans adapted from Loe *et al*. 2014.

slightly different result: the one the archaeologists preferred suggested fifty-two skeletons – and forty-seven skulls. If fifty-two men had been executed that day on the hill, five of their heads had not been buried in the pit.

By the end of the project, only one skull had been linked to its skeleton. We shall see that this particular man was quite significant. But for the rest of the victims, identity remains a nebulous concept. Thus it is in the ancient past. Without written records, not only can we not name anyone, but we cannot see personalities. The individual minds, voices and experiences of people who made up prehistoric and the great bulk of early historic communities are all irretrievably lost. On the other hand, the Weymouth remains represent a narrow range of humanity. It makes sense to consider them as a group, alive, as they died, together. In this way we can hope to approach some form of communal identity. And more widely, by studying both human remains and the debris that people left behind, we can follow the changes in culture and identity that have occurred through the hundreds of thousands of years in which people have lived in these islands.

Of the fifty-two Dorset skeletons, it proved possible to judge the sex of thirty-six, most of them 'strongly male'. Of the skulls, forty-three were definitely male, and the remaining four young heads, still growing, were judged probably so. Without a single female suggested, it's a strong bet that all fifty-two individuals were men.

The age range was limited, too. While by and large it's possible to say if a skeleton is male or female, age can only be estimated along a continuum. Archaeologists talk of age categories, such as young adult (eighteen to twenty-five years) or older adult (over forty-five – osteology can be cruel). The heads in the Weymouth pit had rested on young shoulders. Nearly half were under twenty-five, and of these, seven might have been adolescent. No more than two were over forty-five. The bodies tell the same story: half were adolescents or young adults, and just three were over forty-five.

So these were fit men, a gang of young warriors perhaps, but they were not the stuff of romantic fiction. They had misshapen toes, broken bones and missing teeth. On the one hand, they were well exercised, with a relatively high occurrence of small injuries commonly caused by physical stress. This was supported by the appearance of muscle attachment sites. Bone grows and strengthens to the extent that connected muscles are used: twelve of the skeletons showed strong changes of this type, some of them of young or adolescent age. Overall, the osteologists describe them as a group of athletic men, averaging 1.72 metres tall – 5 feet 8 inches – who had been performing repetitive strenuous activities from a young age.

On the other hand, life seems not to have treated them with equal generosity. One man suffered from a bad case of osteomyelitis, with an inflamed thigh bone caused by an infection that began in childhood, and which would have oozed foul-smelling pus – to say nothing of the discomfort and impaired mobility it would have caused. Another had a sizeable stone in his kidney, bladder or gallbladder. About a third of the men had at least one healed fracture, most commonly in their legs and feet. In one instance a broken thigh bone had shortened by 4 or 5 centimetres as it healed – about 2 inches – leaving a man with a limp. Eight men suffered from osteoarthritis. Two had bunions.

Though several had missing or malformed teeth, dental health was generally good. Just one man suffered severely from bone loss caused by gum disease, and perhaps not surprisingly he was one of the oldest; he was also one of the few with a cavity, and he had lost six of his teeth. At least one man, however, had received the attention of a sort of dentist, and here we move into a new area.

Who were these men? Were they local, native but passing through from elsewhere, or distant migrants – or a mixed bunch of outcasts and travellers from all over? And if not local, where were they from – and what were they doing in Dorset?

The answer – to where they had come from, at least – soon came, clear and strong, from a variety of scientific data. But there is one find that brings home the reality more immediately than anything else. It has to do with the man who, alone among all the fifty-two individuals from the pit, is represented by a complete, identifiable skeleton, from head to feet. In particular, it concerns his front teeth.

Skull number 3736 lay face-up in the middle of the heap of heads. The body from which it had been detached, numbered 3806, was sprawled on its front near the pit centre, feet to the north and shoulders to the south, flexed arms seeming to reach towards the skull a little over a metre away. The skeleton was among a handful completely covered by others, so the body was among the first to be thrown in.

# Chapter 1

Depending on where the cuts had been made, different neck bones had stayed attached to the head or the shoulders. Many splintered vertebrae were found scattered loose in the pit, key evidence to show that the men had been beheaded on the spot, and not carried in having been killed elsewhere. In the case of 3736 and 3806, not only do they bring together the right number of vertebrae, but the reconnected bones fit each other well, and share similar signs of joint disease – bony lumps that indicate osteoarthritis.

This man, then, was in his later forties – one of the more experienced in the group – and strong and tall. He had good teeth. Three are chipped, probably caused by the sudden clenching of his jaws at the moment of decapitation, a feature seen in more than half the men. Two other teeth, however, had been marked before he died. They are the only such teeth in the pit; indeed, to date they are unique in Britain. His jaws have been displayed in the British Museum, and are now in the museum in Dorchester, near the man from Maiden Castle felled by a Roman spear. These are teeth demanding to be seen.

When we move data wirelessly over short distances, we use a technology named after a Viking; the logo is a combination of the initial rune letters of a Danish king named Harald Bluetooth. We don't know how he got that name. The most popular idea is that he had a rotten tooth – 'blue' meaning 'dark'. But there is another explanation, more respectful perhaps of his royal status: his teeth had been deliberately marked.

That Vikings did such a thing has only recently come to light, before which it was thought of as a practice found only outside Europe. Two dozen teeth have been excavated in Denmark and Sweden with grooves filed across the front with care and skill. All are from the top of the mouth, all from the heads of men, and all from Viking cemeteries. The grooves are not obvious from a distance, so it may be they were filled with pigment to create dark stripes. And even then, to show off their filed fangs, these Viking men, these Bluetooths, would have had to have opened their tattooed mouths in a wide smile...or a great scream.

The two decorated teeth in skull 3736 – like the others, central upper incisors – each have two filed and polished horizontal grooves in the crown enamel. There could hardly be a clearer sign that this man was a Viking, and – though we have no idea what the grooves

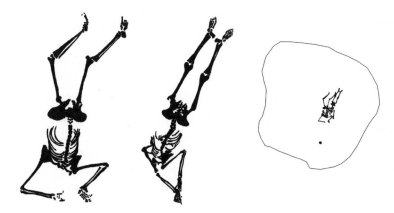

Skeletons 3806 (left), with fitting skull in the pit, and 3804,
lying on the pit bottom.

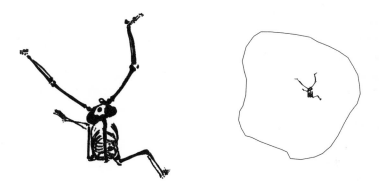

Skeleton of a man aged 20–30; his body lay on the east side of the
heap, above four others and under four.

Skeleton of a man aged 25–44, on the west side of the heap
above five others, one of the last to be placed in the pit.

actually meant – in some way distinguished from most other men. Taking his age and physique into account, one naturally wonders if he might have been the gang leader. For it seems the other men in the pit were probably Northmen too.

We know this principally from a scientific process known as isotope analysis. Applied to human bones and teeth, it is an ingenious way of investigating how people might have moved about during their lives. We will come across it often as we pursue our journey back into the past. It is still a relatively new technique, accounting for continuing surprises when it is applied. Dominant ideas about early migration, laid down in the second half of the last century, were developed before isotope analysis became commonplace. These ideas – in the absence of clear evidence to the contrary – emphasized local population stability. Isotopes are revealing a very different world.

A good starting point to understand the technique is radiocarbon dating, a fundamental tool for archaeology, which depends on the existence of a particular carbon isotope. Elements are defined by how many protons they have in their nucleus. Carbon has six, nitrogen has seven, and if there are eight protons the element is oxygen. The number of neutrons in the nucleus is usually the same as the number of protons, but it can vary, and different atomic varieties are known as isotopes.

There are three carbon isotopes. Most carbon has six protons and six neutrons, and is thus known as carbon-12, which makes up 99 per cent of all the carbon on Earth. Almost all the rest is carbon-13, which has an extra neutron. Carbon-12 and -13 are stable: they don't spontaneously become something else. But there is another, relatively extremely rare carbon isotope, which is radioactive.

Known as carbon-14, it has eight neutrons. It decays, turning into nitrogen-14 (with seven protons and seven neutrons) at a known rate over thousands of years. There is carbon in every living thing, with the proportion of isotopes reflecting their relative occurrence in the atmosphere. At death, an organism's carbon-14 continues to decay, but is no longer replaced as it was during life. Any bits of preserved plant or animal (or human) excavated by archaeologists can be aged directly by finding out how much of the original carbon-14 is still there.

Little radioactivity is involved in looking at where people grew up: the isotopes we will be considering here are mostly stable. They include forms of strontium, oxygen, carbon, nitrogen and lead. As people ate, drank and breathed, their skeletons absorbed these common elements. The body takes no notice of isotopes, but we can see how they varied by extracting them from bones and teeth. A key determinant of such variation is the local environment – geology, climate and geography. The relative amounts of strontium-87 and strontium-86, for example, reflect the type and geological age of rocks (absorbed indirectly through food and water). The quantity of oxygen-18 (acquired through drinking water) is particularly related to temperature, altitude and distance to the coast. And so on.

You can see that this can get quite complicated. First we need to determine the amount of relevant atomic isotopes in an individual's skeleton. This is done by carefully grinding up a small sample of bone or tooth, and treating the sample with chemical processes that will allow isotopic values to be measured.

These figures then need to be compared to maps of what would be expected for the isotopes in different regions. Modern groundwater, for example, has more oxygen-18 in the west of Britain and Ireland than in the east. A map of British variation in strontium-87/strontium-86 is a map of Britain's geology: there is relatively more strontium-86 in the southeast than in the northwest, though with considerable local variation.

Typically an isotope result will point to a broad area rather than a precise location, and allow for more than one source. A great swathe from northwest France to southern Scotland has very similar strontium values. Another complication is time. As oxygen-18 is affected by things like temperature and rainfall, you'd expect the map to look different when the climate was different to today's. An estimated map of oxygen-18 in groundwater 10,000 years ago shows lower values across the board. Furthermore, such analyses depend on the maps being available. Not every part of Europe is as well studied as Britain.

Isotopes can sometimes point to significant journeys between the type of landscape in which people grew up and the place where they died. They do not provide detailed itineraries with precise routes. It can be easy – as confused press stories testify – to misunderstand the results. However, when combined with other types of evidence, such as skeletal characteristics or associated artefacts, the science can be extremely powerful. And there is a further clever twist.

Various parts of the skeleton grow at different times of life. Most permanent teeth form between before birth and around nine years old. Bones grow and remodel continuously, but not all at the same speed: much of the chemistry of a thigh bone is laid down in adolescence; ribs remodel every two to five years. So it's quite possible, if long journeys were taken at the right time, for someone's teeth to show that they grew up in one place, their legs that they spent their early adult years somewhere else, and their ribs to point to a third location – all of which could be some distance from where they were finally laid to rest.

What story, then, did the Weymouth isotopes tell? In a word: Vikings! When it comes to travelling about Europe, few people in history can claim as much enterprise as the Vikings. The men buried in the pit came from all over the place, but none – with a few possible exceptions – from Dorset.[6]

Samples were taken from the ribs or femurs (thigh bones) of forty-five skeletons, and the teeth of thirty-one skulls. The 'skeletons' included isolated limbs and other part-bodies, and derived from a minimum of forty people. So in theory, because we don't know which head came from which body, these samples could represent anything from forty of the men (if all the analysed heads are from the bodies) to all fifty-two – if not certainly everyone who died at the pit, the large majority.

A team led by Carolyn Chenery, who works at the British Geological Survey, looked for isotopes of oxygen (reflecting drinking water) and strontium (geology), and, to consider diet, carbon (plant foods) and nitrogen (meat and fish). On the evidence of oxygen and strontium, most of the teeth, which formed when the men were aged six or seven, could only have grown in parts of the world colder than Weymouth. For some, the possibilities ranged from Iceland and Arctic Norway to further east in the Baltics or Russia. A further twenty-one men had their homes in places not quite so cold, but still far from southern England, from different parts of Sweden and Denmark to eastern Germany or the Czech Republic. The remaining five men could have been born in Britain, two of them locally – but they might also have been born in Denmark or, in two cases, Scotland or Norway.

It was clear from this that the men were not local, and broadly fitted a picture of Vikings scattered over a wide area. In 2018, as I was completing this book, Carolyn, Jane Evans and their colleagues published a further study, focusing on lead isotopes and using a new way of analysing the data. Lead mostly reflects the amount of metal in circulation in things like water pipes. The lead levels in the bones of the Weymouth men are comparable to those seen in prehistoric people, and mostly far below the normal level in Britain at the time of their death – consistent with them having origins elsewhere. But at a finer resolution, the isotopes had more to say.

Combined with the earlier data on strontium and oxygen, the lead outlined a restricted zone within which twenty of the men were likely to have grown up. Surprisingly, perhaps, this excludes not just Britain, but all of Iceland, Norway, Denmark, Sweden and Finland, leaving a wide band from the southern Baltic Sea down to the Black Sea, taking in all of Poland and Romania, and parts of the Czech Republic and Ukraine. The others of the thirty-one analysed seem to have come from further north: three men perhaps from Denmark, three from Russia, Arctic Scandinavia or Iceland, and five whose origins are unclear but are unlikely to lie in Western Europe or the Baltic states.[7]

Femurs throw light on where the men spent the decade or so before their deaths. If five of them had been born in the very cold north, even more had subsequently lived there – twenty-six in northern Scandinavia or east Russia, of whom six were in extremely cold Arctic regions. Interestingly, the ribs, which reflect where the men had been for the last few years of their lives, describe a different story. No one had spent time in the Arctic (nor, for that matter, had any of them lived in Britain), and most of them had been in less cold parts of Scandinavia.

Changes in the men's diet can be mapped in the same way, by comparing nitrogen and carbon isotopes in teeth and bones that grew at different times. Nitrogen-15 increases as a person consumes more animal protein, from fish, meat and dairy products, while carbon-13 increases with the consumption of marine foods. The varied figures from the Weymouth men show diverse diets, consistent with them having grown up in different places and moved about during their lives. The scientists compared their nitrogen and carbon figures to those obtained in other studies for groups of people in England on the one hand, and in Iceland, Sweden and Denmark on the other. These confirm the Weymouth men's northern origins:

they map close to the latter group, and show significantly more nitrogen-15 than the English. These men, it seems, ate better than the people whose lands they invaded, growing up on a high-protein terrestrial diet, and several of them increasing their consumption of marine foods late in life.

Yet more lines of evidence confirm the men's northern origins. Only one skull was sufficiently complete for its ancestral features to be assessed. Compared to existing sets of measurements, the closest fit was with a group of prehistoric skulls – from Denmark. Likewise, the heights of the men were compared to medieval groups from Britain and Scandinavian countries, and the closest match turned out to be with Danish Vikings.

A remarkable result, then, that paints a vivid picture of men growing up and moving about in a wide area of, perhaps, Poland and the cold north of Europe, far from where they died. But if we dig into the pages of figures and tables in the scientific studies, we can find something else. Something that reminds us that this was not just a faceless crowd, but a group of individuals, each with their own hopes and stories.

Differences between the men's isotope values for ribs and femurs confirm that six of them had moved from very cold to less cold regions before reaching Britain – these are the six noted above who had earlier lived in extreme Arctic conditions. They all seem to have moved to enjoy similar and significantly warmer temperatures some two to five years before their deaths, most likely somewhere in south Scandinavia (but not the far south), Belarus, western Russia or northern Iceland. Five of them had returned to where they had begun.[8]

Carolyn and her colleagues noted something about these six men's ages. The group includes two of only three older men in the whole pit (perhaps the oldest), and range down to what might have been the youngest, aged possibly no more than eleven. Could they have moved together? Were they related? These questions become more pertinent when we realize that the one man aged forty to forty-five – a group leader, perhaps, drawing on the wisdom of two elders and responsible for two young teenagers – is skeleton 3806: Bluetooth.

What else do we know about these six men? One of them, an elder aged over fifty, lay apart on the edge of the pit, where his remains had been badly disturbed by the mechanical digger. We can

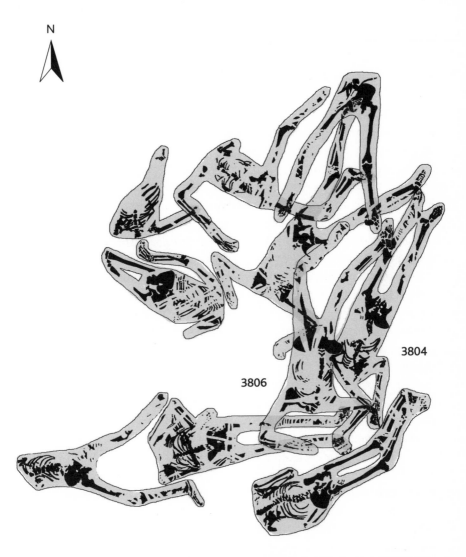

The ten more or less complete bodies on the pit bottom, the first to be thrown in (some on the north side were partly removed by the mechanical excavator). 3806 (Bluetooth) and 3804, one of the oldest men in the pit, lying beside each other with their feet to the north, may have spent much of their lives together.

say no more about him. The rest are mostly typical of the whole group. The older adolescent had a minor elbow injury. A twenty-five- to thirty-five-year-old had particularly strong legs and bunions on both big toes. Bluetooth, who we have already noted was taller and stronger than most of those found in the pit, had robust shoulders and upper arms and legs, and healed fractures in both feet and one of his shinbones. There are two things, though, of particular interest, given the possibility the men might have been hanging around together for some time.

Two of them, the better preserved older adult and the older adolescent, suffered from Scheuermann's disease, a spinal deformity that had caused the older man to lose a little height. The disease is not fully understood, but it is thought to have a significant hereditary component. No one else in the pit showed this condition.

The same older man and Bluetooth had both survived brucellosis. This is an infectious disease picked up from animals. It might be a coincidence, but they were the only two in the group with reasonably clear signs of brucellosis, and it could be they contracted it at the same time. Signs of the disease occur on the bones of only one other man in the pit.

The six bodies were scattered throughout the pit, suggesting the men were not executed and disposed of together. Two, however, lay side by side, feet to the north, on the bottom of the pit beneath a mass of corpses. One was the old man who survived brucellosis. The other was his fellow sufferer, Bluetooth. Here, perhaps, are the two men the others looked up to, who were recognized by their killers as leaders, and who were among the first to die in a long parade of slaughter – the older man, uniquely, taking a stab to his buttocks so deep that the archaeologists think at that point he must have been flat on the ground.

*

Remarkably, this stretch of Dorset coast is where the first Viking attack in Western Europe occurred – or at least, the first to be recorded. Around the year 789, three Danish ships appeared offshore, at a place thought to have been near Portland. Beaduheard, a royal official, was in Dorchester when he heard the news. He rode down to the water, and tried to persuade the uninvited strangers to see his king. They murdered him and his men.

Could the executed men on the hill above Weymouth have come from those first three ships, the first Viking attackers becoming the first Vikings to die in battle overseas? It would be a good story: fifty men could crew a longship, so perhaps there might be two other gruesome pits out there, waiting to be discovered. But archaeology tells us otherwise. The original radiocarbon date was confirmed by two more. Together they suggest that, almost certainly, the executions occurred at a point between AD 970 and 1025, some two centuries after that first Danish visit.

These were anxious times. The carbon dates' fifty-five years span the reigns of six kings: Edgar the Peaceful (who died in 975); Edward the Martyr; Ethelred the Unready; Sweyn Forkbeard (Harald Bluetooth's son, who battled to replace Ethelred but died almost as soon as he'd succeeded, allowing Ethelred to return from exile); Edmund Ironside (who survived seven months before, according to one story, being murdered while he sat on the toilet); and Canute, who came to power in 1016.

Within that period, however, there is a greater radiocarbon probability that the executions took place between 980 and 1020. By this time, the north and east of England were ruled by Scandinavians; Vikings were settling down and building up businesses. Thanks largely to King Alfred (r. 871–99), southern England remained in Anglo-Saxon hands, and was a greater draw for overseas raiders seeking booty and land of their own. Vikings resumed their attacks in the 980s, having not been seen in southern England for fifty years; they continued until the Danish king Canute conquered England. Radiocarbon and history, then, point to the reign of Ethelred the Unready (978–1016) as the likely context for the Weymouth executions.

Not every skirmish or attack during those four decades was recorded. Even when they were, we are given few details. But surviving texts do describe warfare, violence and destruction. The fragmentary histories show us the sort of world in which the fifty-two men on Ridgeway Hill lived and died.

Ethelred's reign was plagued by political confusion, in which both king and rebellious compatriots sought strength in alliances with Vikings. People changed sides at the dip of an oar. Norse bravado, interpreted in popular modern culture as noble and heroic, seems often to have been no more than male swagger in a world where hollow boast was followed by backtracking and betrayal. A Scandinavian in England a thousand years ago could be attacked by another Scandinavian (a concept that embraced a wide range of geographic origins), and both they and English people might have mixed ancestries that within only a few generations reached back into each others' territories.

The scientific evidence from the pit, however, leaves us with two probable explanations for why the men died. In both, Anglo-Saxons ordered the death of Northmen. Perhaps, we might think, one of the few skeletons not yet analysed came from a Welshman – a term originally applied to 'native' Britons. But that takes special pleading. We assume that all the men in the pit were Vikings, and that leaves room only for native English attackers – if, at an unlikely stretch, joined by the odd mercenary accomplice from elsewhere.

One possibility is quite specific: that the men died in 1002, on 13 November – a Saturday. On this day dedicated to the otherwise little celebrated St Brice, Ethelred, for reasons unknown, feared an attempt on his life and kingdom, and ordered the death of all Scandinavians living in England – more bluster than practical reality. Danes, said the king, had 'sprung up in this island, sprouting like cockles among the wheat' (a reference to a now rare agricultural weed with a pretty little purple flower). They should be 'exterminated'.

If the 'Danes' targeted by Ethelred were all soldiers who had recently settled in England – as some historians argue – those in the Weymouth pit might qualify (though only a single adolescent had a wound that might have come from an earlier fight). But evidence suggests Ethelred had a looser focus in mind. Looking back from less than a century later, historians (admittedly writing in what by then was a Norman, or quasi-Scandinavian, kingdom) condemned the massacre for targeting innocent men, women and children; the Norwegian queen Gunnhild and her young son were said to be among the victims.

Following his claim to be justly exterminating cockles, Ethelred described an incident in Oxford: Danes sought safety in a church, only to find themselves burnt to death along with everything around them. Remarkably, recent excavations in Oxford found a compact mass of male human skeletons identified by isotope studies as possibly

Scandinavian, and some of the bones showed signs of burning. Like those in Dorset, these men – young, tall and strong – had been thrown into an old hollow, in this case a prehistoric ditch. The deposit had been partly removed by later building, so we don't know the full scale of the atrocity, but there were at least thirty-five deaths.

Sean Wallis, the archaeologist who directed the dig, is convinced the men were St Brice's Day victims. They were less systematically dispatched than their Weymouth contemporaries. Sword wounds, notably in the head, back, sides and legs, were far in excess of anything needed to kill them, but they were not beheaded. The remains suggest men fleeing a murderous mob more than a systematic execution. It's possible bodies were collected from various places and dumped from a cart; in the ditch, arms and legs lay straight, in line with torsos.[9]

There is something else that distinguishes the two incidents. While the isotope data seem unequivocal about the Dorset men's scattered European origins, the indications from Oxford are less strong. Of thirteen sampled individuals, at most six, but possibly only one, have oxygen isotopes pointing to a clear origin outside Britain. Five of the same individuals' teeth were analysed for strontium isotopes. This suggested that none was local to Oxford; but while one might well have been Scandinavian, the others could have come from Britain.

Which brings us to the other explanation for the Dorset murders: that the men were a gang of Viking raiders whose plan had gone disastrously wrong. We have a scene of composed horror. No one flees. The bodies lie in all directions and positions, arms and legs flung out or flexed. The archaeologists saw the same thing in France, at the First World War Fromelles graves. There, they thought, bodies had been thrown in by pairs of German soldiers, one holding each end. I visited that dig, and was struck by the curious sense of freedom conveyed by the bodies: not hunched in fear, but expansive and open, limbs spinning like falling angels.

On Ridgeway Hill most bodies appear to have been swung into the pit from the southwest, southeast or northeast sides. This suggests to me three executioners, perhaps each assisted by two men, who delivered and held the victims, then slung the corpses onto the growing heap. This was no easy task. Decapitation took up to seven blows, about three on average. They had been delivered from all directions, around half from behind, others from the sides and front. There were many other cuts across the bottoms of jaws and into shoulders. There were also several in hands, wrists and lower arms, where victims had tried to defend themselves; one man's wrist and all five digits in his left hand had been sliced through. This suggests their arms were not tied, which is confirmed by the sprawling limbs in the pit.

Five of the men had other sword cuts in the head. Perhaps they fought. One, aged twenty-five to thirty-five, suffered four such injuries. Three of these could have been delivered from behind by a right-handed executioner, but the fourth implies attack from the left side – another assailant, perhaps. This blow cut clean through the side of his skull. Brain would have oozed from the gaping hole, but it was probably a sword through the neck that killed him.

Vikings, no less than any other people, liked to tell each other stories. Several survive, written down in later centuries and known to us as sagas. Though nothing like the systematic executions seen in the Weymouth pit has yet been found anywhere else in early Medieval Europe, there is, in one saga, a description of an event that sounds eerily close to what might have occurred on Ridgeway Hill.

The incident appears in the Jómsvíkinga saga, a compilation of anecdotes about Scandinavian kings reaching back to the late

A large cut to the top of a skull.

900s, written down some two centuries later. Historians debate how much of it is record and how much entertainment. It is rich in treachery, heroics and sorcery, and Old Testament-style visions and prophecies. Its interest to us now lies in the saga's unusual ending: a mass beheading.

If there is fantasy in the saga – one warrior turns into a gold-hoarding serpent – there is also verisimilitude. Young men form gangs of warriors and go on summer raiding expeditions (this is the real meaning of the word 'viking'; it was adopted to refer to early Scandinavians as a whole, rather than a particular activity, only in recent centuries). Athelstan, another Anglo-Saxon king, Harald Bluetooth and Sweyn Forkbeard make appearances. Finally, a long-brewing confrontation with a group of troubling fighters, the Jómsvíkings, occurs in the south Baltic Sea, with much loss of life. The battle ends with the Norwegian army taking seventy Jómsvíkings prisoner.

The men are roped together and their possessions seized. The Norwegians sit down to eat, and brag about their victory before returning to the captives. They behead three badly wounded warriors. Then they work their way down the rope, untying the men one by one, challenging them to express their lack of fear, holding their heads by twisting sticks in their hair, and executing them with a sword.

Each death is a story. One man asks to take a piss. As he does up his flies, he says he'd hoped to sleep with the Norwegian earl's wife – with the predictable rapid result. Another says he wants to be executed from the front, so he can see the blow and show his true bravery. He did not blanch, says the saga, but his eyes closed at the moment of death.

More men die. Then things start to unravel. The eleventh turns his head as the sword swings and the executioner removes the arms of the man holding his hair. The earl talks to the prisoner, finds out he is seventeen, and takes him into his own army. There is a scuffle when the next man is approached, and the errant blade cuts the rope. The intended victim grabs the sword and executes the executioner. The earl, impressed again, takes on a second Dane, and then releases them all.

In Anglo-Saxon England you could be sentenced to death for treason, theft, trespass, dishonest property deals and more. Legal execution burials are not uncommon, and the location of the Weymouth pit would be typical: the site is beside a major road near an administrative boundary, away from settlement and among prehistoric burial mounds, high and remote, all features that attracted gallows throughout Anglo-Saxon England. Missing heads are also seen at legal execution sites, and are thought to indicate the presence of *heafod stoccan* – heads on stakes, fly-blown reminders of the penalty for transgressions.

But such cemeteries are not like the Weymouth pit. Individuals have their own graves. Hanging is more common than beheading. On Ridgeway Hill, by contrast, fitting the narrative of the Jómsvíkinga saga, removal of the head in itself seems to have mattered. In the rains of blows, several of the men would likely have died without being decapitated. The separate heaping of heads on the shallow south side of the pit emphasizes this theft of person, of isolation of will from bodily action, in life and death. Perhaps up there on Ridgeway Hill, or down in Weymouth by the shore, a local, vindictive triumph over the continuous fear of thieving, murdering young men from overseas was marked by the now missing five heads raised in the air.

It's possible that the fifty-two men were killed by another Viking gang, but that seems unlikely on English soil. They could have crewed a middling warship. The Anglo-Saxon Chronicles, key historic texts for these times, are packed with incidents of raiding fleets, sometimes numbering hundreds of ships. There are battles, betrayals and 'great slaughter', and occasional descriptions of crews' fates. In 992 a ship was captured in the Thames Estuary, and the crew all slain. In 897, after a bloody battle in which sixty-two Anglo-Saxons were killed, two marauding Viking ships were wrecked on the Sussex coast. The crews were seized and taken to Winchester – a good two days' walk – where the king ordered them to be hanged. By comparison, the marching uphill of fifty-two men from Weymouth, in three or four hours perhaps, would have been nothing much to record.[10]

When I was in Dorset to walk the Ridgeway, down by the sea in a Bridport street market I found a children's picture book about Alfred the Great. It tells the story of a hero king repelling invaders, building a British navy, writing books and mapping out the old shires – the school-history saga, complete with the moment when Alfred was scolded by a woman for letting her cakes burn while he plotted how to beat the Danes. Vikings loom darkly, 'fierce sea-raiders from the North who came in their long black ships and attacked the peaceful English farmers'. But Alfred beats them in a great victory, and 'England became a free country', where 'English law and English justice are known and respected throughout the world'.[11]

The atrocities on the downs above Weymouth and in the streets of Oxford don't fit that narrative. We see the villains abused by the good. But that simple inversion may itself be too pat. The English – depending on how you read history – had perhaps themselves only recently invaded Britain. Britons, Angles, Saxons and Vikings were not so different, in their cultures, their languages and their histories, from each other. School curricula celebrate the Norman Conquest, a Viking invasion under another name (the Normans – men from the north – were recently settled Scandinavians in France). Among the massacred men in Oxford, however, it's not obvious who was Anglo-Saxon and who was Viking.

On Ridgeway Hill, the new three-lane bypass sweeps below me in the summer heat. White chalk shows through slowly spreading scrub on the steepest sides of the cutting, but otherwise the works are now overgrown. Grasses that bind new, thin soils fade from green to brown. Delicate downland flowers – mostly absent from the older grazed turf – are everywhere in the disturbed ground, spatters of red and mauve, white, yellow, orange and deep purple. The names are as rich as the colours: corky-fruited water dropwort, common knapweed, horseshoe vetch and dyer's greenweed.

The language of this celebration of returning peace, issued from the earth with the bones of the dead, reaches back to the world of Ethelred, Sweyn and Canute. 'Wort' is Old English for root or plant; it is also found in Old Norse, Danish and Old High German. 'Weed' is an Old Saxon word, and 'knap', a knob, is found in Old English and Old Norse. 'Vetch' comes from the Latin via Anglo-Norman French. A thousand years after the tragedy, rivalries are forgotten in a jumble of flowery tongues. Wild thyme, restharrow, pyramidal orchid and clustered bellflower – otherwise known as Dane's blood.

# The Staffordshire Hoard

*Hammerwich, AD 600–700*

Terry was standing outside the house, waiting for Duncan to arrive. It was a warm summer's evening on 13 July 2009, on a street of 1950s semis with cars on patches of concrete that had once been small gardens. Duncan had been to Terry's metal-detecting club, but on the phone earlier he'd realized he'd not met him before.

Duncan Slarke, then a thirty-year-old graduate in archaeology and religious studies, and Terry Herbert, fifty-five, unemployed, living on disability benefit with his two cats in a council flat, are typical of people in modern Britain drawn together by a fascination with old artefacts. They are rewriting history.

In a couple of months what Terry was soon to show Duncan would become public, and there would be a surge in detector sales. But the hobby was already growing. People were being drawn in their thousands by the lure of history, of making that special find. Detecting needs much patience, but little money and no contacts or qualifications.

Duncan was a regional Finds Liaison Officer working for the Portable Antiquities Scheme, a project run by the British Museum (in England) and Amgueddfa Cymru – National Museum Wales. It is building a unique record of British history, and has attracted

international praise and imitations. Its staff help detectorists understand their discoveries, advise on the best way to look after them, and
record them in a national database. Finders do not have to hand anything over. There is a legal obligation to report particularly significant
finds, which are classed as Treasure, but all other communication
is entirely voluntary. Since its launch in 1997, the scheme has
recorded well over one and a quarter million artefacts. The impact
on knowledge of so much new data from across England and Wales
is profound.

There were six detecting clubs in Duncan's patch, and countless
independent searchers. He was constantly fire-fighting to keep up,
but, he thought to himself, all this hard work is beginning to pay off.
I can make a long-term difference. The collectors trust me, and I
know what to expect when they bring me boxfuls of mud-covered bits
of old metal. On that July day he reached his office in Birmingham
Museum and Art Gallery at 10 o'clock, and his mobile phone rang.

'My uncle's found some Anglo-Saxon things,' said John, no one
he knew, who proceeded to read out a long, ridiculous list of treasures. Duncan wrote down the details and promised to come and
look at them that day. He phoned three colleagues he trusted, to
warn them of something big. It must be a hoard, and they agreed
that they needed to take it in immediately, assuming the finder was
happy with that. If it was the half of what it was said to be, it plainly
came under the terms of the Treasure Act, which meant it belonged
to the Crown – the British nation. In due course the finder would be
fully compensated, but the priorities were identification and security.

Eventually, Duncan took the train back home, got into his
car with his forms and notebook and camera, and drove north.
He reached the house, just across the border into Staffordshire, at
about 7 o'clock.

Terry was waiting for him, arms hanging by his sides. He suffered from heart trouble, angina and high blood pressure, and was
unable to work. He lived less than two miles from where he had
found the hoard. He enjoyed his detecting hobby, but he liked to
chat. 'If he turns up for a dig at 12 o'clock,' said a fellow club member
later, 'he'll normally spend an hour with his metal detector out and
the remaining four hours talking.'

Terry's angina gave him chest pains, brought on by physical
activity and worry; the past week had had plenty of both. He didn't

feel safe with the hoard in his maisonette, so he had kept it at a relative's house. He and John led Duncan into the dining room.

The table, draped with a pink cotton cloth, nearly filled the space. At its centre was an open, white plastic pot, big enough for a pair of boots. It was full of clear, sealable bags, and even as he walked in, Duncan could see the glare of gold. This was real.

He looked quizzically at Terry, and Terry nodded back. Yes, go on, have a look, that's why you're here. There was the cross John had mentioned on the phone, and the sword fittings. It wasn't just the volume, it was the breathtaking beauty of each piece: this was like something nobody had ever imagined. And there it was, on Duncan's patch.

This is big, he thought, swearing to himself. He looked up at Terry again. Terry looked at John, and they nodded at each other, and smiled. Terry spoke.

'Shall we bring the rest of the stuff in now?'

And in it came. Five identical boxes, one at a time, all full of sealed bags holding Anglo-Saxon treasure. Duncan's acceptance of the find was moving back into incredulity. Wow, he said, opening another bag, his eyes bulging. WOW! Then down to work.

Each box had a day and a date on it, written in capitals with a felt-tip pen bought for the occasion. 'Day three, search one, Tuesday 7th July 2009', read one. The labelling mapped the progress of Terry's search, from Sunday 5 July (when he had made his first find, a crumpled piece of gold from a sword), to the Friday when John had phoned Duncan. Friday was day five; Terry had taken one day off. He'd braved wind, rain and mud. He'd mused to himself, while standing in the field in a thunderstorm, what people would make of the singed body of a man with Anglo-Saxon gold in his pockets. But on one day, the pain and the stress were just too much to continue and he had stayed at home.

John had helped Terry identify pieces by searching the web, but they had to guess what much of it might be. Terry was shattered. He lay awake at night, or dreamt about the hoard if he slept. Excitement at the discovery turned to fear that someone would hear of the gold and plunder his field. It had to be important, and he was responsible for it. Were they right? Was it really Anglo-Saxon, were those really pieces of sword? Now the experts would take control, and they could rest.

Using the men's felt-tip marker, Duncan wrote a new number on each bag, running from 1 to 244. It wasn't just the find that was extraordinary, but also the way Terry had collected it. He hadn't presented Duncan with a bag of gleaming gold pared down to its bones by solvents, scrubbing and hammering. What I am seeing now, he thought, is only part of it: much of the finest antique detail is hidden by red earth, perfectly preserved. This was what all his work was for. He snapped a few photos in the fading light, but he couldn't take it in.

'It would have been nice to have heard about this a little earlier,' he ventured. The Act obliged finders to declare a Treasure discovery within fourteen days, so Terry was within the law. But he had been working on this unique hoard for nearly a week, when he might have called the archaeologists in after day one.

It was just kicking around in the ploughsoil, said Terry. All an archaeologist could have done was watch him at work. Anyway, he'd thought, the gold would stop coming. But it didn't stop, and there came a point when they knew they had to involve the archaeologists.

Duncan had been at the house for three or four hours. 'Is it OK to take this away tonight?'

'Absolutely,' said Terry, without hesitation. 'It can't stay here another night!'

So Duncan got out the Treasure Act form, completed it in duplicate, and he and Terry signed both copies and each took one. Duncan drove back to his flat in his blue VW Passat, the boxes packed into the boot with obsessive care. He always drives in silence, and during the forty minutes it took to return home, he thought about what to do next.

The two men were very different, but he liked the detectorist, and had trusted him instantly. When Duncan had left, Terry had been visibly exhausted by their evening together, but Duncan felt powered by adrenaline. His mind was racing. He knew they had to think about excavating the site. What was the farmer like? The landowner? Who else should he tell? It was obvious they needed to keep it secret if they were to mount a full recovery without interruption and almost certain theft, but how could they do that? And anyway, what did all this gold mean?

It was pouring with rain when Duncan reached his flat at around midnight. It didn't feel right, but he couldn't think of a better way. He reversed his car as close to the door as it would go, opened the boot, covered the material up, took a box in, locked the flat and returned to the locked car for the next box. He had to repeat this six times, locking and unlocking the car and his flat over and over again, as the rain came down. If I have to fight for this with my life, he thought, I'll do it.

John had given him a CD with a photo of every piece laid out on the pink tablecloth, a school ruler for scale and paper labels saying what each was and when it had been found. Duncan selected some on his computer and emailed them to Kevin Leahy, the Portable Antiquities Scheme's national advisor on early medieval metalwork, and Barry Ager, a British Museum curator. Now there would be eight of them who knew about the Anglo-Saxon gold.

He went to bed and fell into a deep sleep. And whatever he might have dreamt, or however Kevin or Barry would react to what they read and saw the next morning, none of them would come close to imagining what was to come. Terry had thought it might be ending. It hadn't even begun.

Terry Herbert knew that the little field between two busy roads had been searched before by other detectorists, and that they'd found nothing. But Fred Johnson, the farmer and landowner, had recently given it a deep and final ploughing before putting it down to grass for horses. They agreed to split any finds. Terry started out at 11 o'clock on Sunday morning. At noon he found what he took to be a piece of silver foil. He looked more closely, and saw it was gold.

Just over a week later, Terry's find, by then much the largest hoard of Anglo-Saxon treasure ever seen, was in secret store in Birmingham Museum. Duncan told the coroner and other relevant authorities as the Treasure Act required, and the following week the key archaeologists had the first of many meetings. They decided that to speed things along, the hoard would stay in Birmingham rather than go down to the British Museum. They agreed to dig a 1 metre-square trench, expecting to clear the field of the last gold.

They found twenty-four more pieces of treasure. They doubled the trench. They were still there the following week. Historic England, a government-funded body, offered £25,000 towards costs, and excavation continued, with the site watched by twenty-four-hour security services. Terry scanned the spoilheap with his metal detector, finding yet more gold.[1]

Terry Herbert, with detector and spade, at the hoard site with Staffordshire County Council archaeologists Ian Wykes (centre) and Steve Dean.

Kevin Leahy and his wife, Dianne, an education assistant at the North Lincolnshire Museum where Kevin had been the archaeologist, started to catalogue the hoard. Dianne weighed and measured each piece with an electronic balance and callipers, wrote the results on the back of a yellow raffle ticket – guaranteeing each find a unique number – and passed them to Kevin, who typed it all with brief descriptions into a Microsoft Access database. It took them two days a week for the next six weeks.

Meanwhile excavation continued, until, exactly a month after Terry had first entered the field, the trench was finally backfilled – and even then, Terry carried on, picking up a few more small pieces of gold. Kevin and Dianne finished the catalogue, which now amounted to 1,345 objects (they had had to buy a second set of raffle tickets); of these, fifty-six were lumps of earth that X-ray images had shown to be studded with further scraps of metal.

That might have been it, but Staffordshire County Council and the Staffordshire police, worried about public safety once news got out,

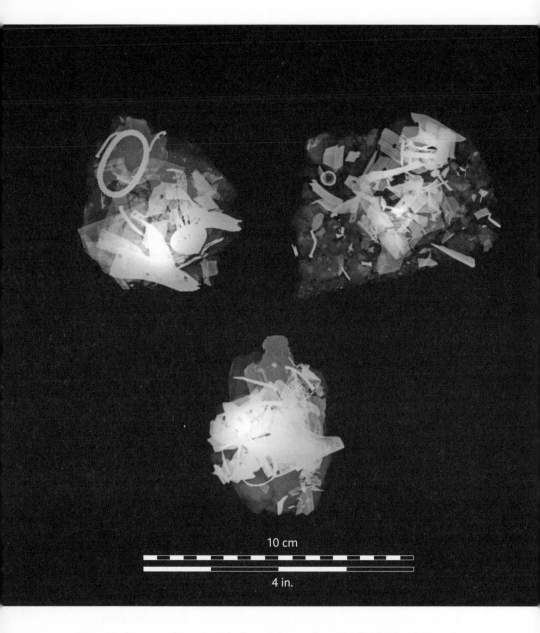

10 cm

4 in.

Terry Herbert saved many packed earth lumps from the field. When X-rayed they revealed jewel settings, decorated plaques and fine filigree work.

brought in the Home Office Scientific Development Branch to ensure the site was completely clean. With military-grade metal detectors and a camera drone, a Home Office team scoured the field, helped by a consultant geologist, another Finds Liaison Officer (Duncan Slarke was now on holiday) and staff from the police's Tactical Planning Unit, Staffordshire County Council and Birmingham University. The fuss attracted a local blogger, who wrote a short post identifying the field's location. All those searchers, he said, as he had been truthfully told, had found absolutely nothing. It was a close thing.

The archaeologists wanted everyone to know as soon as they were ready. 'Our responsibility', said Kevin, 'is to make this available to the scholarly world as soon as possible.' They chose a date for the release, at which point, with unprecedented speed for a complex process, the coroner would determine the find legally Treasure, and they would relinquish their privileged positions.[2]

The week before this was due to happen, Leslie Webster, a former British Museum curator and specialist in Anglo-Saxon art and culture, saw the hoard in Birmingham. Late that night she circulated 1,500 words of analysis among the covert clique of experts.

'This is going to alter our perceptions of Anglo-Saxon England in the seventh and early eighth century', she said in her email, 'as radically, if not more so, as the 1939 Sutton Hoo discoveries did. It will make historians and literary scholars review what their sources tell us, and archaeologists and art historians rethink the chronology of metalwork and manuscripts. It will make us all think again about rising (and failing) kingdoms, the expression of regional identities, the complicated transition from paganism to Christianity, the conduct of battle and the nature of fine metalwork production.' This was, she added, 'the metalwork equivalent of finding a new Lindisfarne Gospels or Book of Kells' – illuminated manuscripts of staggering detail and beauty, and pinnacles of Celtic art.

Finally, on 24 September at 11.30 a.m. at Birmingham Museum, the press were invited in. The Staffordshire Hoard, so named in the vain hope its find spot might remain secret, created headlines around the world. 'Archaeologists', said the *New York Times*, 'tentatively estimated the value of the trove at £1 million – about $1.6 million – but say it could be many times that' (it was valued on 25 November at £3,285,000 – over $5 million). The discovery was compared to that of Tutankhamun's tomb. Terry was an instant if reluctant star.[3]

'This hoard', I wrote in *The Guardian,* 'will change lives. It represents that cultural maelstrom between the departure of the Romans and the formation of England: think iconic kings like Penda and Aethelbald, carving out Mercia as it becomes one of the most powerful kingdoms in Britain.' But no one, I added, knew what it meant. Kevin ended his press presentation by quoting from the great Anglo-Saxon poem *Beowulf,* in which the warrior king was buried with his riches: 'They let the ground keep that ancestral treasure, gold under gravel, gone to earth, and as useless to men now as it ever was.'[4]

'Well,' said Kevin, 'it's not useless now.'

*

Among the manuscripts in the Laurentian Library in Florence is the oldest complete medieval Latin Bible known to have survived in the West. Named the *Codex Amiatinus*, it is truly enormous: some five hundred calves are said to have given their hides for its vellum pages. It was presented to the Pope by Ceolfrith, an Anglo-Saxon abbot. It reached Italy – poor old Ceolfrith died on the way, but his colleagues delivered the gift – in AD 716, twenty-four years after being commissioned.

This historic English monument was created at the twin monastic foundation of Monkwearmouth and Jarrow, in present-day Tyne and Wear. A third of the way into the Book of Numbers – telling the story of the Israelites' journey into their promised land – one of Ceolfrith's scribes wrote out words spoken by Moses as the Ark of the Covenant, a gold-covered chest holding the Ten Commandments, is carried ahead of his people: 'Rise up, Lord, and let thine enemies be scattered; and let them that hate thee flee before thee.'

Perhaps even as the Northumberland monks worked, someone else set out on a different mission nearly two hundred miles to the south. Their task was furtive and hazardous, and conducted outdoors. They bore something heavy. It could hardly have been more different from the *Codex*'s handwritten pages, yet the burden and the book shared a cry to God. Hidden in a carrier among a mass of loose metal was a strip of gilded silver, engraved – twice, with a few spelling mistakes – with the very same words from Numbers.

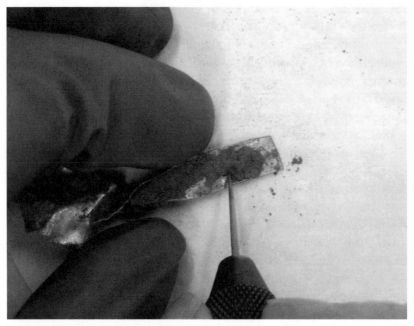

Garden thorns donated by the public were used to clean soil from gold without risk of damage.

The shadowy figure dug a hole, concealed their package and slipped away. They never came back. Nobody else knew about the secret treasure, buried in wooded and heathy wasteland on the edge of the Cannock Hills. Fifty generations passed before Terry Herbert found the first of its contents. After years of slow, painstaking conservation and research, as every tiniest item was cleaned and examined and the earth around it was prised out with garden thorns (a novel device that ensured the soft metal was not damaged), the tally of pieces closed at 4,600.

This was not, however, how the Hoard had been buried. It had been exploded by a season's deep cultivation before Terry found it: a few more years of ploughing, claimed Kevin Leahy, and the delicate treasures would have been atomized. The huge task of putting each piece back together was undertaken by teams of conservators working at Birmingham Museum, under Pieta Greaves and Deborah Cane, and at the British Museum.

As work progressed, the lead specialist, Chris Fern, an independent Anglo-Saxon archaeologist whose career had taken a spectacular turn, tried to read the objects' stories – which, given how much was new, was no mean task. When they began, there were some obvious things, such as the gold cross, its arms folded. Most of the fragments had come from weapons: the first count included 354 sword-hilt fittings. As the conservators reconnected the loose bits, however, and the number of these fell, the object count rose. It reached 600, the greater part of 5 kilograms (11 pounds) of gold and 1.5 kilograms (3 pounds) of silver, decorated with 3,500 red garnets.

We can read the *Codex Amiatinus*. But how do we read these martial jewels? The technologies and styles can be traced back to Roman times, whence they developed in distinctive ways. Inspiration – smiths, even – from southern Scandinavia, northern Germany, the Netherlands, Belgium and France fed into native British traditions and channelled the politics, religion and myths of changing times. But none of that tells us what the designs mean.

There are a few early texts – most famously *Beowulf*, which may have been composed at the time of the Hoard's burial – that elaborate on contemporary gods and heroes, the values of the battlefield and the power of craft and gold. These provide essential contexts for the Hoard's artefacts, and, along with Christian writings, suggest specific meanings for some of the designs. The other half of the equation is the Hoard itself and, not to put too fine a point on it, Chris Fern.

In his early thirties when the Hoard was found, Chris had been thinking since university about the sort of things it holds, and he retains the air of a student discovering new worlds. He saw the press conference on breakfast telly, he told me, and was 'astounded and amazed'. He watched Kevin in his bow tie quoting *Beowulf*. 'I felt very jealous then,' he laughed, 'thinking I wouldn't get a piece of it.'

Chris had studied at York University to learn from some of the country's leading Anglo-Saxon archaeologists, inspired by a book by George Speake, an artist who had researched Anglo-Saxon art. Intrigued by the drawings of stylized miniature boars and serpents, Chris started a doctorate on animal art, worked on excavations, and soon went freelance; he and his wife (an Anglo-Saxon historian, now a school teacher) moved to Norfolk, and he continued to head out to fields and building sites, earning a living as an excavator and project manager. But what he really wanted to do was write about the Anglo-Saxon stuff, and in 2010 he got a phone call. Was he interested in the Staffordshire Hoard?

At the beginning, it was in the hands of the Portable Antiquities Scheme – the British Museum has a statutory role administering the Treasure Act – and organizations local to the find; there were a lot of interests, not all archaeological, in a very high-profile project. As research and conservation continued at different sites, various selections of objects were also on show to the public, some at permanent displays in Birmingham and Staffordshire, others in travelling exhibitions (one at the National Geographic Museum in Washington DC). Meanwhile, with further excavation and surveys and Terry's continued searching, the collection was growing. It was hard to know who was in control.

Some archaeologists were sceptical of the whole thing. 'Any seasoned digger', pronounced one, 'knows that these objects must have been deliberately put there within the last half-century or so....This is an Emperor's New Clothes story.' 'The mood of many scholars now', wrote Martin Carver, excavator of Sutton Hoo, site of the great Anglo-Saxon ship-burial whose treasures have some close parallels in the Hoard, 'is more nearly one of outrage that the science of archaeology in England has sunk so low in professional and public esteem.'[5]

By June 2010 the Hoard was in the ownership of the museums in Birmingham and Stoke-on-Trent, the purchase price quickly raised through grants and public donations in a whirl of intense local pride. Public as well as academic interest demanded that attempts be made to refit the many fragments, but there was a bonus to the pulverization. Treasures in graves were buried in good condition, so the Hoard offered a unique chance to get inside the crafts, to see how the tiny, complex assemblages of gems and precious metals were made. A proper study of the Hoard would take far longer than had first been thought – and would also cost much more.[6]

Historic England had contributed further grants, and it was agreed that it should oversee future work on behalf of the Hoard's owners. It appointed Barbican Research Associates to manage the project, which under Hilary Cool brought in over fifty archaeologists. This was the end of many of the original staff's involvement (Kevin's work was immortalized in the catalogue, where every piece has a K number). And it was the start of Chris Fern's.

Chris's first task – after recovering from the shock of the sheer scale and complexity of what lay before him – was to compile the definitive catalogue, advising as he went along on special pieces and important questions. In February 2014, for the first time since its protracted discovery, the entire Hoard was brought together in one place, on black-cloth-covered tables laid end to end at Birmingham Museum, where there was a back room big enough for the occasion. Over ten days, timed to coincide with his family's half-term holidays, Chris studied the complete collection and found many new joins. The project then entered its second stage. As conservation progressed, what remained was to tease out the objects' stories, to be told in a scholarly book, with further details online, which would be published in 2019. This is when, for Chris, things got really interesting.[7]

Since the 1970s archaeology has transformed our understanding of Anglo-Saxon England. The study of lost cemeteries and villages, with public buildings, houses and workshops, has thrown much unexpected light on the very origins of England – on immigration and colonization, status and trade, costume, lifestyles and values. Yet for the finer crafts, there had been nothing to touch the scale or brilliance of the Sutton Hoo treasures – excavated in 1939, seventy years almost to the day before the Staffordshire Hoard was unearthed – and a handful of hallowed illuminated religious books.[8] It was almost as if Stonehenge had just been discovered.

When was the Hoard buried? And why? Two things made these questions hard to answer. The Hoard's age could be determined only by comparing its contents to known, dated objects, but much of it had no comparison. And initially, because Terry had not washed everything (for which he was much praised), the delicate and minuscule artwork was covered in mud. Much informed guesswork went into the early assessments.

The press were told that the Hoard had been buried between AD 675 and 725. This confident-looking attribution, spanning the reigns of five Mercian kings, masked an awkward compromise. Most objects seemed to date from around 650. The inscribed strip apparently offered a quasi-historical date. The trouble was, the two experts who should know came up with quite different answers: one thought it was written after 700, or even after 800, and the other *before* 700 – hence 675–725, the extremes of conflicting opinions. A more inclusive date might have been 550–850, or the rules of some thirty Mercian kings. Pundits seeking to tie the Hoard's burial to a particular battle – there were many, pundits and battles – were at once chastened and emboldened.

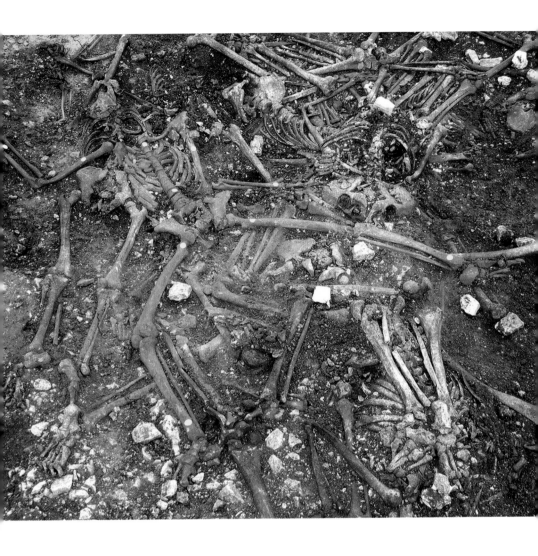

i ABOVE Skeleton in the Weymouth pit of a man aged 20–30, coloured in the photo to distinguish its bones.

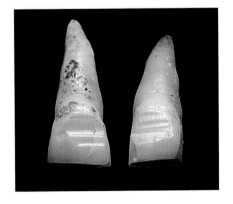

ii RIGHT Incised grooves in the upper front teeth of skull 3736, the first instance of a distinctive Scandinavian practice seen in the UK. The skull and skeleton 3806 are together characterized here as Bluetooth.

**iii, iv, v** A collection of objects from the Staffordshire Hoard. BELOW Gold sword pommel (see diagram, page 56). RIGHT Gold and garnet hilt assembly from a seax, a large, single-edged fighting knife. BOTTOM Gold strip inscribed in Latin with words spoken by Moses, an item that attracted much interest at the discovery press conference: 'Rise up, Lord, and let thine enemies be scattered'. OPPOSITE Imaginative reconstruction of the Hoard's helmet, preserved in over 1,000 scraps of gold and silver.

0            2 cm

0            ¾ in.

**vi** ABOVE, TOP Excavation at the Bloomberg site in 2012 can be seen in the foreground, soon after the demolition of Bucklersbury House. Most of the Roman writing tablets would be found beyond, towards the north end of the site. The prominent building on the left is No. 1 Poultry, site of an earlier large excavation.

**vii** ABOVE Fragment of a tablet bearing the phrase 'Londinio Mogontio' (In London, to Mogontius…). It is one of three tablets from Bloomberg featuring the word 'London'.

**viii** OPPOSITE A complete tablet with a message from Taurus to Macrinus preserved in scratches in the wood (bottom), and imagined as it may have looked (top), with pale wood showing through words written with a metal stylus in black wax (14 cm/5½ in. wide).

... magino domino
carissimo salutem
scias me domine ... ... ...
quod tu sisinnicam cupio
cum cuniurat catapiusliit
luminta aduxit at contudit
quia mallidus tribus pur capu
non possum adrepeta uixi...
no didumunum siti illi
sutuqumpit umumadiuit

**ix** ABOVE Pit 3666 at Cliffs End. The feet of the old woman in the pit lay under the body of a teenage girl, whose head lay on the head and neck of a cow. The woman's right arm is covered by the arm of a bound child. The bones of two lambs were found in the soil around the woman's hips.

**x** OPPOSITE The woman had been killed by several sword blows to the back of her head.

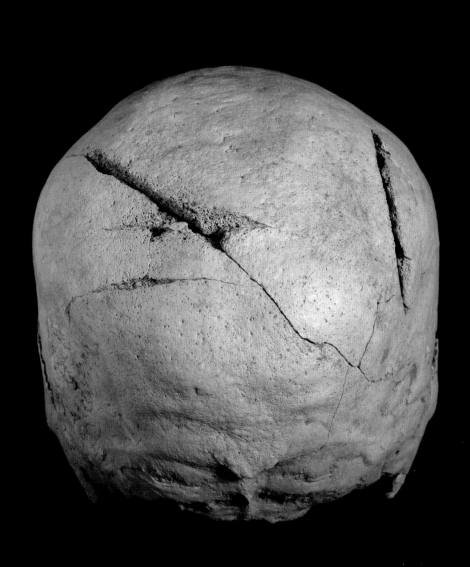

**xi** Roofing a replica of Black Loch's Structure 2 at Whithorn, near Wigtown.

Some key features were clear from the outset. Across England, more discoveries of Anglo-Saxon fine metalwork are associated with women than with men, delicate items typically made from copper alloys melted in little crucibles and cast in intricate moulds.[9] Men took metal to their graves, but most often in the form of sword blades, spear tips or shield fittings, hammered out of iron by muscular smiths. Yet there was nothing feminine about the martial Hoard: there was not a single item more commonly found with women. A second obvious feature was the Hoard's value. In materials or craftsmanship, nothing came close. The exquisite artistry at Sutton Hoo was expressed in gold weighing a third of that in the Hoard. And here was another distinctive feature. At Sutton Hoo, the gold was but a small part of a collection of luxury objects and materials. The Staffordshire Hoard contained nothing but gold, silver and gems.

Originating at 'the very highest levels of Saxon aristocracy or royalty', said Kevin Leahy, the Hoard could not simply be loot. Perhaps it was a collection of trophies, from a battle or a successful military career, offered to pagan gods or hidden for safety. Helen Geake, another Portable Antiquities Scheme early medieval adviser, wondered if it derived from a victory by King Penda, burying the symbolic might of his enemy. Martin Carver proposed that it might have been a high-level compensation or peace payment (weregild); it is recorded that Oswiu, king of Northumberland, tried to buy off Penda's aggression with 'an incalculable and incredible treasure' in AD 655 (Penda sniffed at the offer, only to be killed by Oswiu). For Nicholas Brooks, a medieval historian, the Hoard was a royal treasury, swollen by weapons or bullion bequeathed to a king by nobles (a form of tax known as heriot). John Preston, a journalist who had recently written a novel about the Sutton Hoo excavation, thought the Hoard had been stolen, not from royalty but from a cathedral treasury. The bottom line, however, was that no one knew. 'This has made us realise', wrote Geake, 'that we don't know anything like as much about the Anglo-Saxons as we thought we did. It really does represent a paradigm shift.'[10]

Chris's study confirmed that almost everything in the Hoard had belonged to fighting men. Hundreds of them: some old and wise, and some, like the younger Vikings slaughtered in Dorset, perhaps barely out of childhood. The metalwork's quality suggests that many of these men were powerful and wealthy, leaders in their fields. How

many knew each other, or were alive at the same time? Was everything picked up from a single battlefield? Or was it collected over
decades, a jumble of heirlooms, novelties, loot and merchandise?

Most of the objects are parts from sword or knife handles (hilts):
plates, rings and collars that had been wrapped around the grips, and
knobs or pommels from the tips. Some have copper-alloy innards,
and in one case there is a snapped-off fragment of the tang of an
iron blade, but otherwise these fittings are gold or silver, prised and
pulled off their wooden or horn handles. The simpler hilts came
from fighting knives with single cutting edges known by their Old
English name of seax (pronounced 'say-axe', like Seat, the Spanish
car brand). Sword handles were larger and more complex, with pro-
truding collars and plates – some under the pommel at the tip, and
some at the lower end above the blade. Both types of handle might
have had further decorative gold features.

The making and fitting of these parts, to create a handle to a
blade on which a man would trust his life, were challenging tasks
requiring considerable skill. But a functioning hilt was just the start.
The outer faces of the pommels and collars are crafted to an almost
unbelievable degree of minute precision and beauty. Every visible
surface is ornament, gold framing garnets carved to fit (in a technique known as cloisonné), set over gold foils textured to scatter light
back through the red mineral. The smiths also needed to understand
the symbols and characters of Anglo-Saxon mythology – pagan and
Christian – and to be capable of conveying them in metals and gems.
Like the biblical scribes in Monkwearmouth and Jarrow, they were
educated story-tellers serving a demanding audience.

Other items in the Hoard are few, though their fragments are
many. After years of conservation and refitting, well over 1,000
scraps of sheet silver with further strips and rivets, mostly gilded,
were determined to have come from a single helmet. Fighting men
kneel and posture in stamped bands than run round the head. Gilded
silver cheek-pieces, elaborately decorated with entwined animals,
hang at either side, and a crest with solid animal-head ends runs over
the top. It's too broken to rebuild, but a pair of spectacular reconstructions, made for the museums in Stoke and Birmingham, show
it as the greatest known example of its kind, with a dramatic red-dyed
horsehair crest, flashing gold in the dimmest light. Surely worn by a
king (a word many archaeologists are reluctant to use), it must once

have been the most precious, famed thing in the Hoard, no less than a crown. It had been reduced to shreds.

There are two small gold buckles, and one silver. There is the great gold cross, displaying wondrous beasts with mounts that once held large gems. A smaller gold cross with a garnet at the centre like a glistening peeled plum probably once hung around the neck of a senior member of the Church. There are three pairs of little solid-gold serpents, and other indeterminate gold and silver fittings that may have been taken from book covers. I have mentioned the inscribed silver-gilt strip, folded in half with a gem setting at one end. And the rest is noise: hundreds of gold or silver rivets, washers, nails, brackets, indecipherable scraps and fragments, and loose gems.

If all this, to those who buried it, was a sacrifice to gods or politics, what was their loss? What the gods' gain? Who died if each sword was once owned by an élite warrior? If bullion, for what might it have been exchanged? Or if scrap, what might smiths, in their imaginations, have made with it for new clients?

It's unlikely the original smiths worked alone. Chris's study revealed several parts with fine scratch marks that would have been hidden in the complete objects. They had been made to record how components fitted together, by, he thinks, one craftsperson telling another how to proceed, suggesting workshops with apprentices. Neither were smiths the only hands involved in the Hoard's production.

The minuscule red garnets that decorate the gold are hard minerals of varying colour, difficult to acquire and shape. Analysis has identified large garnets from India and small ones from Bohemia in the Czech Republic, and compared with typical cloisonné work elsewhere in Europe, the Staffordshire garnets are purer. Some of them at least are likely to have been reused from objects already in circulation, selected with perfectionist care.

Occasionally, red glass has replaced a missing garnet. In other rare cases, glass was part of the original work: blue or green shapes adding variety to a carpet of red, or tiny millefiori panels, showing red, blue or white squares. This is the first time this complex process has been seen in apparently new Anglo-Saxon glasswork, rather than in recycled Roman material.

A scrap of textile preserved in a hilt collar turned out to be linen, perhaps from a wrapping cloth. A few silver and gold items encased fragments of horn or wood, the latter including ash, field maple and hornbeam. British Museum scientists identified animal and plant gum in the cloisonné work; analysis in Birmingham identified beeswax and calcium carbonate in the cells, the former thought to have helped correctly position garnets, the latter added to prevent the molten wax shrinking as it hardened. The niello, a black paste to highlight engravings, is silver sulphide, unusually found on silver as well as gold. And there is a mysterious green inlay that no one can identify.

All of these materials would have passed from sources to traders to workshops, to be handled and shaped by different artisans, and brought together by more. The Hoard is a repository of lives and skills. And the metal, of course, in such features as snake-like animal filigree made with gold wire less than half a millimetre thick, is evidence of astonishing craft and knowledge.

Gold is rarely entirely pure, being too soft to be at its most useful without a little alloying, typically with silver and copper. Most of the Hoard's gold is above 75 per cent pure (18 carat), characteristic of its time – and, indeed, of fine jewellery with stone settings today. A pioneering study, however, revealed a secret effect. Most of the gold had been treated to make it look purer than it really was, to enrich its surface colour, sometimes highlighting design features by leaving background gold unaltered. This was achieved by removing silver from the surface metal during manufacture, the first time the process has been seen on a large scale in Europe at this date.[11] Future research will tell us much new about the technology, craft and materials used.

While the last of these would ultimately have come from across Europe and beyond (French Merovingian coins probably being an important source of gold), the designs are firmly Scandinavian or Germanic. Academics still refer to styles of animal art defined in 1904 by Bernhard Salin, a Swedish archaeologist. The first evolved in late Roman times on the borders of the Empire. Romano-Brits saw and copied realistic images of buildings, animals and people, but Scandinavians developed more abstract representations of mythic creatures. Jewellery and weapons decorated in Salin's Style I feature people and animals taken apart and mixed with geometric shapes in a sort of alphabet soup, designs that could be read but only by those in the know.

Reaching England in the later 400s, Style I developed its own regional quirks, especially in metal brooches worn by women. The Hoard contains just a single pair of silver hilt collars in Style I. They are among the oldest pieces, for by 600 Style II had arrived from southern Scandinavia, with a more closely packed way of representing animals (often unidentifiable beasts known as zoomorphs) in curving interlaced lines. Some of the finest pieces from Sutton Hoo, where the great ship burial was probably for King Redwald who died in 624 or 625, are in Style II. The other dominant style in the Hoard, seen in most of the garnet-decorated cloisonné gold, is pure geometric.

Chris says the Hoard's contents were mostly made between 600 and 650. This seems to leave the inscribed strip, even by the older of the two proposed dates (650–700), out on a limb. However, its style and construction – notwithstanding the actual writing – is compatible with the rest of the Hoard, and Chris decided that it was the Hoard that should now date the inscription. Likewise, he would use the Hoard to date the Book of Durrow, an early illuminated gospel, to before 650, rather than after, as had previously been widely accepted. Like a great glowing ball dropped into the waters of early medieval England, the Staffordshire Hoard is unsettling all around it.

In *Beowulf*, as in the Hoard, swords figure prominently: stories of battles and the men they have killed are as precious as the gold on their hilts. Half way through the poem, having defeated the monster Grendel, who had been slaughtering warriors and innocent villagers alike, Beowulf kills Grendel's mother. He achieves this feat with an ancient sword he finds in her armoury. He might then have presented the weapon to his lord, or passed it on as an heirloom, to be wielded by new hands. But the blade melts away, dissolved by the beast's blood. All that remains is the golden handle, decorated with jewels and interlaced patterns.

Beowulf gives it to the king, Hrothgar, who examines it closely. Engravings tell how war first arrived, how the Lord sent a flood to drown the world (biblical themes lurk in the poem, as they do in the Hoard). Runes spell out the sword's first owner. Its glistening blade could have reflected back stories of its triumphs – but only the hilt was capable of telling them.

The swords whose fragments ended up in the Staffordshire Hoard were surely read by their owners in this way. Like Chris Fern, they would have known that a cast silver pommel with a bearded head on one face had been made in Scandinavia and was an antique – by the time of its burial it could have been over a century old. They would have recognized Salin's styles, and known that some pieces were newer than others. They would have understood that hilts came from different kingdoms: Chris sees most as East Anglian, with a few from northern England (for a while, until he found enough comparable material, the latter was simply 'the lost kingdom').

We might guess that Anglo-Saxon warriors and smiths would have read more than this, whether to identify (wrongly, perhaps, in hopeful awe) a particular craftsman or king, or the history of a weapon that had changed hands and travelled across England. Who knows what stories were once evoked by the animals and imagery hidden in the gold and gems, partly carried by the designs, partly by association? But this artistry is far from silent for us. And no one in modern times, I think, has come closer to understanding it than Chris Fern – now working with George Speake, drawn too by the Hoard's riddling radiance.

The ornamentation is tiny. If you see pieces in books or on your screen, they are often hugely enlarged. In exhibitions, the objects are accompanied by great blown-up photos, or viewed under bright light through enlarging lenses. Chris admits to using a magnifying glass, mostly to look at microscopic aspects of manufacture, such as solder marks on filigree wires. Otherwise, he tells me, he can see the art instantly just by looking. The Hoard's craftsmanship is 'fundamentally an intimate art'.

There is purpose in this privacy, these miniature galleries that fit in the hand. From a distance, a gold-ornamented sword speaks of a warrior aristocrat – a man to target and to fear; as you approach you see more, and you might, for example, realize your opponent's allegiances. To see the detail, however, you'd need to be as close to the weapon as its owner, at the point of the capture or death of you or him: art and story-telling as taunt and danger.

It was recognized early on that five superbly crafted gold fittings came from a single seax handle. A collar for the base has a slot for the blunt-backed steel blade, and another at the top, in three parts, for the tip of the tang to which a gold pommel was attached with a concealed pin. The quality of the garnet cloisonné compares with the best at Sutton Hoo. The faces of each collar are divided into panels, four at the top, two at the base, by strips of perfectly fitted interlocking little garnets. The panels contain eight creatures, four above and four below, exquisitely drawn with around 120 individually carved gems. Each knotted and limbed snake – these are anonymous zoomorphs – has an eye made with a minute drop of red glass.

An entire beast in the top row is no more than 15 millimetres (½ inch) across. To see it you have to examine the hilt like Hrothgar, but I need a translator. Apart from a head identified by the glass eye, it looks like abstract knotwork, and only Chris's enlarged drawing and explanation – there is the body, there a hind leg – convinces me, I think, that this is an animal. In another piece, one of the two cast silver-gilt helmet cheek-flaps, a writhing mass of creatures tumble in four stripes, like animated rainbows. With no glass eyes to guide me, separating one animal from another is hard. Even with Chris's diagrams, I struggle to understand everything he sees – twenty-six creatures, he claims, including ten serpents and a beast with a bird's beak, a serpent's head and the body of, perhaps, a horse or a wolf. On a pair of pyramid fittings made for a sword scabbard, two lizard-like birds in cloisonné garnets sit face to face; but the design, says Chris, can also be read as the head of a helmeted warrior.

A love of riddles is consistent with what we know from Anglo-Saxon literature, and distinguishes English art of the time from other parts of Europe. But the metalwork is about more than animal-spotting.

Most of the sword pommels are cocked-hat shaped, with a flattened triangular panel on each of the two main sides. One pommel, argues Chris, features a pair of garnet cloisonné fighting horses (the educated eye can see that what at first look like entwined snakes are in fact the stallions' front legs). On the other face, by contrast, is a geometric design, rounded arches and triangular pediments flanked by crosses. On the end of a lethal, golden-hilted sword, pagan and Christian celebration lie back to back.

Likewise, the arms of the overtly Christian great gold cross are decorated with lovely entwined animals, classic pagan beasts with which one finds a parallel at Sutton Hoo – where extravagant pagan ceremony and regalia are accompanied by a few Christian artefacts – so close as to make a common pattern almost certain. Warriors have always carried their gods with them into war, says Chris. Christian-era armour bore crosses, pre-Christian arms fantastic creatures that

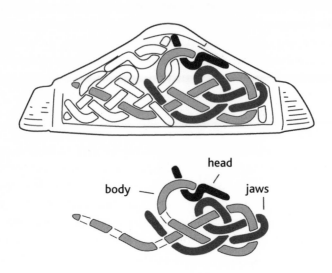

body — head jaws

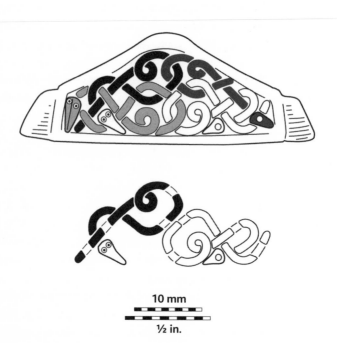

10 mm

½ in.

Filigree zoomorphs (above, top) and serpents (above) on opposite faces of a gold sword pommel, in standard schematic designs drawn and identified by Chris Fern.

people believed could protect them. At a time when faiths were in flux, such animals were transferred onto the gold cross as marks of power.

If we can recognize Christian symbols in the Hoard, another example being a golden fish, pagan ones are more prominent. Birds are likely to represent ravens or eagles, associated with the god Woden, as were boars. Serpents echo the monsters in *Beowulf*, and in literature can also be linked to magic and medicine. Two fighting horses might be Hengist and Horsa, the founding figures of Anglo-Saxon England. And at a simple level, says Chris, this art was meant to entertain.

It is deliberately asymmetric, he says, making it more pleasing to the brain. Figuring it out brings its own mental gratification, as we might enjoy a crossword or a puzzle. Combining this with sacred beliefs and wider narratives inspires you to think about what it means. The art was 'a strategy for legitimizing power for those who understood it'. Its 'complexity and genius', adds Chris, saying his life's work has been dedicated to trying to uncover its power, 'is to a large extent under-appreciated'.

I've referred to but a handful of objects from the Hoard, but we need to remember there are hundreds. Each must have had its own stories and associations, to be understood fully only by a few. As the items were collected, and then buried, much of this was lost. But new myths were created, and it is to this we finally turn: the story of a hoard.

*

We can separate the burial of the Hoard from the acts of collecting what went into it, something that was less obvious in 2009. This is fundamental to how we read it. The early focus was on Mercian history, on battles, warrior élites and the growth of a kingdom that controlled well over half of what was to become England. This offers essential context for the making and use of things in the Hoard; but it may have less to do with why it was buried. The distinction will prove of great help when we try to understand it.[12]

We have seen how most objects in the Hoard can be dated to between 600 and 650: some were made in the early 600s, many of them later. A few others probably survive from the later 500s, including the pommel with the bearded head and other silver items, and the Style I collars. Significantly, these older pieces are more worn. If everything had been collected around the time it was made – on a succession of battlefields, say – we'd expect all pieces to be in more or less the same condition. The pattern of wear, however, suggests well-handled heirlooms that saw action beside less ancient pieces.

This gives us our first insight into the Hoard, suggesting it came together over a relatively short time. Could it all have been collected at once? Probably not. First, so much treasure is unlikely to have been wielded on a single battlefield: as well as the exquisite goldwork, requiring luxury materials and exceptional skills, there would have been far larger amounts of forged steel, delivered by quite different smiths with their own highly valued talents and reputations. There could only have been so many élites in one battle.

Furthermore, Chris believes that decorative styles suggest different regional origins, most simply explained by a number of aggressive encounters across the length of eastern England, from Northumbria (Yorkshire and further north) to Kent. And there's another thing: the Hoard may have been buried in the centre of Mercia, but what's in it was not made there. It seems to be a haul of military treasures brought together over a few decades, between 630 and 650 perhaps, through seizure and tribute by Mercian armies from eastern neighbours.[13]

We are then faced with the inescapable fact that between around 625 and 655, Mercia expanded its territory and strengthened its identity under one of Anglo-Saxon England's most successful warring kings: Penda. We may be looking at material derived from a royal treasury, accumulated in a period of successful political sparring. Some of the gold mounts, a pair of eagles flanking a fish for example, may have been on shields. The great gold cross, with its East Anglian beasts, could have been carried by a Christian army defeated by a pagan one – a possible scene involving Mercians and Anglians at this time.

The collected weapons would have taken on a whole new repertoire of meanings and stories, symbolizing new-won allies and the dead and defeated of enemies. In *Beowulf*, Hrothgar builds a great hall (archaeologists have found many examples of the timber foundations of such halls), gleaming with gold. Perhaps somewhere in Mercia was a royal hall resplendent with the glittering swords and seaxes of alien aristocracies, a gallery of spoils growing with its owner's power.

What happened next is altogether different. The absence of anything in the Hoard more recent than 650 suggests that collecting ceased at that time. Perhaps within twenty or thirty years, we can only guess, with the kingdom under a new peace or ruled with changing ambitions, the purpose of the shining military display passed. If we take the proposed association with Penda literally, the treasures might even have been hastily stripped from hall walls in 655, when news arrived that the king (and, according to Bede, nearly all his thirty 'royal commanders') had been slain at the Battle of the Winwaed. The hoard's value had turned from associations to bullion.[14]

Hilts were stripped from blades, to be recycled in different workshops. The delicate gold and garnet cloisonné is spattered with cuts, rips and scars from pliers used to tear the metal from wooden and horn grips: 'No respect', says Chris, 'was shown for the craftsmanship at all.' Silver, gold and garnets were randomly bundled together; the gems would later float in the goldsmiths' crucibles and could be picked out easily. The only care shown, perhaps, was to bag up the tiniest pieces of metal, mostly silver and many from the helmet, which had been sliced with total disregard for its artistry and power. This is one explanation for the metal-studded soil lumps, which might have been a layer of hard earth at the bottom of a pit, raised and fractured centuries later by the plough.

The presence of so many tiny pieces is a powerful argument against the items having been taken in the heat of battle. The Hoard was merely precious metal awaiting recycling. By analogy with Viking hoards of scrap silver, we might call it hack-gold. Viking hack-silver can consist of anything from ingots and coins to Roman dishes, the larger pieces cut up for ease of carrying. A Viking hoard found recently by a metal detectorist near Harrogate, Yorkshire, had been buried inside a silver-gilt cup, and, along with ingots, arm rings and bits of brooches, contained 617 coins, mostly from Anglo-Saxon and Viking England but also from France and the Middle East.

The absence of coins in the Staffordshire Hoard indicates to some that it was not scrap. This can be explained, however, if we imagine the story I have outlined, in which weapons were taken down from the walls of a hall. Though these had been accumulated over time, the Hoard itself was put together, perhaps literally, overnight. This could also account for another puzzling feature of the Hoard. While hundreds of swords and knives are represented, there are few other parts of a fighting man's kit – belt buckles, so spectacular at Sutton Hoo, and scabbard fittings. This again could be explained by the Hoard's manner of collection. Swords and knives, rich in story and symbol, were retained and displayed. Baldrics had been taken apart and recycled long before the hilts were stripped for the Hoard.

It is a curious fact that the nearest settlement to the burial site was Hammerwich, a village whose name may commemorate a smithy: 'hammer' suggests metalworking, and 'wich' is a common Anglo-Saxon suffix associated with industrial and trading towns. Curiously, the only other early medieval artefact found in the Hoard field after all the searching was a metal object of the same age as the most recent items in the Hoard. Three pieces of a decorated copper-alloy horse-harness fitting were found a hundred metres away from the Hoard site. They had been kicking around in the ploughsoil for some time, and could be all that survives of another, smaller smith's hoard.[15]

\*

At Sutton Hoo the body of a man was laid in a ship and equipped with everything that marked him as a powerful leader in the afterlife. He had his shield, sword and helmet, but arranged around him – on his bed, on the floor and walls of the ship's chamber – was so much more, from cauldrons, feasting dishes and vessels to a lyre and board game, treasures from across the known world. Not everyone was buried in a ship. At Prittlewell, Essex, a tomb for an unknown king or lord was excavated in 2003. A square room had been created underground, filled with arranged luxuries.[16]

Such graves are the silent residues of great colourful ceremonies of remembrance, mourning and the assertion of power, and of drama and saga. By contrast, the secret burial of the Staffordshire Hoard was a dying scream, the uncaring destruction of stories and art. But as the pieces once evoked kingdoms, battles and deeds, so recreated they speak to us of another world: of stunning craft and design, of fish and ravens, of the roots in these isles of Christianity and nationhood, and the origins of England.

We saw how the art drew inspiration from across the seas, from France to Scandinavia. This was not just a flow of ideas. Materials came from a yet wider area, and people were on the move too. Archaeology, languages and place names, DNA (considered in the last chapter), history, even – all show significant numbers of new settlers arriving in Britain at this time. The smiths' crucibles held more than gold and silver: they melded traditions and affirmed identities in changing times.

But whose identities? According to the children's book I quoted in the previous chapter, this was an era of little kingdoms where people kept close to home, and led happy, simple lives, an idyll broken only by the arrival of Vikings. It's a pervasive myth created over a century ago that lies behind many of our ideas of ancient Britain: a timeless, unchanging place of honest superstition and empathy with nature, stripped of the worst excesses of barbarity by four centuries of Roman rule. A land of daffodils and roses, unsullied by strange flowers.

Without archaeology, such a vision could never be disproved, though an understanding of human nature might have made one suspicious. But we now have the fruits of a century of scientific excavation boosted by an explosion of new discoveries and analytical techniques. As we continue back into the past, freed from myth, we find worlds whose complexity is matched only by their unsettling strangeness. Roman London, our next stop, though only a few centuries before the England of the Staffordshire Hoard, was a very different place.

Chapter 3

# Roman Occupation

*London,* AD *45–400*

A thriving city grows like an ant heap. It needs stone and timber for its buildings beyond anything it can find within its limits. It imports materials for industry, often from great distances. More people walk its streets than live or were born there. Goods are also exported and people leave, but with time and decay, the city gains more than it loses. One generation's walls become the rubble foundations of another's. Every leather offcut, rusted nail, broken cup and lost penny finds its way into the teeming earth. Slowly, imperceptibly, the ground rises, covering the traces of the past even as the city buries its dead in the crumbled memories of its ancestors.

Fire and war speed the process. Deep across the City of London are layers of red earth littered with the remains of burnt buildings and artefacts, indications of two conflagrations that devastated the Roman city. When fire swept London in September 1666, it left 100,000 people homeless, having brought down the places where they lived, worked and worshipped. The city heaved a great breath, thousands of tonnes of building materials were carted in, and new walls rose on the levelled debris.

Nothing, however, changed the London ant heap as dramatically as the Second World War. On the night of 10 May 1941, bombing disrupted 8,000 streets; over 1,400 people died, and a further 1,800 were seriously injured. In one city block, a triangle part way between St Paul's Cathedral and the Bank of England, there had been over 350 businesses: accountants, cafés, a bookseller, a tailor, a dentist and more – even a postage-stamp perforator – crammed into a warren of high Victorian terraces and narrow alleys. After the fire of that night, only a few buildings at the tips of the triangle survived, guarding a hollow core of fallen girders and smoking ruins between Queen Victoria Street and Walbrook. This is where, in 2017, Bloomberg, a New York-based financial media company, opened its new European headquarters.

Walbrook takes its name from a minor Thames tributary. It was bridged and channelled in the Roman city and now seeps through mud and forgotten drains deep below the streets. Its filled valley, passing straight through the centre of both Roman and modern London, is – where not removed by foundations, basements and tunnels – an unmatched archive of lives and work across nearly two millennia. By permanently excluding oxygen, the stream's waters have preserved wood and other remains that normally perish. When Queen Victoria Street was built in 1869, a Roman mosaic was discovered that caused a public sensation: 10,000 people queued daily to see it, and it's now a prized exhibit in the Museum of London. When the walls came down on Walbrook in 1941, a great window was opened onto this subterranean story. Peter Grimes was waiting.

A famously charming, skilled archaeologist, Grimes was head of what was then the London Museum, but he also had a spare-time job as director of an excavation council set up by archaeologists to exploit opportunities offered by bomb sites. He knew this one had great promise, and when an architect tipped him off about coming works – completed in 1957, Bucklersbury House would be one of the city's largest post-war office developments – he mobilized his volunteers.

In spring 1952, picking their way around bombed foundations and weed-covered rubble, the archaeologists laid out their trenches and found the Walbrook – a small stream 4 metres (13 feet) across. It had preserved Roman wooden floors, gutters and drains; an old pipe still worked, helping to flood the excavations. And in one trench, after hammering through a concrete basement floor by hand, they found standing Roman masonry.

# Chapter 3

It was not until late 1954 that they were able to return and expand the excavation. They uncovered the lower walls and foundations of a complete temple, with a rounded apse at its west end and a straight façade looking directly onto the Walbrook street at the other. Inside had been two colonnades, whose parallel rows of seven pillars were indicated by circular base stones.

This was reward enough, but there was more. Out of the mud came the greatest group of sculptures from Roman Britain. Marble fragments ranged from a huge hand to a head, of a handsome, foppish young man with a distinctive soft cap folded down over his curled hair. He was Mithras, the focus of a mysterious cult popular with Roman soldiers. The temple had been a Mithraeum, where male rituals originating in Persia were practised under the gaze of a sacred bull with a dagger in its flank and a scorpion nipping at its genitals. City workers queued in their thousands to see the dig. The press waged a fruitless campaign to save the temple from development, and excavation continued only with the intervention of the prime minister, Winston Churchill.[1]

From then on, whatever else might remain of the Walbrook's waterlogged deposits and anything linked to the temple lay buried deep beneath Bucklersbury House. Until one day, in 2010, another developer knocked it down.

*

Peter Grimes managed to record the Mithraeum through luck and public pressure. He had no legal right to be there. The developer allowed a few extra days' excavation and pledged to rebuild the temple foundations within the new office block (they ended up at street level above a car park, wrongly orientated, a Mithraic cave transformed into a weed-grown pavement ornament collecting food wrappers wafted up by passing buses). With this gesture the government could save face, claiming a solution to the problem without having to find vast sums to compensate for construction changes and delays.

It was a warning to businesses and the authorities – don't uncover spectacular ancient remains. For decades, archaeologists across the UK struggled to record the nation's heritage as new roads and buildings ploughed it away, relying on diplomacy, media pressure and the co-operation of developers to gain access to construction sites. Then, in 1989, it happened again. This time it was Shakespeare's Rose Theatre, discovered during another London office development.

As before, the government was powerless in the face of huge compensation bills; after a public stand-off, archaeologists were allowed in and adjustments were made so that remains could be preserved in the new basement. But now, in keeping with the times – and the howls of celebrity actors – things changed. Under new planning policy, developers would pay archaeologists to record a site's remains before construction began. Thanks to this, archaeologists are now part of the system, working beside engineers, demolition contractors and builders. The policy led to the discovery of an ancient atrocity near Weymouth, and it brought well-prepared archaeologists to the Bloomberg site in London. But, as Sadie Watson told me, however much you plan, 'You can't imagine what you're gonna find.'[2]

Sadie directed the excavations at Bloomberg. She's a project officer at MOLA (Museum of London Archaeology), an experienced, skilled archaeologist whose work around the UK and beyond ranges from producing tenders and liaising with builders and councils to researching and excavating. I meet her at her desk in an enormous archaeological store in Hackney. Almost everything now dug up in London – apart from human remains, which are curated by a separate Bioarchaeology Centre – ends up here.

Anticipating future development, MOLA had evaluated Bucklersbury in the mid-1990s, to see what might still survive; Sadie calls such work 'e-vals', which in this case consisted of looking at the results of earlier investigations in the area. At that time, they were digging on a large building plot just to the north, across Queen Victoria Street where No. 1 Poultry now rises like a post-modern Titanic ploughing the city waves. Among the waterlogged timber, with unusual details of centuries of Roman building, industry, fires and demolition, they found a wooden writing tablet whose last message could be read. Inscribed around AD 100, it was a deed of sale for a slave-girl from northern France called Fortunata, described much as we might list a pet dog (named Lucky), in good health and guaranteed not to run off. She cost 600 *denarii*, the equivalent of two years' pay for a Roman soldier – and she was bought by another, more powerful slave.

Archaeologists, then, had high expectations of the Bucklersbury site. Planning consent for offices and shops was first granted in 2007, with a probably unique item (described between an underground train station, and servicing and plant) among the approved floor spaces: Temple of Mithras (643 square metres/6,900 square feet). To comply with Historic England's listing, which gives protection to historic buildings, the developer proposed to move the remains into a new permanent exhibition.

All that – along with much archaeological work across London that MOLA was hoping to pick up – was wiped out by the recession. Bloomberg stepped in at the end of 2010, acquiring the site and appointing Norman Foster as its architect. The new design would be architecturally more ambitious, notably upping its local engagement. Rising 41 metres (135 feet) above street level, it was a little lower than Bucklersbury (which broke a London record at the time) and half the height of the recession-victim tower proposed earlier. Two triangular blocks would be separated by a retail passage on the line of a Roman road. And down in the basement, back in its proper place, the Temple of Mithras would be treated to a larger 835 square metres (9,000 square feet) and further displays.

The planning application was approved in March 2012. By then, MOLA had already spent time at the site. On her screen, Sadie brings up some black-and-white photos of the 1950s development. They show a gaping hole in the ground. The just-excavated temple is perched on a cliff edge, and the pit below swarms with men in cloth caps, shirt-sleeves and cardigans. Around the edge are what Sadie calls blocks of standing archaeology, where thick, dark deposits still remain, undisturbed by previous building. In 2012, thanks to the e-vals, she knew that much of those deposits were still there.

Sadie had narrowed her sights on the plot's northeast corner, where the deepest layers survived. There was to be a new entrance to Bank Underground station, another planning requirement for Bloomberg. A great inverted L-shape would be dug out deep into the underlying gravel by London Underground Limited. This was where MOLA conducted its main excavation, on and off between July 2012 and May 2013. They called it the LUL box. The prospect was the most exciting to greet London's archaeologists for decades.

Empty offices were being taken down around them as they worked. It's difficult to imagine conditions less like those enjoyed by the archaeologists in the Dorset countryside. A priority for McGee, the demolition contractor, was to ensure that Walbrook (the street) didn't fall into the excavation, taking with it the lovely St Stephen Walbrook, one of Christopher Wren's best churches. They supported the back of the trench against the street with a steel wall, braced by huge tubular props spanning the corner. More props were added as the ground fell to as much as 15 metres (50 feet) below pavement level.

Following the remains down, the archaeologists moved back in time, uncovering progressively older deposits. The builders of Bucklersbury House had removed higher layers, and with them all but the most ancient history; almost at once, MOLA was in London as it was before AD 200. Everything else, including later Roman material, had been machined away in the 1950s and dumped somewhere in Essex.

The early city was built of timber. MOLA expected a lot of finds, and pumped up the conservation budget. 'But,' says Sadie, 'we were still overwhelmed.' Why so much stuff?

By the time the dig was done, they had excavated Roman layers an exceptional 7 metres (23 feet) thick, and sifted 3,500 tonnes of earth. They found substantial building remains, mostly wood, a haul of international significance in its own right. Where people lived or worked, you also find refuse and industrial waste – unattractive as that sounds, it's the sort of informative material archaeologists crave – but that alone does not explain what happened at Bloomberg. The people of Londinium had dumped cartloads of landfill in the valley. Some of this was to create solid, level foundations for buildings; some of it probably just needed to be out of the way. And with it all came not just dirt, but the debris and litter of a thriving city. The LUL box was like a library of random news from across Roman London – 'the Pompeii of the north', as the *Evening Standard*, London's oldest daily paper, called it. And that, Sadie tells me, was not what they had expected.

Very large sums of money are committed to a development like Bloomberg's. In a mind-bogglingly complex programme that brings together many specialist contractors and consultants, time is critical. Archaeologists respect this: they do not want to delay construction. Thus coping with the unexpected wealth of what they uncovered was a challenge. It was Sadie's job to sort it out.

Sadie had fifty or sixty staff on site, all graduates. Most were on contracts only for the project's duration, and most came from outside London – half from the UK and half beyond, mainly but not only from the EU (at a London dig during the 2012 Olympics, the archaeologists joked that they could run site tours in every language represented at the games). Diggers gather for one project and move on to the next, giving an excavation the feel of a drama production, a temporary community of skilled enthusiasts on a story-telling quest where friendships are made and discoveries shared. Bloomberg was a once-in-a-lifetime job. Bloomberg was Broadway.

Sadie faced long delays while shoring and props were installed. The archaeologists were further slowed by rain and snow over a freezing winter, working under a tent roof that was more for the protection of remains than staff. They would start the day by pumping out water, sometimes having to break ice first. When the pumps couldn't cope, they just dug underwater. At the deeper levels, circular concrete piles of the old Bucklersbury House rose up in the confined space like elongated versions of the eggs on the floor of the derelict spaceship in the film *Alien*. By the time they had finished, these reached far above the diggers' heads, enveloping them in a dark forest under the tent.

'We were hacking through stuff,' says Sadie. 'We had twenty-six weeks – we took twenty-seven in the end. We just worked longer hours.' They dug at night in shifts, emerging onto Cannon Street covered in mud, rediscovering the passing world of a modern city. Sadie organized weekly meetings at which the diggers could tell each other what they were doing, what they had found. 'Normally,' she says, 'one person, one nice find. Here everyone finds nice things every day.' She installed a covered on-site processing area, where finds were triaged, hosed down in bulk or treated like antique jewellery (some *were* antique jewellery), stored in bins, laid out in trays, or removed immediately to a secure lab.

And so they worked the LUL box through a cold, wet winter, dozens of archaeologists squeezed into the concrete forest, uncovering all manner of things last seen when Britain was under Roman administration. London was already the most extensively and expertly excavated capital in the empire outside Rome. Yet the dig put unprecedented stuff into the Hackney store. The Bloomberg HQ now has an extraordinary archaeological gallery – both building and gallery have won awards – and the Roman displays in the Museum of London will have to be updated. This turned out to be the most productive single excavation of a British Roman site in modern times. London's earliest history has been rewritten in scribbled Latin.

\*

'Pompeii of the north' was a throw-away remark from an excited archaeologist, but it has a grain of truth. Though no Roman citizens died in the LUL box, as so many did at Pompeii, buildings were entombed, in this case by the actions of Londoners who periodically dumped earth and rubbish over the whole area and then laid out new buildings. Combined with the very British effects of waterlogging (not generally found at Pompeii), the result is a sequence of snapshots – of rooms, walls, fences, paths and yards that we can be certain were in use together, along with the things found among them. And for reasons that will become clear, we can be almost as precise in dating the sequence as we can be in saying the year in which Pompeii was destroyed.

There was no London at all before Rome invaded in AD 43.[3] The Thames then was twice its modern width. High tides flooded further large areas of marsh and mudflat, exposing temporary islands when they fell. People had been trading with the continent for generations, particularly from harbours in east Dorset and Hampshire protected by the Isle of Wight (where, perhaps, were it not for the Roman Conquest, our capital city might now be). But no great Iron Age town claimed this eastern waterscape, thought to have been a boundary between kingdoms or tribes with capitals elsewhere. Silchester in Hampshire, St Albans in Hertfordshire, Colchester in Essex and Canterbury in Kent, all to become Roman towns, were already – unlike London – prehistoric centres of power and trade.[4]

Starting at Bloomberg's lowest and oldest levels, the story begins with a bit of Roman ground-levelling and some simple banks and ditches. These marked out an area in which at least one of the activities was metalworking, indicated by copper-alloy sheet clippings, unfinished castings, fire-pits and slag. A head of Mercury cast as a steelyard weight may have been made there, and an unfinished

figurine showing the abduction of Ganymede – another unmistak-
ably Roman-inspired image – was probably brought in with landfill.

Further south, down towards Cannon Street, Sadie found oak
piles, great tree trunks hammered into the wet ground to support
a bridge over the Walbrook, at least 6.3 metres (20 feet) wide. Tree-
ring dating tells us this bridge was built sometime between AD 48
and 61. Named Road 12 by MOLA archaeologists, the route has been
identified in other excavations; it was perpetuated by the 18th-century
Watling Street and Budge Row, and is now reflected in the layout
of Bloomberg's HQ.[5] Just beyond the site to the north is a larger,
parallel road (Road 1). This was the main east–west route through
the early town, continuing west towards Silchester (Roman Calleva
Atrebatum). When archaeologists excavated part of this road on the
No. 1 Poultry site, they found a timber drain underneath it that had
been cut from a tree felled in the winter of AD 47–48 – the earliest
date yet for London.

Imagine these two roads, crossing the stream on bridges engineered from oak poles and carpentered timbers, creaking with
pedestrians, carts and animals. The town is young. It overlooks the
river from a small hill above a single crossing, where London Bridge
is now, and at this stage the Walbrook marks its western boundary.[6]
There is no city wall – there is little masonry of any kind. Grand
public buildings, such as baths, temples, a theatre or a market place
that we might think of as essential parts of a Roman city, do not yet
grace its compact street grid. Who are these people hunkered down
in the damp of the Walbrook, or passing busily overhead? In a city
less than ten years old, none but the children can have been born
there. What language – or languages – do they speak? How do they
dress? Are they Romans? Are they Britons?

There was no great living there, over the century or so it took for
the preserved deposits to accumulate, but the city sent some of its
finest refuse into the valley. Some 15,000 artefacts were of sufficient
interest to be individually bagged and numbered, including Roman
London's largest collection of leatherwork, with some 250 shoes in
a variety of styles. More finds were carted off in bulk, among them
2.5 tonnes of animal bone and 2 tonnes of pottery.

There's a lot of nice glasswork and ceramics, pieces of fine
wooden furniture, a panelled door, a large willow basket, a chicken
wing-bone showing a healed break (the bird was nonetheless later

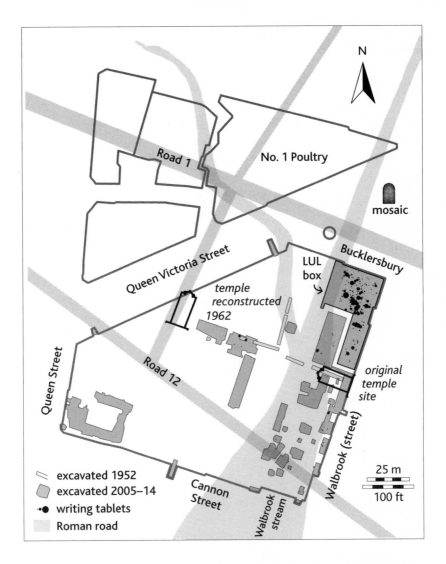

The Bloomberg site (lower polygon; others had been investigated previously), showing excavated areas with ancient remains, the Roman temple and the places where over 400 Roman writing tablets were found (larger dots, more tablets); courses of the Walbrook in early Roman times and of the Roman roads are partly conjectural. Data from MOLA.

eaten) and fragments of painted wall plaster. Pewter bowls and cattle heads were thrown into abandoned wells. There are egg cases, found in a bakery, from cockroaches that made their way to London from the Mediterranean or Africa. There's a tiny amber amulet in the form of a masked gladiator head that might have been carved in Italy. There's a fine and rare copper-alloy flask. Made in several components and decorated with distinctive Celtic-style coloured enamels, it probably held imported perfume or oils; only a dozen are known from the entire empire, all probably made in Britain. The best, however, is yet to come. It does so first in the words of a concerned citizen: 'They are boasting through the whole market', a writer warns a man called Titus the poultry-keeper, 'that you have lent them money. Therefore I ask you, in your own interest, not to appear shabby. You will not thus favour your own affairs.'

The wooden tablet preserving this Latin message was discarded between AD 43 and 53. Remembering the tree-ring date linked to a key road suggesting the town had begun by 48, when Titus received his telling-off London may have been no more than five years old. And the message was about finance.

Some of the words are missing and the sense is not always clear; *turpis*, like the English 'shabby', could have meant scruffy or dishonourable. But I can't help thinking of my Dad, who started off as a poultry-keeper, and like all business people spent considerable time worrying about where the money was coming from. That was not a traditional way of doing things in Britain in AD 50.

There would certainly have been exchanges, gifts, tributes and debts, in an atmosphere of socially prescribed rules. There were coins too, first appearing two centuries before as the idea rippled out from the Classical world and into southeast England. How they were used is unknown. In places like the Dorset coast, where there was Channel trade, it seems likely that coins served commerce. Perhaps mostly, however, they expressed wealth and power, their shiny gold and silver faces stamped with religious and political symbols of identity. In Iron Age Britain successful leaders hoarded gold, from around 50 BC writing their names on their coins – AM, ANT, TIN, VER, mnemonic abbreviations for an illiterate audience.[7] In the new town of London, by contrast, wealth was in what you could lend, and you worried not about the look of money but the bureaucratic account of your dealings.

Titus's tablet, a slice of wood on which his message is inscribed, is exactly the size and thickness of my old iPhone. A raised border surrounds a flat rectangle into which beeswax, darkened with lamp-black, was poured and hardened. Words were written into the wax with a needle-point stylus, exposing pale wood below. Two or three tablets were commonly tied together with string, and they were mostly bearers of short legal or financial documents.

The Bloomberg archaeologists looked for tablets. It was difficult. The artefacts were small, fragile and the colour of mud, and without the rims, which had often broken off, they looked like carpentry waste. MOLA expected a handful: they recovered 405. This is far more than had been found in London before, and the eighty with legible texts compare with a previous nineteen from the whole city. They also found some two hundred iron styluses and a number of spatulas, which would have been heated to smooth wax. The collection is of international significance.

Sadie was extremely fortunate – as are we all – to have Roger Tomlin on hand to decipher the slivers of wood. An elegant Oxford Fellow in his seventies, Roger has studied just about every hand-written Roman text found. Wax survives even less than tablets, but the stylus left marks in the wood. The writing is fluid and informal, often without spaces between words, and, in intermittent scraps, is particularly hard to read. Worse, tablets were recycled. Beneath a clear message in a smooth sheet of wax lurked the fractured scribblings of earlier missives – and the latter are all that remain. And anything that *can* be read is in Latin – sometimes abbreviated, sometimes grammatically incorrect.

The tablets were conserved by a standard process of replacing the water in the wood cells with polyethylene glycol ('peg') followed by freeze-drying – made for wax, saved by wax. Roger looked at them before this was done. He picked out a hundred, which were photographed by Andy Chopping with low light shining from a variety of directions to emphasize the shallow marks. In his well-lit antiquarian-artist den of books, Middle Eastern rugs, sculptures and watercolours, Roger examined the still-wet wood with a microscope and enlarged the photos on his laptop, turning his readings into drawings on a digital tablet. 'You have to have an imagination,' he says in a video, 'but' – and he gives a flicker of an impish smile – 'you must control it very rigidly.'[8]

Concrete piles from the 1950s rise over Roman timbers in an area dubbed 'the office' by archaeologists because of the many writing tablets found there.

Titus's is one of the twelve oldest tablets. Most convey little, but one is dated, to 8 January AD 57 ('on the sixth day before the Ides of January'). This is the first written date from Roman Britain, which is to say the country's first. Again, it's a financial document – the city's original IOU. Tibullus confirms that he will repay Gratus 105 *denarii* for merchandise he has sold on. We know no more about the lives of these men and their contemporaries. But we do know something that they don't. Many are about to die.

\*

There were sixty-odd towns in Roman Britain, of which about a third stood out as being of particular significance. They had varied origins and characters, and we know the names of most of them – or at least as they were written down in Latin. All have been partly excavated, some extensively, especially in those rarer cases where they were abandoned early and not built over. Three show a peculiar and distinctive feature. We know them today as Colchester, St Albans and London.

Wherever archaeologists have investigated these towns, there is evidence for great fires: reddened earth, the incinerated remains of house foundations, walls and roofs, and burnt and broken possessions. The fires can be dated by the artefacts among the debris, and in each case the coins, the styles of pottery and other diagnostic finds point to the same, quite precise era: between AD 50 and 70.

What could explain the coincidence of three such conflagrations? We have texts that suggest they were connected. In AD 60, we read, Camulodunum (Colchester), Verulamium (St Albans) and Londinium (London) were attacked and burnt to the ground.[9] The parallel evidence of archaeology and literature is too much to be dismissed as chance: it reveals the first event that can be confidently documented in both these ways, with Romans and Britons named. It is a story of deals with an empire based in the Mediterranean, an occupying force and an uprising in which thousands died. As we journey backwards into the past, this is the end of nearly two thousand years of testable recorded history, beyond which personalities and politics fade irretrievably into oblivion.

There are written accounts about Britain before AD 60, including descriptions of Julius Caesar's two invasions in 55 and 54 BC (of which the second and more successful attempt resulted in a treaty with a confederation of tribes in southeast England); of the conquest that began under Claudius in AD 43; and a wealth of detail about native customs, political incidents and tribal names and leaders. We would infer a Roman invasion even without literature and inscriptions, as the evidence for forts, soldiers, imported goods and Mediterranean-style buildings is overwhelming. But the revolt that led to the destruction of these three towns is the first occasion for which we can identify material in the ground with the actions of particular people at a particular time.

Tacitus, a perceptive Roman historian writing some fifty years after the events, tells us that emperor Nero was given the lands of the Iceni, a powerful kingdom in East Anglia, when their then leader, Prasutagus, died. Prasutagus had hoped to safeguard his family and property, but it didn't work: locally based Roman soldiers attacked his people and brutalized his daughters and his widow, Boudica. The queen sought revenge with an army garnered from an alliance

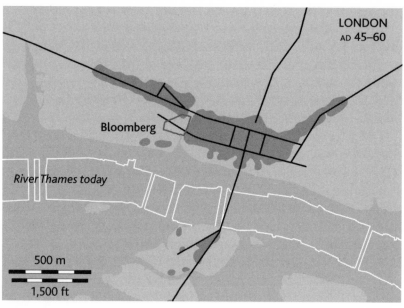

London before Boudica, AD 45–60. The Thames was tidal and is shown at high tide. Data from MOLA.

of oppressed kingdoms. Targeting Roman institutional buildings but sparing nothing or nobody in their way, they laid waste to Colchester and continued south towards London.

Suetonius Paulinus, the Roman governor of Britain, came to warn the city. It was a place of merchants and trading ships, says Tacitus, but the general abandoned those who wouldn't leave, or couldn't, to die – women, the old and the stubborn. Boudica then led her rebels out of London along Watling Street to repeat the slaughter and devastation in St Albans. The 14th Legion, which had been furiously marching east from Wales, finally caught up with her and annihilated her massed forces and encircling war chariots in a pitched battle. That's the last we hear of Boudica, who appears to have died then or soon after (efforts to locate the battlefield, or even the queen's grave, have failed).

Cassius Dio, writing of the incident a century after Tacitus, thought money was behind Boudica's rebellion: emperors had financed conquered élites, he says, and had decided to call in the

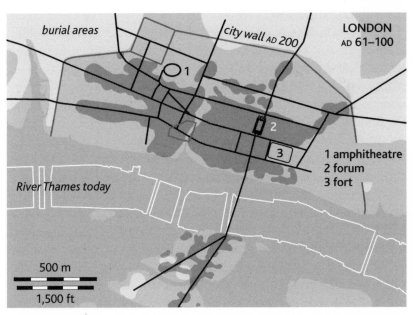

London AD 61–100, after Boudica's attack. The eventual Roman city is similar in area to the modern City; the course of the wall (with a fort in the northwest corner) meets the river at Blackfriars railway station to the west, and the Tower of London to the east. Data from MOLA.

debts. Meanwhile, before the Roman army met Boudica it had been on Anglesey suppressing a Druid revolt. It's all hearsay, but native protest was clearly in the air. London had been wiped out.

Titus, a money-lending, Latin-reading and -writing foreigner in a new town of unfamiliar architecture, dress and values, was perhaps just the kind of person Boudica had in mind when she rallied fighters in East Anglia. We can only guess if he survived the attack. Astonishingly, however, London and its business did. Quite how well was not realized until Roger Tomlin deciphered the other Bloomberg texts.

The wooden streets were easy targets for Boudica. Flames engulfed the town and spread beyond through roadside houses and workshops. We can't see the fire at Bloomberg – there were no buildings there yet to burn – but ditches silted up, suggesting a brief pause in activity. Whether the bridge survived or had to be replaced is not clear, but the stream bank below was revetted with timber. Then, over the next decade, the first landfill was brought in and two simple clay and timber buildings were erected on the platform. A boardwalk is tree-ring dated to AD 63.

The two buildings were buried beneath another layer of landfill, great oak frames were laid down to hold more earth, and further rubbish was dumped over these. A range of long buildings was raised in line with the frames. In one room was a circular bread oven, with outside hearths to fire it. Beside another was a wattle pen, perhaps for animals – the skeleton of a piglet lay nearby.

More dumping occurred. Posts were driven in to hold plank supports for the rising ground. More buildings followed, with hearths, storage pits and wells. Fence lines imply formal property divisions. More dumps, more buildings. Then around 90 or 100, a building went up on a different scale. A raised wooden floor covered much of the area. At first, Sadie thought it might have been part of a water mill; they found wooden gears, and other signs of a large mill had turned up in neighbouring excavations. But after analysing soil samples and a huge collection of butchered bone, especially from cattle, they decided it was more likely part of an abattoir or butcher's shop, draining its fluids into the fetid urban stream. And then, around AD 180, apart from the bottoms of wells and deep foundations dug from above through the earlier deposits, it all stops: Victorian cellars, Bucklersbury House and other developments had removed the rest.

Perhaps the first tablet to be written after Suetonius turned his back on the city bemoaned the fire. The first we have, however, is a contract.

On 21 October AD 62, Marcus Rennius Venustus confirmed that he had agreed that Gaius Valerius Proculus would bring him 'twenty loads of provisions' from Verulamium to Londinium by 13 November at a specified rate. Google Maps recommends driving this route along the M1, a meandering 26 miles (40 kilometres). On foot, however, two ruler-straight sections of what are now relatively minor roads will get you to the city in 21 miles (34 kilometres), or some seven hours: that's Watling Street.

We know, from Tacitus and archaeology, that Boudica had torched both towns, perhaps eighteen months before. This tablet bears unique witness to their apparently rapid recovery. Another tablet dated late in AD 64 records a slave, Florentinus, saying his master has received rental payments for a farm. Around the same time one Atticus pleaded 'by bread and salt' for 36 *denarii* to be sent urgently. Before Boudica, writes Tacitus, London had been famed for its many merchants and expansive merchandise. The revolt caused loss of life and property, but business resumed rapidly.

The tablets also show us the first known references to London, predating Tacitus's descriptions by fifty years. 'Londinio' appears on three tablets – meaning 'in London' as an address – and all were found in contexts no older than twenty years after the fire.[10] The clearest was on a tablet sent to one Mogontius, a man with a Celtic name, and conceivably (though not necessarily) a native Briton. We read of Catullus and his house (used as an address for Junius the cooper, who could be found opposite), London's first identified householder. His is a Latin name, possibly commemorating a famous poet from northern Italy who died around the time of Caesar's invasions. It's unlikely, but you can't help wonder if Catullus ran into Mogontius in this city of migrants. What would they have discussed over a mug of diluted wine?

On one tablet the alphabet had been written out; columns of large numbers filled another, both perhaps the work of apprentice scribes. Roger assembled examples of each letter from every tablet. His drawing would make a good poster: here in London, nearly two thousand years ago, when most of Britain was prehistoric and Christianity was an unknown, distant cult, messages were being written with the letters we use now. One find is particularly intriguing. There were nineteen tablets – three of them parts of a triptych – in a single room at the back of a range of industrial buildings, erected in the 80s just south of the main road bridge; the archaeologists tentatively refer to the room as an office. Even without these, more tablets were found in this area of the site than anywhere else. Why there?

Perhaps it was a writing room. Below the bridge, where they could have had a stall, literate workers might have serviced the new city, making and recycling tablets, archiving legal documents, perhaps reading out messages to those who needed help and inscribing dictated replies on the rewaxed tablets. If the excavated tablets give a voice to early Roman London, what stories might those who worked there have known, eking out a living in the murk of Walbrook, framing snippets of conversation thrown into the wings of the London stage?[11]

Tablets themselves were skilfully split from recycled wine casks made from silver fir, native to the alpine region of central Europe – the pale wood made an effective backing for black wax. Offcuts and chips from shaping wax recesses were found at Bloomberg, along with saws, chisels, awls, bradawls and the blade of a plane. Damian Goodburn, a woodwork specialist at MOLA, estimates that 420 tablets could have been made from a single cask.

It seems the Roman army was there to support the post-fire recovery, and with their presence London became Britain's capital city, growing to half as big again as the next largest towns. Around the turn of the millennium MOLA archaeologists investigated a large area at Plantation Place, an office development at the heart of the early Roman city. Road 1 cut across the site, heading out to the Walbrook bridge. Supporting Tacitus's claim that the British garrison was reinforced, a small fort was raised there with recycled burnt timbers and bricks in its walls. Big enough for 500 foot soldiers, it didn't last long, perhaps because the land became too valuable to business. Its men may have been billeted around town, until a larger fort was built at Cripplegate to the northwest in the 120s.[12]

Construction debris from the early fort may have been dumped at the Bloomberg site, where a few pieces of broken military equipment were found. It's also possible that some of the tablets refer to men who were based there. 'Classicus, Prefect of the Sixth Cohort of Nervians' is thought to be a military commander related to the new procurator of Britain, Julius Classicianus – an imperial chancellor, his predecessor having fled to France after Boudica's revolt. Classicianus is described by Tacitus (who disapproved of his failure to support the governor, who wanted to revenge the insurrection) and is represented in the British Museum, where chunks of a large marble tomb can be seen. The tomb's inscription implies that Classicianus was a native of what is now Germany, and identifies his wife, whose father was a continental tribal leader. Another tablet names Rogatus the Lingonian, perhaps a soldier from a cohort formed by another Celtic tribe in France.

All these people could have been migrants. But surely not everyone could read or write. What about the rest? And what about women? Archaeology can tell us about other Londoners.

In tune with Roman practices and regulations, most of the city's dead were buried beyond its borders – outside the walls once these were built around AD 200 – in formal cemeteries. They reflect London's mixed society. To the north, a burial ground in the upper Walbrook valley was seasonally flooded, and graves were washed out; people came there to tip refuse or dig for sand, and horses picked their way through the reeking swamp in search of browse. Elsewhere, individuals were treated to monumental tombs. Across the bridge to the south, temples, inscriptions and signs of now missing statues proclaim the wealth of a particular community.

This last site – at Lant Street, not far from Borough Market – is interesting because archaeologists analysed oxygen isotopes for twenty-two of the excavated men and women.[13] As with the Weymouth men in Chapter 1, the isotopes threw light on where these people might have grown up. For nearly half of them, this was far from Britain. Two had Asian origins, four African, and at least four more came from the Mediterranean region (one of the last group, a man, was buried with two children; perhaps they succumbed to the cold). The two Asian men were found to have skull shapes suggestive of Indian or Chinese ancestry. They are matched by only one instance – in Italy – in the whole Roman empire.

Two of the African individuals had been laid on a chalky substance, possibly a north African practice. Showing that nothing is simple in this area, such chalk was found in a further seven graves. The isotopes in four of these were not studied, but three were: one was Asian, one Mediterranean and one local. An artefact in one grave, however, seems to point unequivocally to Africa or Asia (it was this object that prompted the isotope study): an unusual folding knife with an ivory handle carved in the form of a leopard.

The owner of this knife – as well as a bronze key, a casket inlaid with engraved bone and a couple of glass vessels – was a teenage girl. She featured in another study, which looked exhaustively at four Roman Londoners.[14] Isotopes suggest she had spent her childhood in the southern Mediterranean, and had moved to London by at least the age of nine; her ancient DNA (aDNA) identifies her as a white European, with southern European or east Mediterranean ancestry through her mother.

A grave on Harper Road, not far from the teenage girl's, contained the remains of an adult woman. That is, her bones appear female, but her aDNA was male – she was intersex. We cannot know what she thought, but she was buried with things that women often took to their graves, so it seems she at least projected herself as feminine. She too was white European. She probably grew up in Britain. She had some imported pottery (including a wine jar) and an Italian mirror, but, with a cultural message as confusing as her gender, she also had a bronze neck ring of a rare and distinctive native design. Born before London existed and dying around the time of Boudica's revolt, she seems to have been picking a way between indigenous tradition and the new world of London: she looked in her Roman mirror, and saw a Briton.

North of the river, at least ten skulls were found in a pit in the upper Walbrook valley, at London Wall (a modern address just inside the course of the Roman wall). They were all from men, possibly unlucky gladiators, and one was analysed. He was white European, and may have been born in London. Finally, from nearby Mansell Street, a man, apparently buried with little ceremony, had also spent his childhood in the London area. He had brown eyes, dark brown or black hair, and dark skin. He was black.

People were writing in other Roman towns, but usually all that survives are the styluses – 160 at Silchester, for example, and just two writing tablets. Scientific studies do show considerable evidence for population movement elsewhere in Britain, including two black African women, one in York and one near Beachy Head, East Sussex, both possibly second-generation immigrants. But London may be unique in its very high proportion of migrants. It was a city of people far from home, often, as soldiers or slaves, there for reasons over which they had little control, clinging on to symbols of their remote and varied identities.

Latin would have been a common language as well as a tool of bureaucracy, and to native British ears it must have been far from the only alien tongue. Many of the names on the Bloomberg tablets are Latin. Of some hundred and thirty, two dozen are emperors, consuls or fathers name-checked in passing, and more are uncertain, leaving ninety-two identified Londoners. These include Domitius Tertius the brewer; Rusticus, a bodyguard; and troopers Agrippa, Longinus and Verecundus. Men given Roman citizenship can be recognized from the form of their names, such as Gaius Valerius Proculus, noted above. Martialis was the son of Ambiccus, who had a Celtic name. There are twenty such names, but these, says Roger Tomlin, are no more likely to indicate indigenous Britons. Soldiers recruited from native tribes would have been Gauls (French) or Germans. Atigniomarus and Namatobogius were likely to be native men from the continent.

The unnamed women – aristocrats, craft-workers, mothers, servants and prostitutes – might have included more local people, but at the Bloomberg site there was a place where the men – the soldiers and bureaucrats – found particular community and a home from home: the Mithraeum.

Sadie was surprised to find more of the original temple foundations surviving than she had expected. They hadn't been entirely bulldozed away in the 1950s, and new remains were found at the east end. Bloomberg's duty was also to the reconstruction, which was moved to the original site, back across the plot and deep below the streets. Here, however, even the little that had been rebuilt in 1962 was a disappointment. The material had been stored in a builders' yard before reassembly, by which time such distinctive items as the round column bases had been 'lost'. Bucklersbury's architects, who went to the trouble of commissioning some fine engraved glass depicting scenes inspired by Mithraic ceremonies, had waved two fingers at the archaeology: the reconstruction's low walls contained medieval and modern bricks, held together with cement that needed a diamond-tipped chainsaw to break it up.[15]

Bloomberg's response was largely to ditch the idea of an 'authentic' reconstruction, and instead to create a permanent display that

The remains of the Mithras temple, rebuilt at Roman level below the Bloomberg HQ, rising on a full-scale print of the 1954 excavation plan.

would convey something of the reality of the temple, at the same depth as the original but to one side to preserve what still survived. New York-based exhibition designers Local Projects (who had delivered exhibits to tell and remember the 9/11 story) worked closely with MOLA archaeologists. Using Peter Grimes's excavation records, a precise replica of the remains was created with bricks and mortar made to recipes identified at Roman excavations. The form of the temple walls is imagined in the darkness with light.

The original Roman ceremonies, known only from the many temples and their sculptures and inscriptions excavated across the empire, are obscure. They celebrated the culmination of Mithras's labours as he killed the primeval bull of life and power, in an atmosphere thick with initiation, sacrifice and astrology. A stone relief found on the temple site in 1889 shows Mithras slaying the bull, surrounded by the twelve signs of the zodiac, the sun, moon and wind gods, and the torch-bearers Cautes (symbol of life) and Cautopates (of death); a snake and a dog drink the bull's blood. Rudyard Kipling, writing in *Puck of Pook's Hill* (1906), understood the appeal to soldiers. 'Mithras, also a soldier', he has a Roman legionary pray: give us strength, keep us pure, and 'teach us to die aright!'

*

In the late 1950s, midway between the close of Grimes's excavation and the cementing of the rebuilt temple walls in the new Bucklersbury House, BBC Television broadcast a drama serial called *Quatermass and the Pit*. It opens with cranes moving earth at the construction of Baldhoon House, remarkably like Bucklersbury. A workman spots something and calls his mates. Machines stop. Men run. 'It's almost 'uman,' says one, as they look at a dirty object, half ancient helmet and half misshapen skull. 'Reckon we oughta report it,' says another, 'you know, to a museum or something?' 'That's right,' says a third, 'like them Roman remains.'

The foreman worries that work will be held up, but is persuaded that revealing the find might earn them cash. Matthew Rooney, a Canadian palaeontologist, mounts an excavation. More fossils are found. He interprets them as evidence for unique, five-million-year-old humans. The developer is about to destroy the site, so Rooney holds a press conference, hoping to stir up public opinion. It works. People queue to watch as Rooney's team continues.

The archaeologists find a strange craft occupied by carcasses of dead Martians. The ancient mission survives, to recreate their species in human form on a new planet. As Martian spirits are aroused in susceptible people, flames consume London (shown with documentary footage of the bombed city). Rooney disrupts the Martians' electrical power, and dies saving the Earth. At the end, Quatermass, a British space scientist, faces the camera. 'Every witch-hunt, race-riot, purge', he says, referring to the slaughter that sent Martians into space millions of years before, 'is a warning. We must fight the ancient destructive urges within us.'[16]

The writer, Nigel Kneale, had been moved by the riots in Notting Hill in 1958, when gangs of young white men had attacked African-Caribbean migrants. The outdoor sequences had been filmed at Bucklersbury, the site only months before of a strange discovery, queues and the timely intervention of the press. His story echoed the incomprehensible mystery of London's buried past, the destruction wrought by Boudica, the city's reliance on outsiders and its power to recover, its feet in the ant heap of time.

Chapter 4

# Living in Round Houses

*Black Loch, 450–250 BC, and*
*Must Farm, 1300–800 BC*

Spectacular discoveries described in this book have changed people's lives and our understanding of British history. But they do not
make sense of the past on their own. That broader picture comes also
from thousands of everyday finds, and the research and science that
connect them. In that welter of stuff, it's easy to miss that something
big has happened. This chapter is about one of those things.

It tells how people lived in Britain for over a thousand years
before the Roman Conquest, and in particular of their houses. The
story finds its climax in two excavations – neither of which is complete as I write – in southwest Scotland and in Cambridgeshire. At
both sites water has preserved exceptional remains of wood and
other materials. Nothing like them has been seen in Britain since
discoveries first made in Somerset at the end of the 19th century.
We begin, however, with Gerhard Bersu, the director of the German
Archaeological Institute in Frankfurt, who was removed from his job
in 1935. His father was Jewish.

Bersu had been befriended by Osbert Crawford, an English
archaeologist and pioneer aerial photographer who realized just
how much archaeology could learn from a higher perspective. By

looking down on marks in soils and crops made by earthworks that had been ploughed flat, he could see things that were invisible from the ground. In 1938 Bersu invited Crawford to Berlin to take part in an exhibition of aerial photography. Crawford was delighted to pass on his expertise in what he thought of as a British invention, and further the cause of international archaeology. He gave a talk in the Air Ministry, which had paid his expenses, with many German military officers present.

They were confusing times, and Crawford – a Marxist who believed in the civilizing power of science, of which archaeology was firmly a branch – was politically naïve. But he may have saved Bersu's life. He hoped the German archaeologist, with excavation skills so admired in Britain, would direct a dig in England. They discussed aerial photos Crawford had brought with him. They chose a site in Wiltshire, and come the summer Bersu was opening up trenches in a field south of Salisbury. He returned for a second season in 1939.

As war approached, excavations in the rest of the UK were closing down. But near the city where Southern Command had its headquarters, one of the most influential digs of the 20th century was being directed by a German. On one occasion, the archaeologists thought Bersu's notes had been stolen by secret police. When war began, Bersu and his wife were put up by colleagues until, in May 1940, they were arrested as enemy aliens and interned on the Isle of Man.[1]

The archaeologists named the site Little Woodbury. In a glossy black-and-white aerial photo of the site, what looked like a giant single-celled organism under a microscope sprawled across a couple of fields, its rounded body containing amorphous dark shapes and its open mouth framed by long thin feelers. The marks were caused by new crops germinating early above deeper soils filling old pits and ditches. It might once have been a fortified prehistoric village.

At the time, excavation in Britain, the best, perhaps, directed by Mortimer Wheeler, had a particular style. Trenches were mostly narrow and sometimes terrifyingly dangerous, designed to reveal the sponge-cake effect of layers of earth thrown up as banks or accumulating in ditches; the goal was to create site histories by deciphering the layers. Germans did it differently. Instead of thin slots that looked like trenches on the battlefields of the First World War (whence their name), German excavations went on forever: they exposed villages, not just a pit or two. State funding had come from a government writing a nationalist history, and British archaeologists were jealous of their profession's higher status on the continent. Crawford wanted Bersu to bring this expansiveness to prehistoric Britain. He wanted a village.

Bersu obliged at Little Woodbury. By the time they had to abandon the project, they'd opened up a good third of the site, exposing a mass of pits showing dark against the white chalk. The ring in the aerial photo (revealed to be a ditch and palisade footing) enclosed about one and a half hectares. Pottery suggested it was Iron Age, around 300–100 BC.

Excavating on a smaller scale, archaeologists had found many pits and artefacts of this date elsewhere. Even as Bersu was digging Little Woodbury, a couple of hours' drive to the southwest Wheeler was at work on Maiden Castle, where swarms of students, press and minor celebrities left the Bersu–Crawford project looking a little sombre. Wheeler found pits dug into the chalk deep enough to stand up in and once, he thought, the subterranean homes of the fort's builders – an old idea known as 'pit dwellings'.

Bersu found pits too, but he said they were for storing food. His Iron Age people didn't hide underground, surrounded by rats, 'squatting in the centre round the fire', as Wheeler put it, throwing 'the gnawn bones over their shoulders'. They lived in round houses, with pitched roofs raised on great posts. One was an apparently simple affair, 10 metres (35 feet) across. Another was half as large again, with two rings of posts around a square of four massive timbers, and a great porch framed by more large posts.

Bersu found only holes in the chalk, and nothing to show what the buildings actually looked like. But his discovery caused a sensation, and in 1944 archaeologists advised on reconstruction of the larger house on a film set at Pinewood Studios in Buckinghamshire. The full-scale home was carefully distressed to look lived in, and ornamented with a boiling cookpot, ponies and sheep, but no people, giving the scene an eerie feel, as if the villagers had suddenly fled. It was the high point in a documentary film about ancient Britain, made for schools by the Ministry of Information.

Archaeologists returned to work after the war, and found more round houses elsewhere. They are now a commonplace of excavation, sometimes large and single, sometimes smaller and clustered by the dozen. One of the few constants, apart from their circularity, is a single doorway. This gives them an orientation, and after a

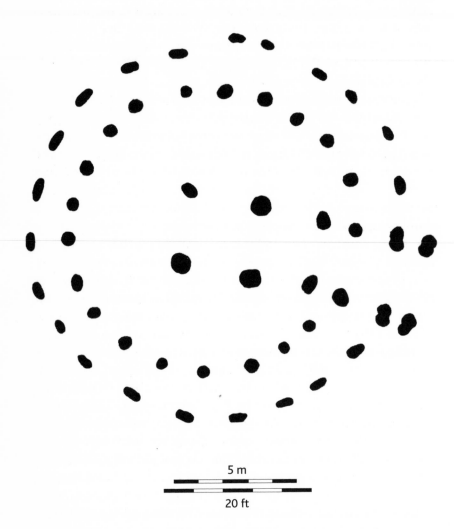

Plan of post holes excavated just before the Second World War at Little Woodbury, Wiltshire, by Gerhard Bersu. Archaeologists saw this as the first demonstration of a large Iron Age round house in Britain.

large number had been excavated it became apparent that there was a strong prehistoric liking for getting up in the morning and walking out to face east or southeast.

That might sound as though the houses' occupants woke to the rising sun, but it's not that simple. Few houses face north of east, where the sun rises in the summer. Perhaps they face away from prevailing winds, which in the UK are mainly from the southwest. But that doesn't explain the scarcity of doorways facing northeast. So archaeologists started to think of less prosaic explanations. Debris scattered on the floors suggested it wasn't just the doors that were orientated, but the use of space inside too: to the left on the way in, people worked at weaving, grinding flour, preparing food and cooking, while to the right were beds and storage. This mimicked the cycle of the sun, with day-time activities in the southern part of the house and night-time ones to the north. Circularity wasn't just a feature of building, but also of life, the houses embodying a perception of time and season, perhaps even of birth and death – a cosmology that reached back centuries and was part of the world that gave people their identity, and in which they felt at home.[2]

Where Iron Age Britain had round houses, in the rest of Europe houses were long and rectangular, often large enough for extended families and their animals. Straight-sided buildings, such as we live in today, can be extended indefinitely by adding extra rooms; they can be wrapped around courtyards, joined together in terraces and raised one floor above another. By contrast, round houses are essentially one-roomed buildings, and there is a natural limit on their size. If you want to extend a round house, you build another one. When Roman architecture arrived in Britain, with its straight walls, windows and rooms of different functions, it was an affront to generations of round living. The change was sudden. The few round houses in Roman towns look like workshops and hovels. They didn't last long.[3]

The reconstructed house and its setting in the Pinewood meadow looked very real. But there were no walls: it was a great pointed roof of turf and thatch, reaching to the ground from the four centre posts, with a grand entrance. Such a design stuck rigidly to the evidence – it could hardly be denied that there would have been a roof – but, from the start, archaeologists felt that there could have been a bit more style, the original having been created by people who, among other things, stood out across Europe for their fine decorative metalwork.

So as well as inspiring excavation, the large house at Little Woodbury and the government film encouraged archaeologists to build more, distinctively British round houses. Often these were experiments to see what would work with the excavated arrangements of post pits and gullies. The structures were impressive, and in several cases parks have opened to the public, where we can look at ancient farming experiments, wince at the smoke from open hearths, and watch staff in 'Celtic' dress work at Iron Age crafts. In 1980, at one of the longest-running such projects, Butser Ancient Farm in Hampshire, they built an actual Little Woodbury house following Bersu's excavation records. Like most of these new round houses, 'the Little Woodbury' has a low wall made of wattles woven through upright posts plastered with brown daub (a mix of mud, animal dung and straw), a simple door and a conical thatched roof.[4]

But there remained a reluctance to push the evidence too far, to make the houses too elaborate – timbers round and simple, walls mud and mostly plain, floors dirt. The only things to go on were those old holes in the ground, dug to take the posts that had long since gone. Debate persisted over whether even the reconstructed buildings were too ambitious. Then, in 2015, excavation began at Black Loch in Wigtownshire and Must Farm in Cambridgeshire. Both projects had been initiated by the discovery of bits of old wood sticking out of the ground. Such apparently inauspicious finds resulted in two of the most extraordinary digs Britain has ever seen.

*

The site at Black Loch of Myrton – on the edge of a former fenland pool in a landscape rich in ancient remains, not far from the coast near Port William – was not new. It had first been noted by antiquaries in the 1880s, when eight or nine small, low mounds were described and one was excavated with little record. It was thought to be a 'crannog', a type of ancient site especially common either side of the Irish Sea in Scotland and the north of Ireland, where an important house was built on an artificial island. When an archaeologist visited Black Loch in the 1970s, no trace of the crannog could be seen.

In 2010 Rory Christie, a dairy farmer who hopes genetics will improve his milk yields and is working to achieve carbon- and methane-neutral systems, was laying drains beside Black Loch when he dug up a couple of oak stakes. He took the wood to the local museum. Word reached Historic Scotland, and archaeologists were sent out to have a look. They could see mounds, and they found more timbers. Two pieces of wood were radiocarbon dated to somewhere between 600 and 300 BC – Iron Age. The crannog was still there.

So in summer 2013, Anne Crone and Graeme Cavers, of AOC Archaeology Group, a large Scottish consultancy with offices in York and London, travelled down from Edinburgh to evaluate the Black Loch. The site was covered in young trees. Anne and Graeme surveyed the mounds, which they could just make out under the nettles and flowery hemlock, cored the earth to take environmental samples, and dug a small trench. They were there for only two weeks, but it was enough to realize that this was no crannog. It was something far more special.

The cores gave the first clue, pulling up long tubes of wet muck from deep below the surface. To build a crannog, people piled up rocks and wood to raise the bed in a shallow lake until a small island emerged above the water. The ground would then be prepared with finer material and layers of brushwood and timbers, and a large round house built, usually just the one, often further protected and enhanced by a timber palisade. But there were no rocks at Black Loch. The cores brought up dark brown peat, and only small bits of wood and reeds. Several metres down the archaeologists hit clay. In the lab, microscopic diatoms (single-celled algae) showed the peat had formed in fen or stagnant pools, and pollen that the land had once been forested. Whatever they were, the low mounds had not been raised in a lake.

Dodging tree branches and roots, Anne and Graeme put a narrow trench across one of these mounds. They found a monumental hearth, its boulders and cobbles held in place by a log frame and covered over with orange clay. It had sunk down into the peat, and another, larger hearth had been built over it in the same way, topped with a large stone slab. This second hearth had also been rebuilt, so that a third lay on top, creating a great sandwich of fireplaces, as if they might trap within memories of the meals and stories that had been shared around them. For the hearth was at the centre of a round house.

The house was marked not by teasing holes in the ground or a gully, but by wood: alder posts and oak planks, lines of stakes, and logs and branches laid flat on the ground. None of it stood very high, but these truncated remains were like nothing the archaeologists had seen. Apart from the exceptional preservation and lakeside location, the site now looked like a typical Scottish Iron Age village. The preservation, however, changed the game.

Only three directly comparable sites had been recorded before, and all were far away in Somerset. For archaeologists they have mythic status. Like Black Loch, these Iron Age villages had been built on wet ground near open water: they had been dubbed lake villages, one near Glastonbury, the other two near a hamlet called Meare. They had been excavated over summers by local archaeologists, starting in 1892, pausing for two world wars, and continuing almost without interruption into the 1950s. When archaeologists visited Meare in 1982, they found the site hut still there. In one corner was a pile of newspapers: on top was a *Daily Telegraph* from 1955, and at the bottom a copy of *The Times*, dated 1890.

Apart from the many round houses, marked like that at Black Loch by great domed hearths that had been refurbished as they sank, an extraordinary range of finds had poured from these lake villages, from wooden bowls to ladders and parts of wheels, and such food items as bread. The discoveries had heavily influenced early 20th-century pictures of life in Iron Age Europe, despite the fact that not much remained of the houses themselves beyond their wooden floor foundations and lines of small stakes. Little now survives of what had been found except for a small selection of preserved timber and the sort of stuff you see everywhere – pottery, metalwork and bones. Much about the villages is now difficult to understand, and were the sites to be excavated today, a huge amount of additional information would be retrieved.

The archaeologists at Black Loch knew all this. I spoke to Graeme soon after they had finished the evaluation. He thought it unlikely that the 'loch village' could be preserved, as the peat was so shallow. 'The drainage threat is real,' said Anne. As the ground dried out the old timbers would perish, but they couldn't stop it. Rory Christie wanted to farm the fields around, and it was his land. 'Eventually all the wooden artefacts will disappear,' Anne added. They couldn't let that happen, and there was only one thing to do. They had to dig it up.

Crannogs, built mostly in Iron Age and early medieval times, are immensely precious to archaeologists simply by virtue of being in lakes: the water preserves a wealth of data about the ancient environment, structures and rare organic artefacts like those found at the Somerset lake villages. But very few have been studied, and in 2015 a group of universities in Belfast and across England launched a project to see if they could get a handle, using the latest science, on exactly what was happening at these curious places. Anne had long been researching wet sites in Scotland, and had just excavated a crannog with Graeme to great effect: her special skill is dendrochronology, building up long sequences of tree rings across ancient timbers to date old wood. The project's timing was perfect for Black Loch, and it was slotted in as a site for special study.

So in 2015 Anne and Graeme were back under the trees to start a full-scale excavation, returning with local volunteers each summer until 2018, when they had to think again about how to fund more work. Their survey showed that the village, with an oval plan 65 metres (200 feet) across its long axis, had been built on a promontory that had once jutted out into a small marshy loch. But for a natural narrow causeway to the south, it would have been a lakeside island. To the Iron Age people who made their first houses there, it must have seemed like a ready-made crannog, but with enough space to accommodate a community more typically sited away from water. All they had to do was build.

And build they did. Anne has found the oldest houses to be three on the northern, most lakeward side (Structures 1, 2 and 5 on the plan), for which the most recent timber was cut down in the spring or summer of 435 BC. These seem to have been the original settlement, arranged in a triangle at the end of a straight wooden track that ran out through a palisade of close-set alder posts and onward to the causeway. There are no signs of renovation, and the houses were lived in for three or four decades, at most. One had suffered a minor fire, perhaps a controlled destruction after key parts had been recycled elsewhere.

A second palisade was built further back inland, with more houses behind it. It was a massive construction made from cleft oak trees, creating an impenetrable façade. That wasn't enough, though, for before long a third barrier was raised just inside the second, a rampart made with bright-orange sand, surfaced with cobbles and faced with stone-packed oak timbers. Gateways where the track passed through were given special attention: they may have

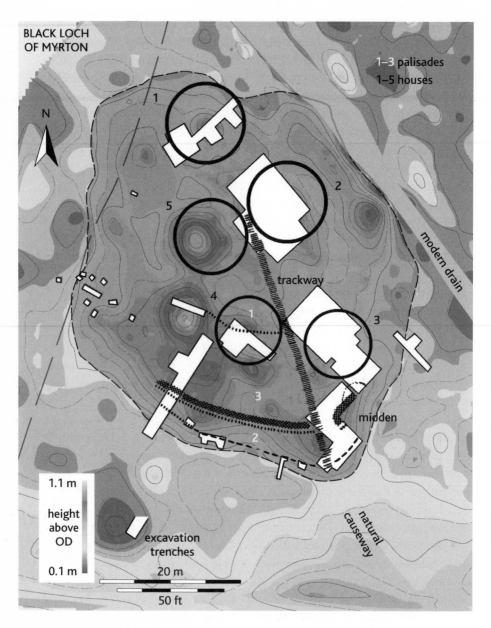

The village at Black Loch was sited on a natural promontory on a lake edge; circles mark the five house structures so far identified in excavations. Adapted from AOC Archaeology.

had roofed passages, framed with dressed timbers and with large threshold beams on the ground. And it seems they weren't there just to impress. An oak post has a hole cut in it to take a horizontal draw bar, redolent of the entrance to a medieval castle.

Anne and Graeme have excavated parts of three other houses, dated by radiocarbon to the 300s or 200s BC. One of these, Structure 3 on the plan, is unlike the others. About 9 metres (30 feet) across, it was flimsier, and where other houses had their great central layer-cake hearths, this one had a succession of eight hearths and domed clay ovens at different locations, separated by renewed floors. It seems to have been a work place. The floor was uncharacteristically dirty, with fly pupae and fresh animal bones. Slag and bits of crucible – and one complete example hidden under the floor – suggest one of the occupants was a bronze smith.

Just outside Structure 3 was a huge deposit of whole, unburnt hazelnuts. It lay nearly 40 centimetres (15 inches) deep and had to be carted out for analysis in five barrowloads; the diggers called it the Nutella factory (using standard archaeological jargon as she

Structure 3 at Black Loch, with floor surfaces and post rings around hearth stones at centre. At top right, the house is passed by the log track.

described it to me, Anne called it 'the hazelnut spread'). Beneath this was an older rubbish dump, an example of the middens so beloved of archaeologists – probably the midden of the earliest houses. As I write they have barely started to dig it out, but animal bones, shells, a massive corn-grinding stone and a wooden bowl, decorated with the sort of geometric design that is more usually seen on pottery, hint at treasures to come. People were growing barley and three varieties of wheat, and chaff from all of them suggests crops were processed in the village; the protective iron tip from a wooden ploughshare was found in the original evaluation.

Such things will tell the kinds of stories about the people who lived and worked at Black Loch that are normally beyond reach. The evidence for houses alone is astonishing. To date, the best under-stood is Structure 2, one of the first built on the site. Among the thousands that have been excavated across Britain, it is surely the first Iron Age round house whose construction can be dated to a precise year.

It was not much smaller than the large house at Little Woodbury, a little over 13 metres (43 feet) across. One of the many problems archaeologists have always had with trying to imagine round houses into post pits is simply knowing where the house was. Is a central square arrangement part of it, or of another building that stood there at a different time? Are two rings of post holes one house, two, or one that had been refurbished? Might the outer wall not have had any posts in it at all, and so be invisible? At Black Loch that was not a worry. The wet timbers were there, glistening a deep-red honey-brown and fresh with the marks of axes and chisels, carved, jointed and fitted together, looking as they had done when someone last walked out through the front door.

Structure 2's outer wall was hazel wickerwork, woven around two circles of stakes, mostly hazel, with a little ash, birch and alder, 40 centimetres (15 inches) apart, the gap between them looking as if it would have contained insulating material such as brushwood. Two metres (6 feet) within this was a ring of oak posts. Each one, big enough to support a roof and carved with a concave base to rest on logs in the sub-floor, was connected by a sillbeam, from which rose a wicker screen. This created two main spaces: an inner area around the great hearth, and a circular corridor between that and the outdoors. Here, perhaps, was the simple solution to a perennial difficulty with

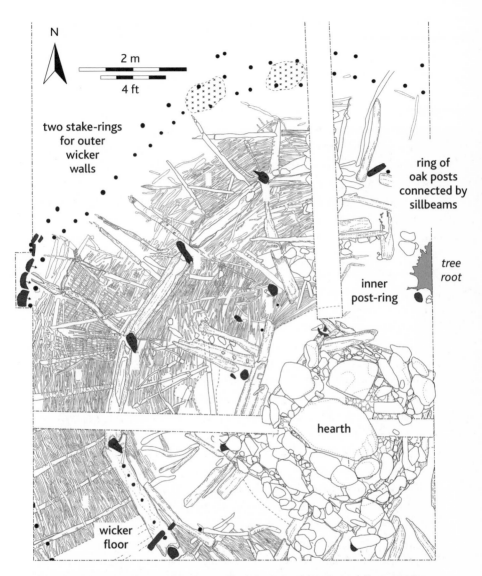

Plan of Structure 2 after excavation at Black Loch in 2015; the entrance was later found to the southeast. On a more typical dig like Little Woodbury, only pits for larger posts would have been found and, if well preserved, the hearth stones.

The labels within the figure read:

N

2 m
4 ft

two stake-rings
for outer
wicker
walls

ring of
oak posts
connected by
sillbeams

inner
post-ring

tree
root

hearth

wicker
floor

The massive approach to the front door of Structure 2, with oak plank walling on left. The scale at the top is 1 metre (3¼ feet) long.

reconstructed houses: the inner wicker wall shielded the fire from draughts, and created a relatively smoke-free zone around the edge. Nothing seemed to have survived from the roof, and interestingly, given its popularity in the minds of archaeologists, there was no sign of daub. But there was a door, and it faced southeast.

Anne and Graeme have described the threshold as a 'truly massive piece of engineering, the scale of which we have yet to fully understand'.[5] The opening was 2 metres (6 feet) across, defined by two large, radial logs on the ground. Between these was a floor of crosswise logs, some with flattened upper faces, jointed together. On either side, against the curving outer wall enhanced with massive vertical oak planks, three large mortise holes had been cut into the radial logs to take squared posts. People entered through an inner porch lined by more oak. It was like the grand entrance to a Georgian city house, with steps, pillars and a hood, but turbocharged with attitude.

Indoors, the floor consisted of wicker panels resting on timber and covered with thick layers of plant litter– sedges, rushes and bracken. Preservation was so good that, at one point, tightly curled bracken fronds lay beneath more open fronds, suggesting that an early spring floor had been resurfaced later in the season. Scientific study of these floors will tell us much about what was going on. Ironically, if there is a limit to what we will learn, it will be because people kept their homes scrupulously clean.

We saw above how some archaeologists came to think of people using space in round houses in a clock-like fashion, with activities determined by sector and time of day. Another way of picturing the homes has been to focus on the distance between edge and centre. Early studies suggest this may be appropriate at Black Loch, where more artefacts, food and fuel debris have been found around Structure 2's hearth, and relatively little refuse in the outer passage, reserved, perhaps, for sleeping and storage. There is little sign that animals were stabled indoors.

How large this house was only became clear in a reconstruction. Before the dig was even over, a new round house had been built by the Whithorn Trust, down the lane from the excavation. It's a full-scale replica of Structure 2, created by an impressive community and educational project. Because the Whithorn site is a Scheduled Monument (an important centre for early Christianity), posts could not be sunk into the ground and engineering adjustments had to be made to sit the house on a concrete raft. But otherwise it is faithful to the original: it's built from oak, alder and hazel (Rory Christie donated timbers for roof rafters and purlins) with a double wattle wall; there is reed on the roof (the only traditional material that had to be bought in, 10 tonnes from Devon and Hungary), and a 1-tonne stone at the centre for a working hearth. The design was adjusted at the last minute as excavation at Black Loch revealed the massive doorway.[6]

The house is just over 13 metres (43 feet) across and 10 metres (33 feet) high at the centre. Inside, Anne tells me, it has the feel of a cathedral, with a roof space soaring around huge, massed posts. In fact, there is so much space that, as I write, the trust is talking about installing a mezzanine floor with ladders – much of the superstructure remains informed guesswork. It could easily have accommodated three or four families, says Anne, with thirty or more people sleeping around the edge. The three-house community could have been as large as a hundred.

*

'Are you sure this is Bronze Age?'

It was 2010, and Peter Carter, the last traditional eel fisherman in the East Anglian Fens – perhaps anywhere in the UK – was looking at a basket trap. Archaeologists had shown him something they'd dug up. It had been made around 1100 BC, but it could have come from his workshop.

The archaeologists had found the trap near Must Farm, east of Peterborough. If the world there today is almost completely flat, it wasn't always so. Early in the Bronze Age it was gently rolling farmland, pasture and scattered forest. In one of the last effects of a warming climate at the end of the Ice Age, the North Sea fingered its way inland as the water level rose. By the Late Bronze Age, a river meandered through the swamp, probably a tributary of what was to become the modern Nene.

All of that is now hidden below further layers of peat and river silt, the organic remains preserved by the wet, and the landscape itself simply by dint of being beyond the reach of modern farming and building. Archaeologists, however, would know almost nothing of it but for the presence deeper still of some of the country's best brick-making clay. A great clay quarry is still active at Must Farm. Since the early 1990s the Cambridge Archaeological Unit (CAU), a commercial excavation practice based at the eponymous university, has been working with the quarry owners to record the unique ancient remains as they are exposed, and to re-imagine and understand the lost worlds.[7]

In 1999 Martin Redding, an independent local archaeologist, spotted decaying timbers sticking out of the quarry face, just above the level of the lake it now contained. A few years later the CAU excavated to see what was going on. They found more timbers, some lying flat in the peat and silt and others standing upright. It was one of the most extraordinary trenches the archaeologists had ever had to squeeze into, a window on a Bronze Age disaster. A home raised over the old river had caught fire, pitching its rarely seen contents – from fine textiles and bronze tools to whole pots, in one case a bowl of porridge stirred by a wooden spoon – into the mud and water that had preserved them.

The discovery was so unusual it was decided that, rather than excavate the rest of it – a challenging and expensive task – it would be better to save it for future generations. Complex arrangements were made to protect the land and to monitor the water table and underground conditions. The archaeologists then continued to study the landscape the ancient community would have known, by excavating remains that came to light as the quarry expanded.

In 2010 they investigated a 60-metre (200-foot) stretch of the buried river channel upstream of the settlement. Deep under the flat fenland fields were felled trees, hurdles, fish weirs and traps, human remains, Bronze Age spears and Iron Age swords. There were nine log-boats. It seemed the water and what it could offer, which perhaps included the best way of getting around the marshy landscape, were highly valued by the prehistoric people of Must Farm.

One of the traps, a tightly woven waisted tube with a pointed tip, was different from the others, and David Gibson, the project manager, invited Peter Carter to the site. The fisherman identified a basket eel trap, probably the oldest yet seen. He took one of his own from the boot of his car – he called it a grigg – and they looked the same. Modern traps, he explained, are made with split willow, which allows the buoyant pith to absorb water and the trap to sink. The

Bronze Age willow was not split, so he suggested it would have been pegged down. It had probably been set between April and June, laid at dusk, and collected the next morning. 'But he didn't come back,' he added. He? Peter's family had been fishing the Fens for over five centuries. It was always the men who set the traps.

And so work continued, scientists measuring groundwater levels at the site of a possible village, and archaeologists inevitably wondering what might lie there while they recorded off-stage activity – fence lines, banks and ditches, and the massed hoofprints of cattle, deer and pigs. After a few years, however, it was clear that preservation was not working. Left alone, the remains would eventually disappear. A lot of discussion and planning took place, but in the end the outcome was inevitable. The village had to be excavated.

They began in late summer 2015 by taking out the upper sediments with a mechanical shovel. This would be an excavation on an altogether different scale from that at Black Loch. Thanks to the earlier evaluation, the CAU knew to expect an unusual amount of finds exceptionally preserved. They could also say more or less where a village would be, and by covering the site with a large, electrically lit warehouse tent, they would be able to open up the entire area and dig continuously regardless of weather and seasons.

Ultimately, the site was at risk because of the clay quarry, and planning regulations obliged Forterra, the brick maker, to save it – and they had anyway always been happy to help the archaeologists. Recognizing the high cost of the project, however, Historic England also made a substantial contribution, bringing the budget to over £1 million. Mark Knight was in charge of a field team that would grow at the end to some twenty excavators, scientists and recorders – who would map thousands of pieces of wood and other artefacts by digitally transforming 3D photogrammetric models. All was in place to deal with the challenges ahead. They had nine months.

One of the key revelations came early on. Must Farm is just south of Flag Fen, a similar location on the fen edge where great quantities of Bronze Age timbers were uncovered in the 1980s and 1990s. The excavations helped make the director, Francis Pryor, along with his regular appearances on *Time Team*, a well-known figure. Flag Fen is now an archaeology park where visitors can see ancient wood still in the peaty ground, reconstructed round houses and an experimental prehistoric farm.

There were a lot of ancient posts and planks at Flag Fen, but, despite early hopes, no houses. The archaeologists found a timber pathway that crossed the swamp between two areas of dry land, possibly substantial enough to take cattle and sheep, and held in place by posts arrayed like massed scaffolding poles. Curiously, while there were few domestic remains, as you would expect, there were hundreds of bronze weapons and ornaments, the former missing their handles – sword and dagger blades, spearheads, knives, pins and brooches. It seemed that people had deliberately thrown the stuff into the water, in a sort of group Excalibur event that ran for generations. The wooden viaduct wasn't just a footpath, which at one end passed through a wide heap of posts and loose timbers dubbed the Flag Fen platform, but a stand for rituals at which people sacrificed precious things.[8]

With its posts and bronzes, Must Farm seemed like another such platform, and that was what the archaeologists called it when they started digging. It wasn't long, however, before they realized they were wrong. Not only was this realization important for understanding the site, but it helped make sense of a great European Bronze Age mystery. Flag Fen was not the only place swords had been cast over marshes, bogs and rivers. What was all that metalwork doing there?

In the original trench at Must Farm, there were two types of post, whose wood was easily recognized: smaller, red-brown ash, and larger, more gnarled blue-black oak. In the narrow confines of the excavation, it was not easy to see how these structures related to each other, but that became clear when the archaeologists opened up the larger area.

Houses had been raised above the swampy riverside on oak stilts, connected to one another by horizontal woven hurdles and a surrounding walkway supported on the inside of an ash palisade. The edge facing the river had long been quarried away, but if the village had been symmetrical, it would have had at least eight to ten round houses. When it caught fire, homes and contents plunged into the water, where a slow current was unable to move debris whose fall had been cushioned by dense reeds. Everything that hadn't been consumed in the flames was still there, reflecting where it had been the day before the fire. The ship had sunk, and if the crew hadn't gone down with her, neither had they returned to collect their things. It was a Bronze Age *Mary Rose*, a few hours from another world trapped in the black wet amber of the East Anglian Fens.

Looking southeast across the Must Farm excavation, December 2015.
Rafters of Structure 1 at centre right lie amid rings of house posts,
with the line of palisade posts along the trench edge at the rear.

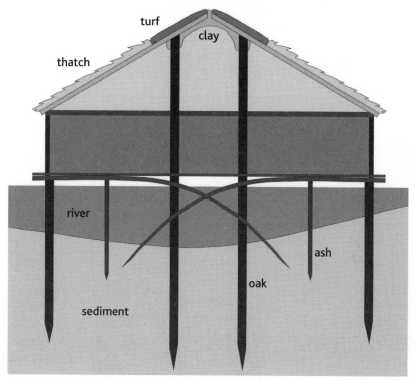

Schematic cross-section through a reconstructed Structure 1 at Must Farm. Adapted from the Cambridge Archaeological Unit.

As the archaeologists dug down, they came to a layer of silt rich in fragments of freshwater mussel shell. Easily recognized, they were a handy warning that the next thing they would encounter would be the village's charred remains. So Mark's first task was to clear down to the top of the shelly silt across the whole site, in preparation for the forensic excavation to come. Already at that level, however, were important timbers: the still-standing posts that had once held the community out of the water now rose above its sunken remains, preserved up to the level of the river that deposited the silt. There wasn't *a* platform. There were many.

Mostly, these were the homes and walkways of the village, marked by the rings of house stilts and the curving line of the close-set palisade posts. But there was another one that had coincidentally also appeared in the evaluation. It crossed the eastern part of the site in a straight line from northeast to southwest, and was now marked

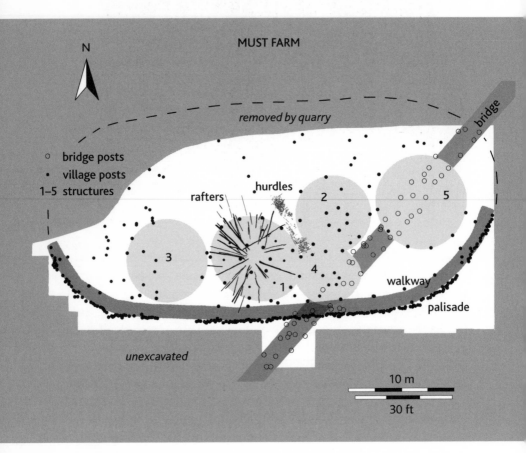

Simplified plan of the Must Farm excavation, showing rafters in Structure 1.
Adapted from the Cambridge Archaeological Unit.

Looking west at Must Farm, July 2016. Most timbers have been removed, leaving posts rising from the river silts. In the foreground, a large plank within rows of posts is part of a footbridge that crossed the site before the village was built.

by dozens of large oak posts. This was a path, narrower and shorter-lived but otherwise exactly like that at Flag Fen, even down to its date of construction between 1290 and 1240 BC – four centuries before the village was built around 850 BC.[9] Its timbers were on a different scale to those used in the village, with some posts hammered more than 3 metres (10 feet) down into the sticky sediments (rough handles had been cut into them to ease moving the unwieldy weights), and a massive plank over 7 metres (23 feet) long. Mark Knight talks of a 'carpenter's aesthetic', an engineered bridge-like structure hewn simply from hard oak with skill and efficiency. And as they dug down, they found metalwork everywhere.

Along the excavated 20 metres (65 feet) of bridge were seven bronze items, all on the southeast side (all metal at Flag Fen had been cast away to the south, too) – spearheads, dirks (long daggers), a sword, a rapier and a 'quoit-headed pin', a large dress pin with an ostentatious loop at the top that may have been continentally inspired, but was unique to Britain. There was even more bronze across the site, in the houses (or now under, having plunged faster through the water). Every home had the same repertoire, about twenty pieces each. Wooden buckets held broken metal, perhaps awaiting the attention of a visiting smith. At a dry-land excavation, the discovery of one piece of bronze in an entire settlement would be a major event.

Objects found at the Must Farm village include axe blades (seven in Structure 1), sickles (typically three or four per house), billhooks, awls, punches, gouges, tweezers and razors (Structure 1 was for a long time missing its razor, but it turned up at the end). There might be a few swords and spears among the homes, but overall the collections were more like the contents of a tool shed than revered treasures or displays of weaponry. And another thing distinguished these bronzes: many had wooden handles or hafts – exciting enough to archaeologists used to seeing thousands of museum bronzes with little idea how the whole implements looked, but additionally significant at Must Farm because none of the pieces under the bridge had handles.

Why do bronzes like these turn up in rivers and bogs? Usually they come with nothing else, as if all that had survived at Must Farm was the metalwork, a jumble of axe blades, spears and swords dredged up in a net. But here in one place, from the same people separated by fifteen generations, is an explanation – or at least a demonstration. When there was only a bridge, people occasionally let the costly bits of weapons and ornaments – emotive, gendered[10] and personal things of high value – disappear under the water. They must have been saying something, metaphorically and perhaps literally, when they did so. I wonder if such bronzes, which often seem deliberately damaged, belonged to people who had recently died, their bodies given to fire (a common practice of the time), and an object that distinguished them, or was precious to them, to water. Could their mourners have looked southeast, imagining the dead leaving their homes for the last time? Who knows. But at Must Farm four centuries later, we can be pretty sure that no one planned to throw away all their tools.

The catastrophic destruction of the village froze its day-to-day contents. Bronze must have been a common material before iron came into use. It's extremely scarce in most excavations, probably due to the fact that villages usually came to an end with less urgency, and people removed things of value. Assuming you're not an archaeologist, you would be surprised by how rarely academics write about prehistoric bronze for home use. This is hugely important for our

Mark Knight holds a socketed axe blade just recovered at Must Farm, still showing patches of shiny bronze.

understanding of the Bronze Age, not least for reasons that will become apparent in the next chapter. At the same time, the contrasting older finds from the bridge confirm archaeological suspicions that bronze could also be ceremonially sacrificed. That knowledge too is an important gift of the Must Farm excavation.

The evidence that bronze was an essential material lies not just in the metal, but also in the village itself. Every post, every rafter and hurdle, every wooden plate, bowl and spoon; boxes, paddles, a bobbin stick shaved out of dogwood down to a width of 6 millimetres ($\frac{1}{2}$ inch); a couple of wheels, one of them the oldest complete example yet found in Britain, and, like fragments found earlier at Flag Fen, made from three boards expertly joined with dovetailed bracers – all these were cut and shaped with bronze blades.[11] The best preserved wood, the posts entombed in sediment beyond the reach of flames, glisten with the fresh scalloping of axes and chisels. So what did the villagers build?

Studies continue, and Cyprian Broodbank, head of archaeology at the University of Cambridge, told me he hopes Must Farm will grow into a twenty-year project. We can already see how the evidence for houses contrasts not just with what archaeologists have imagined for Little Woodbury, but also with what they are even now excavating at Black Loch. How much of this is due to the nature of the site, with houses on stilts over water rather than on the ground, and how much to the passage of at least four centuries and the different Bronze Age and Iron Age worlds, remains to be seen.

At Black Loch the archaeologists peeled away peat from foundations and thresholds, and gazed up into the trees above to imagine the standing houses. At Must Farm they looked down onto roofs, and like time-travelling burglars worked their way through coverings and rafters into the homes, cleaning grey silt from the remains of exploded walls and floors and revealing the possessions and stores that no one had been able to tidy or claim.

In each house – there were at least five – was a pile of raw, grey clay, spread around the centre and associated with turves. Nothing like this clay had been seen before. Microscopic analysis showed it was not the kind used in pottery, and the heaps could not have been from hearths or they would have been fired. Perhaps they had been part of the roof at the apex, providing a weather-resistant cap to a turf covering and possibly also a fire-proof flue, with reed-thatch lower down.

This massive weight was supported by closely spaced rafters resting on a jointed ring-beam or circular wall-plate. The best preserved and largest house, Structure 1, was 8 or 9 metres (28 feet) across. Early in the dig its exposed rafters, the ribs of a great broken umbrella, lay flat in the silt; soon the roofs of the other houses appeared, touching one another like giant lily pads. Bevels on the rafters' ends suggest Structure 1's roof was pitched at around 30 degrees. Another plate ran round at floor level, and walls were made from wattle panels – like those at Black Loch, and again without any daub.

The wall posts rose out of the water from deep in the sediment below, as did the biggest posts of all, in a smaller ring in the centre that would have supported the tips of the rafters high above. These posts were all of oak. A third ring of ashwood posts ran between them, supporting the floor. The floor itself, mostly burnt, was not planked, but seems to have been formed of more woven panels. The houses would have sagged and creaked as people moved about, feeling like tethered boats at night with the sound of water in the reeds.

A cluster of round houses – Structure 4 relatively small and flimsy, and looking more like an annex than a house – is the sort of thing archaeologists are used to seeing in the form of rings of small post-pits on dry land (though the Must Farm houses don't seem to have the usual porches, so it's not obvious which way they opened). But the details of construction and materials are wholly exceptional. And so are their contents – this is not just about bronzes.

Animal bones, when conditions are right for preservation (the many factors include the state the remains were in when buried and the type of soil), are common on digs. Typically, however, they are scattered and weathered, all that's left of centuries of living and then of decay. At Must Farm it's different. Because, as we shall see, the village was abandoned soon after it was built, the rubbish outside the houses came from just months of activity, and what was inside from even less. This will make the evidence much easier to read. Still-articulated bones from lambs and calves in the southwest part of Structure 1, for example, suggest joints hung in the roof space there; or, perhaps – and this is supported by the presence of carbonized lamb droppings – young animals were kept indoors.

Opposite, in the northeast part, was the crockery – simple, plain Late Bronze Age jars, bowls and cups. Sometimes shattered by the fire and the fall, sometimes whole and lined with charred food, they look so similar and distinctive that they may all have come from the same large batches, whole sets potted for every house in the new village. Each house also had a stone quern, a grinder assumed to be for grain, and there are many cereal remains – though where food was cooked or bread baked is not immediately clear.

There is no space here to describe everything, and studies continue – not least of beads, in amber, jet, stone and glass, found in clusters as if necklaces had slipped from hooks. The glass beads form the largest group of its kind; analysis suggests they were made from distinctive sand found only in the distant eastern Mediterranean region. And there are textiles. Almost unheard of in the UK ('We don't find textiles,' says Mark Knight, 'do we?'), the evidence is among the best from anywhere in prehistoric Europe, and the textiles the finest.

Fabric-making was clearly an important, highly skilled operation. There are tools – clay weights from spindles and looms, and wooden cloth beaters. There are materials, all made from plants, mostly flax (a crop probably brought here by the original Neolithic farmers), as well as nettle and lime bark – balls of unspun fibre, and thread in hanks, around wooden spools or wound into balls. And there are products – over a hundred charred scraps of woven fabric, including linen with threads the diameter of human hair, and fragments of knotted-string nets or bags.

'And then,' says Mark, 'there's this fire.'

On my third visit to the site, they've been digging for nearly a year – before they began, Mark had had to defend a budget that assumed a huge quantity of finds, and he hadn't been wrong. The white tent has become a sort of home, with well-worn paths and familiar spaces, dark posts that first appeared as little stumps now waving in the air after the silt and loose timbers around them have been cleared away. A surface outside the palisade, excavated early and pitted with Bronze Age footprints, is green with lichen and moss, life reclaiming the earth even as the team works.

I stand on a raised scaffolding walkway with Karl Harrison. Rings of posts and a line down one side mark the ancient structures, like the bones of a great beached skeleton. Karl is a lecturer in forensic archaeology at Cranfield University. He has worked on thousands of modern crime scenes, including high-profile murder cases. Below us, an archaeologist is digging out deep oak piles, some of the last house remnants to be examined and removed.

Karl's doctoral thesis was about archaeology and fire science, and we've been talking about the village's end. The evidence seems to be pointing to one conclusion.

'So do you think,' I ask, 'the village was deliberately burnt?'

Karl's smile says it's early to be quoted, but he nods. 'I think it's intentional.'

By now, scientific analysis is saying the village was less than a year old at the time of the fire. Trees for the palisade and houses were felled in the same winter, and the wood was still green when it burnt. Among the preserved insects are very few synanthropes, bugs that gather wherever there are people, nor any that invade dead wood. There is little refuse, and there's a curious distinction: while domestic animals – alive or dead – were kept inside, skilfully butchered remains of wild boar, red deer and roe deer had been thrown into the water.

Perhaps as the new community built its home, it had resorted to hunting to obtain meat, unable to trade or farm. The lambs might have been the germ of a new flock, and pots full of barley, wheat and flax seeds destined not for eating but for sowing. Like the fresh timber piles hammered into the clay, this was a village without established roots, of people newly arrived with their stories and possessions, planning new lives

Building or modifying houses, says Karl, would have been the riskiest time for a village like Must Farm, with piles of timber and roofing materials stored on site. The excavation was littered with chips of oak and ash: structures had been carpentered on the riverside, not in the woods to be brought in for assembly. But flames had spread through a living village, with roofs sealed against rain, food on the table and a dog – indicated by a skeleton the size of a Jack Russell terrier – apparently tied to a post. The fire had been intense, fuelled by air coming up underneath the raised structures ('Like Brighton Pier,' says Mark), turning thatch into slag, cremating animal bones and polluting the river silt with clouds of charcoal. 'There's a lot of charring in all the houses at a low level,' says Karl. Fire was set in every home. The Must Farm village was torched.

But who by? It would have taken twelve to eighteen minutes, says Karl, for the fire in a house to reach the extreme heat achieved – time enough for people to remove things. But they didn't. Why not? And who were the villagers? They could as easily have been colonists from the other side of the North Sea, says Mark, as local families staking out new ground. There may be a clue.

On an earlier visit to the dig I'd seen a human skull. It was easy to miss, tucked in the corner of an excavated area, stained dark red-brown by the mud and hidden under an excavation cloth. Just the top of the head and the beginning of an eye socket were visible, and it looked as if it had belonged to a woman. I imagined the rest of her skeleton splayed in the silt. I found it hard to take my eyes away, wondering what she might have known. Had she died in the flames? Or drowned under collapsing timbers?

In fact there was no body, so an alternative explanation might be that the skull had been fixed in the roof, perhaps over an entrance – it lay on the southeast edge of Structure 1. The head of a woman, preserved and displayed over the threshold into the finest house, suggests a founder figure, a matriarch. Isotope analysis won't prove she was local. But it might show she wasn't.[12]

As evidence grows for a comprehensive and uniform fire, Mark sees attack. Maybe there was a big falling out, he says, with another valley group, a local feud. He recalls a massacre in the Vietnam War, when US troops took South Vietnamese people out of their homes before burning a village, or set fire to houses and waited for occupants to flee.

If Must Farm was assaulted, it may be that we've got one thing wrong. We look at the houses, the footprints and the wood chips in the mud, the food and the possessions and all the things that excite archaeologists as unique insights into prehistoric lives, and we think, this is Must Farm. This is what outstanding luck has preserved, and this is what modern forensic resources and skills allow us to wonder at. Yet if the village was attacked, and everything its people owned destroyed, what was the real story? Why did no one return to collect the bronze? Were they killed, taken into slavery or transported to another district?

And if they died, what happened to their bodies? As we shall see in the next chapter, death and burial in the Bronze Age could be, to our eyes, unexpectedly varied and gruesome.

Chapter 5

# Paths of the Dead

*Cliffs End, 900–300 BC*

You may have noticed press reports about some of the excavations described in this book; it was hard to miss the Staffordshire Hoard when it was announced, and Stonehenge revelations come and go with phases of the moon. Cliffs End, however, is less familiar, despite being one of the most extraordinary, puzzling discoveries of our times. It conveys something of the dark otherness of the prehistoric past combined with hints of a world that was more complex – more thoughtful, even – than we often imagine.

Had the remains been excavated in the 19th century, I suspect we would now take little interest in them, saying that early antiquaries had made a muddle of it. Today, skilled forensic excavation has revealed critical details that may well have been missed even a few decades ago. Scientific analysis whose results were initially questioned, delaying the project, added an unexpected angle to an already unique set of finds. In doing so, it put the site into a world of semi-mythical events that defined England for generations of school children, and whose theme lies at the heart of modern British identity.

It's not over yet. As I write, analysis of ancient human DNA is being planned, and the scientific search for evidence of

The burial hollow at Cliffs End, overlooked by housing. The Bronze Age grave pit
is being excavated in the foreground.

mummification is likely to follow. But here, until more research is done, is the story of Cliffs End.

Like any excavation, it began with bureaucracy: desk research, meetings and, because the cause was construction (as at Weymouth and London), a planning proposal. In 2002, Millwood Designer Homes, a Kent housebuilder, asked for permission to develop some land in Cliffsend, a hamlet near the shore of Pegwell Bay. It hoped to build twenty-seven houses, convert some old barns into a further five homes, and, in keeping with the spirit of it all, create a village cricket field.

When Millwood got the go-ahead, the council asked for archaeological evaluation before construction began. If any important remains were revealed, they had to be preserved, or excavated and recorded. Wessex Archaeology, an established consultancy comparable to MOLA and Oxford Archaeology, which we met earlier, brought in a mechanical excavator to dig fifteen small trenches across the site. They could see some ditches and a few pits, and they collected sherds of ancient pottery. So they worked out what to do, and started to excavate. And this is when the plan unravelled.

Wessex Archaeology asked Dave Godden, one of its experienced project officers, to run the dig. 'We had six weeks to do it,' Dave told me. 'It took a year.'

It wasn't a particularly large area – an irregular rectangle about 100 by 120 metres (350 by 400 feet), overlooked on three sides by housing and opening up on the north into an orchard. Dave's strategy was to machine-strip the top, allow the exposed ground to weather, and return to clean it and map what was revealed. Starting in July, they began with a 10-metre-wide (33 feet) zone on the southern and eastern sides, which they then used as a place for their spoilheaps. The growing piles, which in time ran the whole way around the site, screened the dig from the neighbours, whose dormer windows peered over the top like the eyes of children behind a panel fence.

The archaeologists could now see a lot of ditches and pits, several of which looked suspiciously like graves. The most tantalizing feature, however, had gone entirely unnoticed in the evaluation trenches. In the northeast corner was a large area that didn't look right, reaching 50 metres (165 feet) into the site and at least 30 metres (100 feet) across. Something had disturbed the ground, and the only way to find out what was to dig holes in it.

Dave machined out a trench at one end of this enigma. They could see the evidence of a hollow at least a metre (3 feet) deep that had slowly filled in – but little else. At the other end, where bits of pottery lay on the surface, they hand-dug a smaller pit, just one metre square, and found human bone. As they dug down, they retrieved several disarticulated pieces, including skulls. When they reached articulated bones, they stopped. They sent a piece off to a radiocarbon lab, which told them it was around 3,000 years old – like the pottery, Late Bronze Age. Clearly there was something important here. The mystery feature, however, lay across the site entrance; digging it first would hold up everything else. Finding out what it was would have to wait until they'd excavated elsewhere. And there was plenty to do there too.

Often, a single location attracted people repeatedly in the past. Cliffs End Farm was one of those places. The first substantial remains at the site consist of six Early Bronze Age (2200–1500 BC) round barrows – or, at least, their ghostly traces, ring-ditches that had served as quarries for long-gone burial mounds and had emphasized their height (the term 'barrow' has nothing to do with the wheeled things used on building sites and in gardens, but is an old word for a hill or mound). Neither had any human bone survived, but there were pits where graves usually are, and these had a few artefacts also suggestive of burials, including Bronze Age pottery known as Beakers.

A few centuries later, larger and less regular ring-ditches were dug in the empty ground between the barrows. These ditches were quarries for matching banks, paralleled by timber palisades; together, these features enclosed spaces for the living. There was an entrance into each enclosure on the east, and inside were a few small pits or postholes and one large pit or hollow, but curiously no sign of houses. The larger, northern pit was 8 metres (26 feet) across, over a metre (3 feet) deep and stuffed with finds – pottery, animal bones (which had survived here possibly because of the way ancient refuse had affected soil conditions), cereal-processing waste and grinding stones, burnt flints, bone tools, and a few ingots and other pieces of bronze. The layering of earth and debris suggested a succession of dumps had been thrown in, the first perhaps linked to a handful of feasting events over a few decades between 1000 and 900 BC, then continuing, on and off, until 600 BC. In the southeast corner of the site were signs of a third enclosure, but most of it was under the spoilheaps or the gardens of existing houses.

Later, people dug a few ditches across the site in Iron Age and then Roman times, and generations after that an Anglo-Saxon community buried their dead in and around the old grass-covered barrows. Some of these men and women may well have been alive when, further north, the Staffordshire Hoard was accumulated and buried.

But our interest here is in the three small Late Bronze Age enclosures; with only one fully exposed and the other two partly outside Millwood's plot, there might be more close by. Why were they built, and what happened inside them? An important part of the answer could lie in the only place on this busy site not covered by barrows, ditches or Anglo-Saxon graves: the disturbed ground in the northeast corner. With the rest of the dig done, Dave Godden and his colleagues prepared to move into the mysterious hollow. Recording it would become one of the most challenging tasks of their careers.[1]

*

Rain had washed silt over the northeastern part of the site, and it was spattered with green weeds. The sides of the trench where they'd found the bones had collapsed. It was November, and a carefully preserved tree that loomed over the top of the site – standing across parts of two of the barrows – had shed its last leaves.

Dave set up an aluminium panel fence to screen the area (now a common requirement of licences to excavate human remains), and strung out a line down the centre of the mystery feature and six more across it. Then fifteen excavators, plumped by scarves and warm clothes under their hi-viz jackets, started to dig in alternate sections. As they worked, picking and trowelling and wheeling out the spoil, their segments lowered and the whole thing began to look like a giant dish of lasagne with alternating slices taken out from the sides. When they thought they'd reached the bottom of the hollow, they recorded details of the vertical sections and took out the other segments.

It didn't get any easier. They found around thirty pits dug into the part-filled hollow or its base. Many were empty, but some were graves, and they also came across human remains that must have been lying in graves they couldn't see – just soft red-brown brick-earth. So they kept digging, and measured the location of bones in three dimensions so that later it could all be put together and they could try to make sense of it.

By the time they'd finished excavating the complete elongated hollow, they had retrieved fourteen articulated human skeletons and over two hundred further finds of scattered bones. There were very few artefacts, so they had to rely on a large number of radiocarbon dates – around fifty, half of those for the whole site – to say which part of Cliffs End's history these people belonged to. Some were Late Bronze Age, around 900 BC, from the same time as the small enclosures. Some were Early Iron Age, 600 to 400 BC. And some were Middle Iron Age, around 300 BC. These period niceties are not insignificant, defined by more or less subtle changes in artefact styles, houses and farming (and at one point, of course, the introduction of iron); and the gaps when there is no evidence for burial seem to be real, though whether it stopped altogether or just within the excavated area (the hollow continuing an unknown distance to the northeast) is impossible to know.

In this great pool of disturbed ground with bodies and bones, there was one place with a clearly defined ancient pit bigger than a single grave: ringed by a small ditch, it was up in the corner where the original small trench had been. By the rules of chance that seem to govern archaeological digs, that random test excavation had gone straight down into the most sensitive part of the site. The pit contained all but one of the oldest burials (and the exception was very close by). Gathered together nearly 3,000 years ago, the bodies seem to have drawn the dead for generations afterwards – as, you might almost think, they had drawn the archaeologists from another world. In the sequence of features across the site, the pit had collected the number 3666. As archaeologists dug down, they might occasionally have paused to think that this was indeed the pit of the beast.

It was large, larger than it needed to be to take the bodies in it: a squashed oval in plan, 4 metres across and 2 metres deep (13 by 6 feet), with almost vertical sides reaching down to a flat base. The ground had already been disturbed when it was first dug, so that the earth that had been thrown back in contained a few bits and pieces that had been buried before. These included loose bones

In a unique Bronze Age grave pit at Cliffs End, a woman's body (top left) was accompanied by a crouched juvenile with a pot above its head (bottom), a teenage girl with her head on the head and neck of a cow (at the woman's feet), a child in front of her arms, and male body parts (top right). Looking southwest.

from at least half a dozen different people – the remains of a foot, a fragment gnawed by a dog, parts of skulls, a kneecap and more. There were also some animal bones, including several sheep horn-cores (or goats'; they are difficult to distinguish) and a wing and a leg of a buzzard.

All this may have been unwitting and accidental, the scattered earth-stained debris from former burials not noticed when the pit was dug (though radiocarbon dates suggest these lost burials were little older than the pit, a generation at most). But other things put there were very deliberate.

And so it was that the first deposit placed in the pit was of two newborn lambs, one complete, one represented by the feet from the left side of its body. These were covered with the ashes and embers of a fire, so that smouldering dung scorched the earth below, and above them were placed the remains of at least two more newborn lambs, whose bones had been burnt.[2]

The pit had already been open for a time; silt had washed in, and there had been a collapse on the northern edge, perhaps while it waited out ceremonies nearby. The obvious place for those is in one or more of the three earthwork enclosures that ring the great hollow. And on cue, these enclosures had preserved some scattered human remains in their pits and ditches.

At least two of the enclosures contained the same thing, as mentioned above: a round pit or hollow with a cluster of postholes to its southwest. The pits were full of the sort of debris – food-processing and feasting waste – also found in the earth of the burial pit, where it might indicate similar activities close by, or fill actually taken from the enclosures. Some of the little pits were paired. Dave remembers that when they were excavating them, the archaeologists wondered if they might have been for carved posts, rising over the scene like totem poles.

Five human bodies followed the lambs into pit 3666, covered by more dumps of earth and debris. They were laid along its southern and eastern sides, leaving half the floor area clear, where it sloped upwards: here, presumably, stood the people who received and arranged the corpses.[3]

The lambs were at one end of this spread of death, and the first human body was placed at the other, to the south. She was an older woman – over fifty, probably elderly for the times, though we have few other remains from Britain of this date to compare (it is thought most people were cremated). She lay on her left side, legs flexed at the hip, arms raised in front of her face. She had lost six of her teeth, had caries in five of those that remained, and had a chronic abscess where her back teeth had worn down enough to expose pulp cavities; an infection in her upper jaw and nose had left slight scarring in the bone. In several places new bone had grown due to muscle damage around tendon attachments. Half of her back bones suffered from joint disease, and she had arthritis on the right side of her body. Age could have been behind all of this, and the conditions would have helped to make her look elderly. But they would not have killed her. A sword did that.

She had four cuts on the back of her head. Two were parallel to each other and close together, 3 and 5 centimetres (1 and 2 inches) long. A longer one crossed them at an angle, and the fourth, the last and also a little longer, sliced into the right side of her skull. While two of the blows lodged in the bone, this and one of the shorter cuts went through into her brain. The blade (or blades) cut into fresh bone, and there are no signs of healing. Neither are there any other wounds on her body – a curious point, if we remember the men buried at Weymouth, many of whom had cuts on their arms, a common sign of self-defence. At least two newborn lambs had been placed with the woman's corpse: when the archaeologists exposed them, the bones had fallen into her pelvic area as if she might have been about to give birth.

The other four bodies followed, though it's not possible to say in which order. Closest to the old woman, in front of her arms, was a child, perhaps a girl, nine or ten years old. She lay on her front with her knees up by her chest, as if the corpse had been bound. Her left leg and arm lay over the woman's arms. An adult foot was near her right leg.

The child's remains had been partly disturbed in antiquity, and a skull retrieved; fragments lay elsewhere in the pit, undisturbed in modern times. Or perhaps those weren't hers? Another, more complete skull that might have come from this body lay at the other end of the pit. In either case, something had separated her head and body before they were completely buried. If the second skull was in fact hers, it's notable that it has a healed wound, which would make her the second of only three people from the entire site to have suffered weapon trauma: there is a depressed fracture in the back of the head, probably caused by a blow.[4] That burial wasn't instantaneous for the woman either is suggested by the bones of a frog found among hers – unless, rather than a live specimen falling into the open pit, a dead one had been placed carefully on her chest.

Next, moving north, was a young woman, seventeen or eighteen years old. She lay on her back with her legs flexed to the right, her right knee under the knees of the older woman, her right arm across her chest and over the woman's feet, and her left doubled up to her shoulder. Her head rested on the head of a cow: that it was fleshed is indicated by the presence of the lower jaw and a neck bone, all articulated, though cutmarks show that its tongue had been removed. The young woman's bones have remarkably extensive lesions where tendons would have been attached. This suggests, wrote Jacqui McKinley, who analysed all the human remains and was lead editor for the dig's study (and from whom we'll hear more soon), the girl 'may have often been engaged in strenuous walking over rough ground and probably carrying heavy loads'. That might account for a healed broken toe.

North again, this time separated from the others and lying over the original lambs and burnt earth, was another child, ten or eleven, possibly a boy. As usual, this was no simple arrangement. With legs and arms bent double, he lay on his right side, his hands together at his neck; they looked as if they'd been tied. His skull was propped up, facing away from the body and into half a bowl – the only even partly complete pot in the pit. Some articulated bones were still attached, so the head could not have been moved long after death; it suffered in life too, as the boy had had an infection or haemorrhage at the back of his head when he died, present long enough to have marked the bone.

The final body, away from the others in the southwest corner of the pit, took arrangement to a new level. It was an adult man's, in his thirties – or, at least, it had been once. Now it was a bird-like bundle that could only be made sense of later in the lab. His skull was there, and his spine, and the left side of his chest with his left hand and arm attached at the shoulder. The bones were articulated in two groups, so must have been held together by at least sinews and ligaments if they were not fully fleshed. A few broken bones suggest the body had been taken apart with a hammer rather than a knife, so it was probably

The man in the burial pit, showing skull and neck bones (A), left arm and shoulder (B), and part of his spine and rib cage. A bone and copper-alloy pendant protrudes on the left, and beneath the bundle is a cattle foot.

already partly decomposed, and may perhaps have been buried and dug up again before reburial in the pit.

Another possibility is that the body had been mummified. Two tightly folded bundles of human bone excavated in the Outer Hebrides at Cladh Hallan, which looked like the complete bodies of a man and a woman, similar in age to the Cliffs End pit, turned out on analysis to be something more macabre: one consisted of parts of three men, and the other parts of two female bodies with a man's head. This anatomical puzzle was solved partly by aDNA. And microscopic study showed that the bodies had been eviscerated soon after death, cleaning them of the bacteria that otherwise would have eaten into the bones and left their mark – a trait of mummification.

Armed with this evidence from Cladh Hallan, Tom Booth looked at remains from across the UK for his postgraduate research at the University of Sheffield. He found little sign of mummification during most of the lengthy period when people were buried (between the Neolithic and historic eras), except in the Bronze Age. As we have seen, inhumations of this date are rare, but Tom's research indicated that half of them were of mummified bodies. On that evidence, it seems not unlikely that the male bundle at Cliffs End was in fact a mummy.[5]

Meanwhile, a curious artefact lay among those bones: a roe deer shinbone, trimmed and polished and capped at one end with a bronze ring, below which was a small perforation. Perhaps it was a pendant – or could it have been some kind of handle or fixture for a long-decayed drawstring on a bag that held everything together? If so, the bag might also have contained the left cattle foot whose bones lay under the body.[6]

There was another curious object in the pit, just beyond the young woman's head. Because they weren't in contact, we can't be sure they had anything to do with each other, though the positioning is suggestive. The object was a small piece of lead, 3.5 centimetres (1½ inches) across, in the shape of a rounded cone. It has a tiny hole at the top, as if it once had a fitting for suspension. At around 150 grams (5¼ ounces), it might be a weight, though there's nothing else quite like it from Bronze Age times. There is, however, another Bronze Age object from the site, found not in this pit but elsewhere in the funerary hollow, which seems without doubt to have something to do with weighing. It's only 1.5 centimetres (½ inch) long, the broken central part of a balance bar – a fine bone tube with a copper-alloy wire loop threaded through a hole. If not unique, this is a rare item of which only a handful have been found across Europe.

I have described in detail the pit contents, as we can see them now, because they are so striking. The unusual evidence suggests that the people represented by more or less complete bodies may all have died at the same time, or at most within a few years of one another. Many other strange burials were made in the larger hollow over the following five centuries or so, and I will not list them here. I will, though, say just a little more about what lay in the ground close to the pit, as it seems to have been connected.

There was another body just to the northwest, a young woman missing forearms and hands who died shortly after those on the pit bottom; she was buried either in the top of the collapsing pit or the ring ditch around it. Nearby lay bone debris from the disturbed grave of an adolescent girl, and another woman's grave, this time from a later era, the Early Iron Age. If these were the only bodies, however, there was a lot of other loose Bronze Age human bone; in addition, the pit was ringed by articulated animal bones, including five cattle skulls and another left foot, and, found together, the charred remains of two newborn lambs – an obvious echo of what was in the pit.

Over the following twenty generations, more bodies ended up in the hollow, some in their own graves, but often as scattered bones. 'It was like a plum pudding,' was how Dave Godden put it to me. These remains were almost all to the southwest of pit 3666, as the long hollow reached towards the older burial mounds, its far end entering the enclosing ditch of the most northwesterly and its alignment continuing to the oldest of the six barrows at the top of the low ridge. And it wasn't just the hollow that pointed that way, but the old woman too – with the index finger of her right hand.

I know of no other burial in which a pointing finger has been recorded, and you might think it was just one of those chance things. But look at the photo and I defy you not to agree: she is pointing, not just with her finger but with her whole being. Dave was so struck by it that he took a photo, when no one else was on site, crouching down on the edge of the pit to record what she – or those who had arranged her body before rigor mortis set in – wanted him to see; to catch the view before it all went and the ground was covered in houses and gardens. There is a spoilheap to one side in his shot, and you can just make out the tops of roofs in the distance. The woman points across empty ground, to the right of the preserved tree and, it is easy to imagine, the first Bronze Age person to have been buried at the site, in the grave under the original barrow – and, beyond, out to sea.

Her left arm looks carefully placed, too. Her hand is against her mouth, and her fingers clutch a small lump of chalk. It's not carved or polished, and whatever it meant to her or to those who buried her, to us it can be no more than a small lump of chalk, an unfathomable mystery held in intimate embrace. We can of course guess, and soon I will do just that. But first, there is another strange twist to add to this story. We saw in Chapter 1 how analysis of isotopes in the teeth and bones of the murdered men at Weymouth helped identify them as Vikings from far to the east of Dorset. The archaeologists thought it would be interesting to see what isotopes might have to say about the people at Cliffs End. They were right.

*

The work for the Cliffs End remains was done by a different team from the one that had studied the bodies from Weymouth, led by Andrew Millard, an archaeological scientist at Durham University who began his career digging at weekends while studying for a chemistry degree at Oxford. Andrew arranged for tooth enamel to be analysed for oxygen at the University of Lyon, France, and for strontium in Durham. Where possible, he took samples from two of each individual's teeth, allowing comparisons between isotope signatures from different times in childhood. Twenty-five prehistoric people are represented in his results: eight from pit 3666, sixteen from elsewhere in the mortuary hollow and one from the northern enclosure. The picture that emerged is unequivocal. There were migrants at Cliffs End.

Isotopes are not boarding cards – they don't name a place of origin. But they can identify people who are not local, and suggest broad regions where they might have grown up. In this vein, by combining the results from strontium and oxygen, Andrew could see three groups at Cliffs End. The largest comprised those individuals whose isotope signatures matched those of animal teeth and a

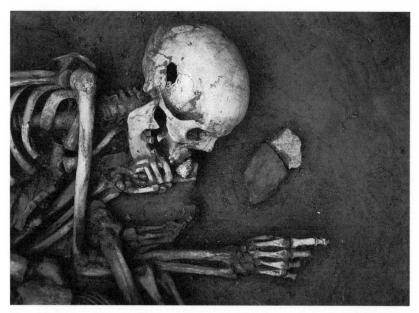

The elderly woman in the grave pit was buried holding a piece of chalk to her mouth and pointing with her right hand.

brickearth sample from the dig, and wider local geology. These are the people who could have been born in the Kent region, or even at Cliffs End, and Andrew called them 'locals'.

Altogether there were ten locals, fewer than half of those analysed. This was, to put it mildly, an unexpected result. However, there was absolutely nothing at the dig that could have caused Andrew to selectively sample foreigners. And while they *could* have been locals, this is not to say they *must* have been: the local signature covers quite a wide region that embraces land on both sides of the English Channel. There might actually have been fewer than ten genuine locals.

Apart from an adolescent man who could be local or migrant, there is no doubt that the other people investigated spent at least their early years somewhere other than at Cliffs End. Some of them have isotope signatures like the Weymouth Vikings: they came from somewhere colder. This might have been east or north of Britain, or in the high Alps, but as no one lived in the north Atlantic islands until early historic times, and Scandinavia is a closer and larger land mass than the high Alps, Andrew called these people 'Scandinavians'. There were nine Scandinavians at Cliffs End.

The isotopes for the final five went the other way. They had been born somewhere warmer, with matching signatures in southwest Iberia (Portugal and Spain) or even north Africa. Not only were more than half the people buried at Cliffs End migrants from outside Britain, but they came from two culturally and geographically quite different parts of Europe.

This surprising pattern was established from the start by the people in pit 3666. The old woman could have been born locally (perhaps she was pointing at her ancestors' graves), as could the boy and the young woman. The man, however, tied up in a bag in a corner of the pit, was an immigrant from a relatively cold part of Europe. And the girl came from the warm south. Any journeys some of these people took, it seems, were undertaken by children as well as adults.

The loose bones in the pit told the same story. One person was local, one Scandinavian (a woman who might have moved to northern England or Scotland when aged ten or eleven before travelling south to Cliffs End, where she died at around forty) and two southern (a young man and a teenage girl). This pattern continued outside the pit: the young woman with no forearms was local, the adolescent girl southern, and the Iron Age woman Scandinavian. And so on through the years as burial continued to the southwest in the great hollow, local and immigrant swimming together in the earthy sea, with a particular Iron Age Scandinavian focus in the centre.

How do we begin to understand this? The great assembly of death; the endlessly imaginative ways in which bodies were taken apart and reassembled; the pan-European origins of the people: each of these on its own is unique. Together they challenge anything we might have thought about the Bronze Age in northern Europe, and certainly in Britain.

A good place to start is geography. Is it even possible that at this time people could have travelled the distances implied, across some of Europe's most challenging waters? And if they could, why should they have wanted to do so? Partial answers to both these questions can be found a day's walk south, along the coast to Dover.

You might think I chose Dover because it's nearby and fits a particular narrative: it's Europe's busiest ferry port, and attracts refugees and would-be immigrants crossing from France like nowhere else in the UK. In fact, the two sites I'm going to describe, one a boat and the other a shipwrecked cargo, are each one of only two such finds made in Britain. In their different ways they are unique.

Remains of Bronze Age boats were first found in the muds of the Humber Estuary at Ferriby, Lincolnshire, in 1937; one of them is the oldest plank-built craft known from northern Europe. The Dover boat, however, is much better preserved. It was found in 1992, during works to build a new road to the Channel Tunnel. It has its own museum in the town, it is the focus of a long-running project managed by institutions in Canterbury, Ghent, Boulogne, Lille and Paris, and a half-size replica has been made and successfully tested at sea.

Archaeologists have taken no less interest in the two shipwrecks, one near Salcombe in Devon, the other from Langdon Bay, just outside Dover Harbour in the shadow of the famous white cliffs. To date, nearly four hundred items of bronze have been found at each site, and despite the fact that nothing of either ship seems to have survived, they are both designated as being of international significance under the Protection of Wrecks Act. Interfere with them, and you could earn a criminal record.

The Dover boat was made in 1550 BC, and the other two ships sank around 1100 BC.[7] They are all older than the burials at Cliffs End, which you'll remember began about 900 BC. But they all come from similar Bronze Age worlds. And anything possible at sea in 1500 BC was certainly possible six centuries later.

It was tremendous luck that the Dover boat had survived. It had been abandoned (or deliberately broken up and sunk, say some archaeologists) in water, and the silts never dried out so that the wood was preserved in the same way waterlogging preserved the writing tablets in London and the houses at Black Loch. It was sliced and partly crushed by a mechanical excavator, and it was lucky that archaeologists were there at the time, in particular Pete Clark: they spotted the bits of wood that survived the initial exposure, and they were experienced and skilled enough to recognize their significance amid the noise and activity at the bottom of a pit dug by contractors deep below street level so they could put in an emergency pump. And it was lucky that this pit was right above the old boat.[8]

The boat had been made from substantial carved oak planks, fixed with wedges and twisted yew withies, its crevices sealed with moss, wax and animal fat – a type of frameless construction not seen in Europe for millennia. Until this discovery, archaeologists had denied (despite protestations from a few amateurs who understood boats) that any known ancient British craft could put out to sea. Now, contrary arguments would take special pleading. At least 14 metres (46 feet) long, the Dover boat was too big for the inlet where it was found – it even had a bit of marine sand among its timbers of a type not found at Dover. With a crew of twenty and capable of carrying 3 tonnes of cargo, it could easily – if not always without danger – have brought the Langdon Bay metalwork across the Channel. In any event something must have. The bronzes were not made in Britain.

Bronze Age Europeans got through a vast amount of bronze. We saw at Must Farm how a small community owned a lot of tools and weapons with metal blades and working bits, but this is a unique insight. Mostly we know about the huge demand for bronze not from the places where people lived, but from hoards. People buried collections of metal, and, for reasons we can only guess, didn't always dig them up again. Such hoards are often composed mostly of scrap and ingots (there were 320 ingots in the Salcombe wreck, 280 copper and 40 tin), or of newly finished items, and it seems reasonable to imagine that many were concealed by smiths.

People were recording prehistoric bronze hoards centuries ago, but with the common use of metal detectors the numbers have risen exponentially. Since the founding of the Portable Antiquities Scheme in 1997, almost three hundred Bronze Age hoards have been found in Britain. They can be small, with just a handful of pieces; hoards with a few hundred bronzes are quite common; and rarely, they are very large: the Isleham Hoard from Cambridgeshire, buried around 1000 BC a long day's walk from Must Farm, disgorged over six and a half thousand bits of bronze. If burials are the plums in the Bronze Age pudding, hoards are the currants, a trail of metal seeding the earth with memories of fire and industry.

Hoards can be enormously informative. Bronze is malleable and recyclable. The demand for particular styles and types of objects changed frequently, so that every hoard carries a story: of things abandoned and things desired, of changing technologies and ore sources, of new ideas from near and far. British hoards evoke continental Europe, and vice versa. The cargo of the wreck at Salcombe included a curious little item made in Sicily. The Nebra disk, a stunning confection in bronze and gold found in a hoard in Germany by metal detectorists and apparently featuring a sky map, was made with Cornish tin.

The Langdon Bay wreck must have been a disaster, even if no lives were lost. Over three hundred and fifty tools, weapons and ornaments make it the largest collection of its particular type known. Some of the objects are familiar either side of the Channel, but most are rarely seen in Britain; of the latter some are common on the continent, others are rare there too. Stewart Needham, a leading Bronze Age specialist who studied the two wrecks and the Cliffs End site, thinks the Langdon Bay ship had been collecting scrap along the southern shores of the Channel and the North Sea. Whether the smiths and fellow travellers intended to end their journey in Kent or back in France, they had expected to set up a workshop and melt down their haul. They might have been heading for Pegwell Bay when they were wrecked.[9]

Gordon Childe, my favourite prehistorian, had something to say about this. An Australian immigrant working in Britain, he was an intellectual giant who migrated from politics into archaeology. In his last book (published in 1958 after he had returned to Australia and walked off a cliff to his death), he argued that European identity lay in a long history of wayfaring sages and craftspeople. This tradition, he said, originated in the Bronze Age. Smiths were itinerant, travelling across Europe in search of ores and customers for their wares. Their rare skills and knowledge, allied to the demand for bronze, freed them from the constraints of local communities and loyalties. And with their goods and technical accomplishments they also brought ideas, stories of other places and different ways of doing things. Bronze was a force of identity and change, a disruptor of conservative ways and oppressive élites, and it derived this power from movement.[10]

Britain and Ireland were producers as well as consumers, with significant sources of gold, tin and copper. A dozen Bronze Age copper mines have been identified in a zone covering the northern half of Wales and reaching into Staffordshire, with more on the Isle of Man and in the far southwest of Ireland. The scale of production, which had begun at Ross Island in County Cork by 2400 BC and had spread to mid-Wales by 2000 BC, seems beyond that needed to meet local demand. Mining apparently ceased by 1500 BC, and by the time of the first burials at Cliffs End, more traffic was moving into Britain, bringing recycled scrap, and metal and ores from the Alps.[11]

The Irish mines face the Atlantic and the British the Irish Sea, giving shipping an almost inevitable role: if the boats weren't already there, they surely would have been invented. In a fast, modern sailboat the Channel can be navigated from, say, Salcombe to Brittany in a long day-crossing. There is no evidence that the Dover boat carried a sail, however (albeit a theoretical case can be made), and it seems likely that a paddled craft would routinely have hugged coastlines and chosen the shortest sea routes – which for the Channel means between Kent and northern France.

Pegwell Bay has long been linked to a succession of iconic, semi-mythic landings. Perhaps it was no accident that the Dover boat was found where it was, and that Cliffs End became the site of a migrant cemetery.

On the bay's south side, across the River Stour, are the remains of a Roman fort at Richborough. If you drive inland and follow some

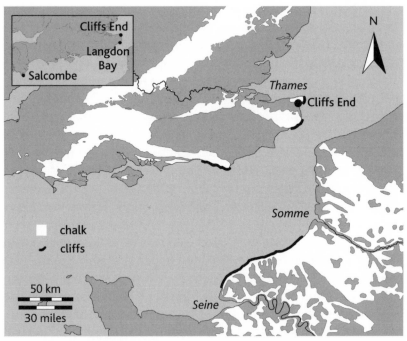

Location of Bronze Age wrecks at Salcombe and Langdon Bay, and of chalk cliffs either side of the English Channel.

narrow lanes, after twenty minutes you reach the north coast of Kent and another ruined Roman fort, at Reculver – half of it has fallen into the sea. The origins of both forts lie in the early years of the Roman occupation of Britain after AD 43; Richborough is often said to be the place where Claudius landed his fleet. The two are now separated by flat land crossed by the wandering Stour, but in Roman and earlier times – and indeed through most of the Middle Ages – this was a sea passage, the Wantsum Channel, sufficient to allow sizeable boats to cut through to the Thames Estuary. The Isle of Thanet, the land to the east, was then a real island. Until a bridge was finally built in 1485, over a river by then narrowed and choking with silt, if you lived at Cliffs End and you wished to see the world beyond your back garden, you needed a boat.[12]

As well as being a safer route compared to navigating the sea around the northeast tip of Kent, the Wantsum Channel offered ships crossing from France a wide sheltered landfall, directed by the chalk cliffs either side. These frame Pegwell Bay, rising high

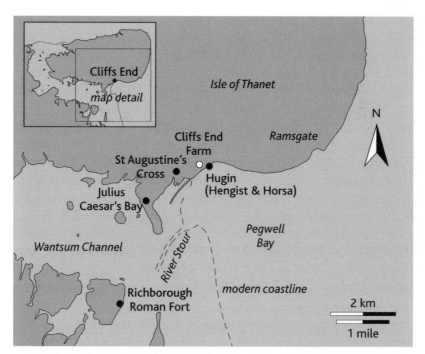

Until early medieval times, the Isle of Thanet was a real island, separated from mainland Kent by the Wantsum Channel.

and white to the north from Cliffsend (hence, of course, the name) and south from Deal and on past Dover. Here, say some archaeologists, is where Caesar made his successful landing with 800 ships in 54 BC, building a temporary fort on what would have been a small peninsula at Ebbsfleet. Ebbsfleet is also where, according to early chroniclers, Hengist and Horsa landed the invading Anglo-Saxon fleet in AD 449. Ebbsfleet, too, is where St Augustine stepped out onto English soil in 597 on his mission from the Pope to convert pagans to Christianity.

The last two events are marked on the ground. A large stone memorial, carved in the ornate style of early medieval Christian crosses, was erected in 1884 at the site where Augustine is said to have met King Ethelbert, and baptized him in the stream now known as St Augustine's Well. There's another stone near the shore at Cliffsend, a small slab commemorating the arrival of Vikings – in 1949. The *Hugin*, a fully working replica of an ancient ship excavated in Denmark, was sailed across the Channel by Danes in horned helmets to commemorate Hengist and Horsa and Britain's support during the Second World War. The ship itself is at Cliffsend too, propped up on concrete blocks and recently restored, having been given to the towns of Ramsgate and Broadstairs by the *Daily Mail* in a nod to the community-building efforts of invading foreigners.

Pegwell Bay is celebrated in English mythology as a haven for migrants and invaders. In that sense, the people at Cliffs End who came from different parts of Europe – and who knows, perhaps some *did* come from the Alps, bringing bronze – are no surprise; if there were travellers and migrants in the Bronze Age, we would expect to see some of them in Pegwell Bay. But that doesn't explain the burials.

It was a good site, Dave Godden told me, overlooking the sea from a headland, a prime position. 'My thoughts when we were digging were mostly practical – how on earth can we do this with the team that we've got and the time. But,' he adds, 'I really didn't like the look of some of the burials. There was a young person lying on their side. But hang on a minute, the lower part of their arms are both gone! How did that happen? A young guy was buried on a horse – but actually it was only some of the horse, its head was gone and there was only one leg left, it must have been a real bloody affair. Somebody had been buried face-down, hands tied, and her legs were

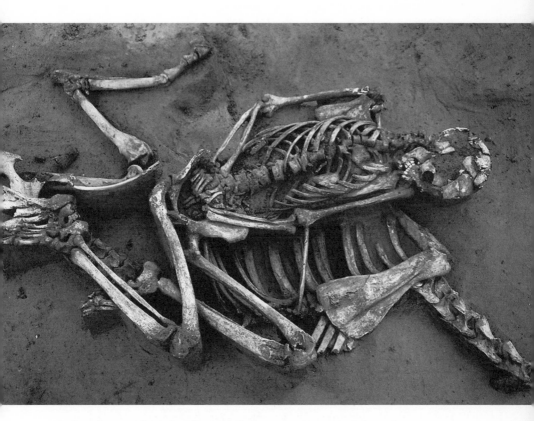

An Iron Age man buried with parts of a horse were among the remains
at Cliffs End that shocked excavation director Dave Godden.

sticking up in the air because the grave was not long enough. If you're going to bury somebody in such a disrespectful way, why would you even put her in the graveyard? What had she done that was so terrible?'

When the dig was over and the archaeologists were analysing the finds, Dave clashed with Jacqui McKinley, who had been helping to run the site from Wessex Archaeology's Salisbury office, and had worked out how to excavate the mortuary hollow. As Wessex's long-standing human remains expert, Jacqui got to examine all the bones and write the report. 'You see a lot of grinning skulls if you're in archaeology,' said Dave, remembering Cliffs End. 'You don't wanna spook easily. But to this day I'm slightly haunted by what I'd seen and what must have happened there.' Jacqui had other ideas.

Like Dave, she's handled a lot of skulls – and more remains still: bodies are not always complete and many were cremated. 'I've seen hundreds of skeletons in the ground,' she told me, 'and I've worked on several thousand.' Even for Jacqui, the Cliffs End burials are exceptional and difficult to explain. But where Dave sees disre-spect, she sees the opposite. All those people over all those centuries, Bronze Age to Iron Age. 'There must've been some familial or com-munity link,' she says, 'pulling people together over generations.'

The old woman – Jacqui calls her 'the wise woman' – didn't fight her death. 'And warriors don't kill off old ladies in battle,' she says. 'She wasn't dispensable, but she gave herself for the good of the com-munity at a time of stress. If the otherworld is a real place, death is not that scary: you're going from one stage to another. She would've been seen as a hero, sacrificing herself to commune with the ances-tors to help others. Her death was ritualized.'

When we die in Britain today we have a choice: burial or cre-mation, normally soon after death.[13] Graves are of standard shape and depth, sufficient only for a body-sized coffin, or, if ashes are not scattered, an urn. It seems a natural way to do things, but of course every aspect is culturally determined (these days, most of it is legally controlled too). We've been doing it for 2,000 years, since the Romans brought formal cemeteries and rectangular graves and small pits for urns, and unless you were extremely powerful like the kings at Sutton Hoo, or the matter was out of your hands, as it was for the men in Weymouth, that has been how everyone's been buried regardless of belief, status or wealth.

As a standardized idea, 'one person, one grave' first appeared in Britain around 2400 BC, with larger pits (more like rooms than doorways) being a practice, as it happens, again introduced by immigrants, as we shall see in the next chapter. But the idea didn't last long, and for most of the Bronze and Iron ages just about the only thing we don't see when it comes to the dead is a coffin in a deep rectangular pit. One way of making sense of Cliffs End – we can of course only guess – is to imagine a community of the living and the dead, and the hollow a place where the dead were at home together and from which they could physically return like newborn lambs to re-join the living; the remains we see now are at that point when, for those individuals, the cycle of burial and retrieval had stopped. Perhaps there was some kind of festival, wonders Jacqui, that brought people to Cliffs End from different areas to exchange women as tokens in political alliances. The traders, the travellers, men, women and children, on the move in life and gone to earth in death, but never apart.

There is a famous painting of Pegwell Bay, done by a Victorian artist called William Dyce. It shows with extreme realism a view from the beach on the north side, looking southwest towards the setting sun. Dyce and his family holidayed in Ramsgate, a popular resort then, and in the foreground he shows himself, his wife, one of their sons and his wife's two sisters collecting shells. The chalk cliffs are drawn with geological precision, and in the darkening sky you can see the tail of a comet.

Dyce left little to explain what he was thinking, but a common modern opinion is that the juxtaposition of his family and a comet was a prompt to reflect on science, humanity and time. It was a real comet, as he shows by the work's full title – *A Recollection of October 5th 1858*. The date has further interest. He sketched the view in 1858, and first showed the painting in 1860. The year between, 1859, saw the publication of Darwin's *On the Origin of Species*, a book that instantly shook popular ideas about the place of people in the universe.

Maybe Dyce's recollection had other references as well as the comet. He knew that St Augustine was supposed to have landed there, and it's likely he knew too about Hengist and Horsa. In the dark across the mudflats is Richborough Castle, where the Roman invasion began, the site of excavations that had been lavishly published in 1850. We can look at his painting now and imagine the burials at Cliffs End, taking the story back into pre-Christian times, hidden behind the cliff. Like Dyce's painting, the ancient burial hollow is a meditation on birth, death and resurrection.[14]

And the old woman? What is *she* thinking, the fingers of one hand wrapped around a piece of chalk held to her lips, like the seashells in the Dyce family baskets, and those of the other pointing to the southwest? The white cliffs of Kent have been co-opted as defences by a particular view of Britain as an island fortress. But for most of our history they were a welcoming gateway framing safe harbours, small at Dover and expansive at Pegwell Bay. Perhaps the chalk is a symbol of arrival, and the woman indicates the coast, the sea that bore the journeys of those she knew, and – who knows – her own, too. If ever it were possible to analyse the lump and say exactly which cliff it came from, I wouldn't be surprised if the answer turned out to be where she points: the white cliffs of Normandy, the Côte d'Albâtre across the waters of the English Channel.

Chapter 6

# Shaped by Beliefs

*Stonehenge, 4000–2000 BC*

The more we learn about Stonehenge, the more we realize how extraordinary it was even at the time it was built. Its meaning, and its origins, tell not just of Salisbury Plain, nor Wessex, nor southern England. It is the creation of islands, of generations of people from Land's End to the Orkneys. It is a memorial to a defining era of British culture and history. It is 2,500 years of identity, a crumbled ruin lording it over miles and miles of buried lives now being exposed as never before. It is a story only archaeology could have told.

This chapter is different from the others. First, while elsewhere I have closely followed the discoveries, spoken to archaeologists and visited excavations and labs, I have not been personally involved in the projects. At Stonehenge, by contrast, I have conducted and published my own research for many years: I bring my own vision to the narrative. Secondly, while at heart this is about one place – Stonehenge – the story is told through many recent excavations and scientific studies, not just one or two.[1]

Most significantly, however, we are entering a past that really was another place from the one we inhabit. I have tried to convey in each of the earlier snapshots how different those times were, not only from our own but from each other – the past is not just us in a long sequence of funny costumes. Yet here we take a greater leap. In later chapters we will move yet further into unknown territory, but when we meet the Neolithic we might truly say for the first time: this is life, but not as we know it.

In a technological sense, in the Bronze Age we seem still to be in familiar country, with wheels and carts, swords and knives, cups, bowls, razors and tweezers and much of the pre-industrial paraphernalia that still serve us well today. In the Stone Age we are in a foreign land. The defining technology of working and using stone for tools is extinct – it exists today almost solely in the hands of archaeologists and craft hobbyists who have taught themselves how to do it (it's harder than you might think). In this and each of the next three chapters, all of which occur in the Stone Age, we will see more variety in culture, technology and lifestyle – even a world with different human species – than was expressed between Anglo-Saxon times and the Bronze Age.

In those most recent 3,000 years there were migrations and profound changes in society. Yet we can still see a thread of continuity, a population that was changing yet constant as it absorbed new people and new ideas, and faced new challenges. We can look back from the present and imagine stories being passed down from one generation to the next over millennia: mothers helping their daughters with childbirth, old monuments recognized as things made by ancestors, the value of good wood and of good earth, the ways of rivers and seas, in a wandering flow of wisdom and gossip. Some of our ancestry will have come from far away; but for all except the very most recent migrants, much of it disappears into that long congress of local antiquity. And then there is the Stone Age.

The Neolithic – the New Stone Age – was a fundamentally different place from the one it succeeded; its arrival was an event, which here in Britain happened 6,000 years ago. In the next chapter we will explore the world it replaced, that of Mesolithic (Middle Stone Age) hunters and gatherers. A summary of what was new will convey the scale of change. Farming – not just new technologies and ways of thinking and living, but new crops and animals, many of which ultimately originated in the Middle East – first reached Britain around 4000 BC. It came with people crossing the Channel into southeast England from northern France and southern Belgium, and, in the west, perhaps a century or two later, up the Irish Sea from Normandy and Brittany. Within three centuries people were farming across the whole of the UK and Ireland.

These people didn't just clear land and dig fields or gardens. They built things. They lived in long, rectangular timber and thatched houses, different from anything seen before or since (the nearest equivalents being Anglo-Saxon halls). Large, complex constructions in the form of long barrows (communal burial mounds) and earthwork enclosures, where people periodically gathered from wider areas, appear within a few generations. Along a swathe of downland from Hampshire to central Sussex, where the deep structure of the chalk and the quality of flint were right, numerous mine shafts were sunk to extract stone for making axe blades, for felling trees and for shaping timber.

Like the houses, mounds and enclosures, the mines were an engineering challenge – with the added risk of injury or death – met with skill and experience gained in earlier centuries on the adjacent continent. Between Britain and the rest of Europe we can see differences in details of houses, pottery styles (no one had made anything like pottery in Britain before) and the rest, and there can be little doubt that anyone at the time would have known which side of the Channel they were on. But for people in Britain, there was a historic cultural horizon that stopped within a few, known generations. Their ancestors were continental European, not British, and for at least a century or so in some way they must surely have known that.

On the face of it, there can be little reason to question this theory of a major new population arriving in Britain at the start of the Neolithic (though, as we shall see in Chapter 10, some archaeologists have done just that). More controversial, however, is what happened at the end. British archaeologists now talk of a Copper Age that came between the end of the Neolithic and the start of the Bronze Age, between 2500 and 2200 BC. As its name betrays, it was a time that saw the first manufacture and use of metal, of copper (and gold), while stone remained an important material for tools and weapons.

Before archaeology was a science, this era was imagined to have been ushered in by migrants, named the Beaker people after distinctive pots placed in their graves. There seemed to be a complete change in culture and technology, including not just the new use of metal, with distinctive new stone tools and new burial rites, but even a different shape of head: the by then indigenous farmers had longer skulls, and immigrants rounder – resembling, as was noted in the 19th century, the shapes of their long and round burial mounds respectively.

More recently, a huge increase in knowledge from excavation and scientific research muddied the Beaker transition and extended its duration. To many archaeologists it seemed less the result of one or more great migrations than of gradual change from within, native farmers adopting continental fashions and ideas. Disparities in skull shape were explained as adaptations to different living environments, or perhaps the result of head binding in infancy. And then, even as I was writing this chapter, everything changed again.

A significant new study of aDNA (at the time, the largest of its kind ever conducted) focused on skeletons accompanied by Beaker artefacts, and in the graves of their Neolithic predecessors. It found a spectacular change in the British genome after 2450 BC. Scientists proposed a minimum 90 per cent turnover of the population. The Neolithic genome never recovered.

This profoundly affects the way we think of the Neolithic in the UK. Now we can say not only that it started with a population change (also confirmed by new aDNA research), but also that it ended the same way. Little pre-farming DNA survived in the Neolithic population, and neither did much of the latter survive into the Bronze Age – and thence into us today. In population terms, this defining era of British history, which began with what Gordon Childe called the Neolithic Revolution and culminated with Stonehenge, was like a huge gasket between remote antiquity and modernity. It changed everything, establishing an economic basis and a relationship with land and property that are still with us. Yet the people who did that are not. Stonehenge may be their memorial. It is not ours.

Unless, of course, it was built by immigrants.[2]

*

Superficially, at least, the world where Stonehenge would later be built was no different from many others of that time in the Early

Neolithic (4000–3500 BC). Partly, it has to be said, this may seem so because we know relatively little about it – as is the case with contemporary landscapes across Britain. There were some significant earthwork monuments in Wessex, but there has not been a lot of modern excavation at them, and we know even less about how and where people lived.

To start with the landscape itself, there was never a single type of natural vegetation cover on the chalk. The open prairie-like fields we see today, turned to permanent pasture around Stonehenge by the National Trust with the help of EU grants, go back no further than the 18th century, when old grassland started to be broken up for arable. Yet neither would that grassland, which until then had preserved so well the ancient earthworks, have been recognized in prehistoric times. On the other hand, our early people would have got quite lost in an alternative but fictional vision of ancient forest in which 'a squirrel could go from Land's End to John O'Groats without ever touching land'.[3]

Whenever there was vegetation – which returned in earnest after the end of the Ice Age some 11,000 years ago to colonize previously frozen ground – there were people and animals too, browsing, felling and trampling, and, along with fires and storms, creating a mosaic of woodland and open spaces, with patches of grassland and weedy, disturbed ground. Not far from Stonehenge, rivers meander gently southwards to west (the Till) and east (the Avon). These would have attracted water birds and beavers, and animals coming to drink through marsh, reeds, and alder and hazel woodland. They would have been places favoured by people too, in a countryside otherwise lacking in streams and springs.

Into this varied landscape walk the first farmers. They bring alien animals – sheep and goats and domestic cattle, and pigs likely to have been bred from European wild boar. They grow cereals, and other crops that are harder for us to see in what survives. From excavations around Stonehenge have come occasional wheat grains, and, from elsewhere in southern England, barley, flax and opium poppy seeds; even, in a unique case from Dorset, a grape pip (whether vines were growing there or dried fruit was imported is an open question). Wild plant foods include crab apples, sloe or blackthorn plums and grass tubers, and, the most common, hazelnuts. Trout bones have been found in one pit near Stonehenge.

I call these people farmers, but it is probably more accurate to think of them as gardeners or small-holders, tending little plots of mixed plants near their homes and penning a few animals. Nonetheless, investing in such resources would have given them a proprietorial interest in the land quite different from anything that had gone before. Not only did they have to put time and effort into tilling, sowing and harvesting, but also their plants would have needed protection from wild animals – birds, red and roe deer, cattle and pigs. Their own beasts, too, would have had to be kept safe: from predators like bears and wolves, and from the unwelcome attention of wild bulls and boars (a particularly intelligent and vicious creature).

The best evidence we have for local Early Neolithic settlement was found in 2016 at Bulford, 8 miles (5 kilometres) northeast of Stonehenge, where archaeologists excavated 13 hectares of downland ahead of new house building for the British Army. Here were many pits on a hillside sloping down to the Nine Mile River, a small tributary of the Avon. Thousands of pieces of flint, shaped and split while making tools and in such fresh condition that many can be fitted back together, show this to be a unique site: nothing so well preserved had been found anywhere near Stonehenge before. Much light will be thrown on people's lives when the remains are analysed. But for now, the most prominent signs we have of this time are relics of a different type of investment in the land: burial mounds.

Long barrows are found in various forms across much of Europe. They have in common their elongated shape, created by heaping up earth and rubble between two parallel quarry ditches; a variety of wooden or stone structures raised within or buried under the mounds; and, usually but not always, human remains, often consisting of body parts or scattered bones. Building and maintaining long barrows demanded more than the efforts of a couple of people – a village perhaps, or a wider community.

There are (or were, a few have been completely ploughed flat) ten of these mounds in an unusually dense group southwest of the future Stonehenge site, three more to the east and others a little further away. There may have been more. Five have only recently been recognized: two small ones now close to Stonehenge (their ditches identified by geophysics), two on the western edge of the World Heritage Site (found in archaeological works associated with plans for alterations to the A303 road), and one at Larkhill Garrison, where the Army is building another large housing estate.[4]

Most excavations into these mounds were done in the 18th and 19th centuries; modern work has been limited to looking into a few of the flanking ditches. We could learn a great deal from new excavation, but in the meantime there is one feature worth mentioning, for reasons that will become apparent. In several mounds, close to human burials, were found remains of large cattle – so large that when antiquarians took the bones to their local butcher, they struggled to know what they were. The remains were mostly of heads or feet. The rest of the beasts might have been consumed in funerary feasts, but it seems there was something ritually significant about these particular parts, at least some of which were probably from wild cattle or aurochs, the largest animals on the plain.[5]

There is another type of communal earthwork found near Stonehenge at this time, as across Britain, where human remains were buried. Archaeologists call them 'causewayed enclosures': irregular ditch circuits with numerous interruptions. In rare cases where banks still stand, they can continue without break, as is the case with Robin Hood's Ball, a double circuit surrounding 3 hectares on a south-facing slope from which Stonehenge can now be seen 2½ miles (4 kilometres) to the southeast. This was the only known example for some distance, until in 2016 archaeologists found another one during the Larkhill Garrison excavations, a little closer to Stonehenge and this time on a slope facing north, away from the monument. It's early days, but perhaps they were not active at the same time: radiocarbon dates suggest the new discovery is older (3700 BC), and was succeeded by Robin Hood's Ball (3600 BC).

What were these sites? They are one of our great prehistoric mysteries. Human bone is often found in the ditches, but so is much else, including quantities of butchered animal remains, broken pottery and stone tools; at Larkhill, archaeologists found a flat stone quern. There is little to suggest that people lived in the enclosed spaces, however, so they are thought to be occasional, perhaps seasonal, meeting points, where communities gathered to exchange goods and gossip, conduct ceremonies and expand their everyday horizons. Elsewhere in Britain there are signs that these sites were sometimes defended against people armed with bows and flint-tipped arrows.

Some years ago I went to a festival in northern Thailand, near the border with Burma and Laos. It was an unusual event, and people had travelled through challenging landscapes to get there, some trekking for days and staying with relatives or at impromptu guest-houses. You could identify different peoples from their talk and their dress (often at its most elaborate and distinctive to suit the moment). There was drinking, feasting, music and dancing, and you could buy or swap all manner of things not usually to be seen. For a few days there was an unaccustomed buzz, and people left with new possessions, stories and occasionally partners. Something like this, I imagine, might well have happened on Salisbury Plain over 5,000 years ago.

Life continued into what archaeologists call the Middle Neolithic (3500–3000 BC), defined by new styles of pottery and flint tools, particularly arrowheads; no obvious reason for the changes has yet been identified, but they occur across the UK and echo events on the continent. We can see these artefacts across the area, especially from recent excavations. An important group of pits has been found close to Stonehenge, at West Amesbury Farm. They held the remains of over fifty pots, some fourteen thousand flint artefacts, shale beads and working debris, butchered bones from domestic animals, hazelnut shells, sloe stones and crab-apple pips – but no cereals. A dozen such pits have been excavated at Larkhill Camp – another Army development site, just west of the garrison – and more at a housing site in Amesbury, where one contained large amounts of burnt hazelnut shells, as well as field weeds and a few grains of wheat and barley; a barley grain was found in a pit at Bulford.

Late Neolithic pits (3000–2500 BC, another change in pottery and arrowhead styles) are still more common.[6] Several have been found at Durrington and on Amesbury Down, east of the Avon, containing quantities of artefacts, bones, hazelnut shells and a few cereal grains; in one were over a hundred flint scrapers, in another a rare antler hammer used to work flint. A few postholes tell us little about houses; one four-post building could have been funerary in nature.

At Bulford, some fifty Late Neolithic pits yielded one of the most significant artefact collections of this era near Stonehenge, suggesting activities that ranged from domestic to ceremonial. Finds include carved chalk, stone axeheads, a fine flint knife, flint-working debris, wild cattle bones and much charcoal. Many of these artefacts look deliberately placed, among them chunky chalk objects archaeologists call 'cups'. They are irregular in shape, and it's difficult to see how they could have held much; an alternative explanation is that they are hollowed lumps left over from scraping out chalk powder. Perhaps people were making body paint.

Significantly, radiocarbon dates make the pottery, an early style of Grooved Ware, the oldest example of its kind yet found in Wiltshire: dated precisely to 2950 BC, it overlaps in age with the oldest such pottery in Orkney, where the style may have originated. Phil Harding, a former *Time Team* archaeologist who works for Wessex Archaeology, was so excited by the Bulford finds that he delayed his retirement to work on them.

So while we may lack details of exactly how people lived (we still have almost nothing that looks like a house, bar a significant exception we'll come to soon), there were clearly plenty of folk about during the Neolithic. In 2014 the discovery was announced of a dozen or so ritual monuments around Stonehenge. The survey, which 'transformed our knowledge of this iconic landscape', was conducted by an international team using cutting-edge geophysical kit, which found many small circular earthworks, now flattened and invisible above ground, represented by pits and ditches. It's an important achievement, though without excavation we can only guess how old the discoveries are: they might be the same age as Stonehenge, older, younger or, quite probably, a combination. In any event, Stonehenge was plainly an important ritual and religious monument, and we might expect there to have been a few echoes in the neighbourhood.[7]

On the other hand, until the new excavations by Wessex Archaeology and Historic England at Larkhill, Bulford, Amesbury and closer to Stonehenge, it was still possible to imagine the downs as being thinly populated, and to explain that as a Stonehenge effect: this was not a domestic landscape, but a ritual one. The discoveries of settlement, and the pits of artefacts and food debris, show how wrong that was. The ritual is there too: archaeologists found a great oval of large post pits on Amesbury Down, of which thirty-one were excavated, 60 metres (200 feet) across. At Bulford are two adjacent henge monuments, ring ditches 16 or 17 metres (55 feet) across; centuries later, both were converted into Bronze Age burial mounds. And

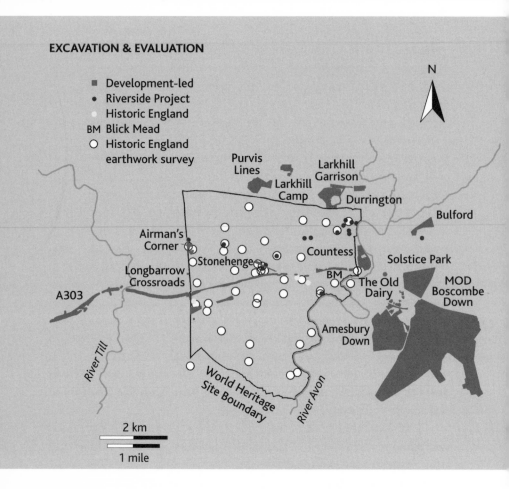

## EXCAVATION & EVALUATION

- ■ Development-led
- ● Riverside Project
- ● Historic England
- BM Blick Mead
- ○ Historic England
  earthwork survey

N

Purvis Lines

Larkhill Garrison

Larkhill Camp

Durrington

Bulford

Airman's Corner

Countess

Solstice Park

Stonehenge

Longbarrow Crossroads

BM

The Old Dairy

MOD Boscombe Down

A303

River Till

World Heritage Site Boundary

Amesbury Down

River Avon

2 km

1 mile

In recent years there has been an unprecedented amount of archaeological fieldwork around Stonehenge, much of it still under analysis. Our understanding of ancient landscapes is changing profoundly.

burials are everywhere. Living, dying and building made Salisbury Plain a very busy place.

And nowhere, at certain times, was busier than Stonehenge.

\*

Stonehenge's original era of construction, use and rebuilding spanned the Late Neolithic and the Copper Age (3000–2200 BC), continuing into the Early Bronze Age (until 1500 BC). Inevitably during those fifty or sixty generations both the world and the monument changed. So can we see the one in the other?

One of the few apparently definitive claims about Stonehenge is that it began 5,000 years ago, before which there was nothing there to notice. Around 2900 BC people dug a perfectly circular enclosing ditch, a little over 100 metres across (350 feet) and threw the spoil up into a bank. It's harder to date what went on inside, but by association we have long assumed that a slightly smaller concentric circle of Aubrey Holes (fifty-six large pits) was also dug at this time. The new consensus is that these pits probably held the first megaliths, relatively small bluestones from Wales.

The pits at Bulford, full of Grooved Ware, flints and animal bones, could be contemporary. These are the only ones of their kind investigated in recent times, but others were found in the last century with comparable hauls of selected and buried artefacts on the Avon's west bank and on King Barrow Ridge, overlooking Stonehenge from the east. Something unusual was going on, but there is growing evidence that it wasn't the beginning of it all.

While the ditch at Stonehenge is firmly radiocarbon-dated by tools used to dig it, made from red deer antler, other remains gave older dates. A few deer and cattle bones, including two ox jaws and an ox skull, date as far back as 3250 BC. Archaeologists have described these old bones as 'curated': they were collected from elsewhere and deliberately put in the ditch when it was dug. But where were they collected? The simplest answer would be more or less where they were found, some perhaps placed carefully in the ditch, some incorporated by accident. Stonehenge before Stonehenge.

One of the site's defining features is a cremation cemetery, the largest of its kind known in prehistoric Britain. Though poor excavation records in the last century and the fact that much of Stonehenge remains unexcavated make it impossible to know exactly *how* large it was, there were probably a good two hundred burials, perhaps many more. The most recent radiocarbon date we have for one of these is about 2500 BC, and it has been assumed that the cemetery began when the Aubrey Holes were dug, where many of the burials are found.

In 2008 I was part of a team that re-excavated a huge mass of cremated human bone, first recovered at Stonehenge in the 1920s and reburied in an Aubrey Hole in 1935. We were surprised to find a previously unknown burial that had not been excavated before. The woman's remains gave us a radiocarbon age of around 3000 BC. Of the twenty-eight cremated individuals for which we now have dates, a good half seem to be a little older than the ditch; three are older than 3100 BC. The Aubrey circle is undated, but if, as many archaeologists believe, its pits and stones were part of this cemetery, then it too may well be older than the ditch circle.[8]

Many other parts of the site are undated. An earthwork survey done recently by Historic England (the first ever full survey of Stonehenge) identified several new, barely visible remains, including a low mound among the stones that appears to be natural. A small earthwork known as the North Barrow seems most likely to lie under the enclosure bank, meaning it was made before it. Unexcavated in modern times, the North Barrow, despite its name, is not a burial mound but a ring ditch with an outer bank – a tiny henge.

The Heelstone, a lone megalith that today marks the rising sun at midsummer, may also predate the ring ditch. By weight (some forty tonnes) it is the largest stone on the site, completely undressed – unlike almost every other stone – and irregular in shape. I excavated near it in 1979, and found a pit crushed on the bottom by the weight of a large stone. Either the Heelstone was moved a little from an older location, I thought, or it is the lone survivor of what was once a pair.

Back then I favoured the latter. Few of us took seriously the idea that there might have been any significant natural stones on Salisbury Plain. Instead, we said, the Stonehenge sarsens (notoriously hard sandstone boulders and slabs) had been dragged from the Marlborough Downs 20 miles (30 kilometres) to the north. Hundreds were used in the megalithic monuments there at Avebury, and many still lie on the hills around.

Excavation of Aubrey Hole 7 in 2008, where cremated human remains
excavated previously at Stonehenge were reburied in 1935. The remains are now
providing key insights into people who travelled to Stonehenge from across at
least southern Britain. Author is on far right.

Recently, however, archaeological surveys suggest that there were indeed some large sarsens closer to Stonehenge – if not (to my mind) anything like enough to build the whole monument. The Stonehenge Riverside Project investigated two undressed sarsen boulders a few miles northeast of Stonehenge, known as the Cuckoo Stone and the Torstone (named after an archaeologist's dog), either side of the River Avon near Durrington. Both stones seem once to have been standing, and had beside them what looked like natural hollows from which they had been quarried.[9]

A problem with my pit by the Heelstone was its size: it seemed too big just to hold up a megalith. Perhaps, then, the original pit was a natural hollow enclosing the half-buried Heelstone, sunk under its weight into chalk that had been broken up and semi-liquefied during permafrost freeze and thaw during the last Ice Age. All the builders would have had to do was scoop out the stone and stand it up. For reasons we can only guess at (did it fall over? Was it adjusted to a different solar alignment? Was it temporarily removed so new stones could be dragged in through the entrance passage?), at some point it was re-erected a little to the southeast.

We know of one other pit at Stonehenge of comparable size to that by the Heelstone, a great hollow northwest of the tallest megalith, Stone 56. No convincing explanation for this pit has yet been found, but perhaps it too once held a great boulder, now lost among the carved sarsens. If this was the case, it is notable that the two pits with their half-buried stones lay roughly on the solstice axis – towards the rising midsummer sun in the northeast, and the setting midwinter sun in the southwest – which was to become such a key and distinctive feature not just of Stonehenge but also of other nearby monuments.

The pit by Stone 56 is near the centre of the Aubrey circle, and the distance between it and the pit by the Heelstone is equivalent to the circle's diameter. The site's basic location and geometry could have been derived from the natural occurrence of two sarsen boulders. Possible candidates for a rounded, elongated sarsen that might have come from this hollow are the curiously shaped Stone 16 – at the back of the sarsen circle beside the solstice axis – or perhaps even Stone 56 itself.

These two sarsens – the Heelstone and whatever had been in the other big pit – could have been part of a pre-Stonehenge focus that included the North Barrow, the Aubrey circle and other, as yet unrecognized features, some of which were there by at least 3200 BC. The combination of a little henge, megaliths from Wales, cremation burials, large cattle bones – some possibly from wild animals (which, as we saw earlier, featured in older Early Neolithic funerary rites) – and, perhaps, the two largest natural sarsens on the plain aligned with the midsummer and midwinter sun make the site unique. Stonehenge didn't so much burst into view around 2900 BC as grow slowly over a long time before.

There are even a couple of tantalizing Mesolithic radiocarbon dates. A cow-like bone has been dated to around 4150 BC, and a piece of charcoal to more than 9,000 years ago – more or less the same age as a few great post pits not far to the northwest of the future Stonehenge site. No Mesolithic artefacts have yet been identified, but these are fragile things that could not have come from far before they became buried. People were there long before Stonehenge was thought of, and at least on one occasion long enough to sit down and make a fire.

It's important to say that none of this would make Stonehenge Mesolithic, a creation of hunter-gatherers rather than farmers. What most of us think of as Stonehenge, what we might call peak Stonehenge – the rings of carved megaliths with horizontal lintels packed into the centre of the site – was created around 2500 BC. It transformed the place. But there had already been a variety of little-understood timber structures, a ring of stones and a ditch enclosure, and who knows what before them, reaching back centuries. When the enclosing ditch was dug around 2900 BC, creating a space within which happened everything else that followed, the site had long been attracting people for different reasons. When peak Stonehenge began, that sanctity, that distinctiveness of place, was memorialized and re-imagined through unprecedented deployment of resources and effort. But it was already a very unusual and special place.

None of this should surprise us, as we've long known that there was something else nearby at this time that was just as remarkable. A little to the north of Stonehenge is a huge elongated enclosure, delineated at both ends and sides by a straight ditch and bank. William Stukeley, Britain's greatest antiquarian and astute observer of the Stonehenge landscape, discovered it in 1723, when it was better preserved than now. He imagined it as the site of prehistoric Olympic

One of many recent research excavations around Stonehenge. Here, the ditch around a burial mound at the east end of the Cursus is being investigated.

games, and gave it the Latin name Cursus, a racecourse. The name stuck, and as more comparable earthworks have been found across Britain (the total currently stands at over a hundred, though only two exceed the exceptional size of that at Stonehenge), we still call them cursus monuments. Stukeley pictured ancient Britons thundering down in horse-drawn chariots. Neolithic people probably had neither horses nor carts, and we have no evidence for what really happened in or around a cursus.

The Stonehenge Cursus starts on a low hill to the northwest of the stones. Its parallel banks and ditches, 100 metres (330 feet) or so apart, run down the valley and up the other side to another low ridge 2 miles (3 kilometres) away, to the northeast of Stonehenge. To put its scale into perspective, its footprint is three times that of the entire proposed A303 dual carriageway and road tunnel as they cross from one side of the World Heritage Site to the other. And while any road-works would today be carried out in an open landscape, the builders of the Cursus may have had to cut down substantial numbers of trees with their stone-bladed axes. Its banks and ditches when freshly carved out of the white chalk must have made a truly monumental impact. And there was another one, known as the Lesser Cursus, 600 metres (2,000 feet) to the north; it's 400 metres (1,300 feet) long, and has been ploughed flat.

Recently radiocarbon-dated to around 3500 BC, the Stonehenge Cursus came at a time when long barrows were still being used but less commonly created. Its plan echoes the mounds' layout, and it's possible it was in some way involved with rituals of death or transitions in life – a larger communal successor, perhaps, to the more localized mounds. How long such rituals continued to be enacted we can only guess, but perhaps the Cursus, and the later cremation pyres and burials, were somehow connected. The mystery further embeds the site of Stonehenge into a deep past, of significance to an area larger than the immediate hills of Salisbury Plain, generations before the great carved megaliths appeared.

That geographical reach has been confirmed by a pioneering new study in which isotopes have been measured, for the first time, from cremated bone, taking samples from our Aubrey Hole re-excavation. Varied ratios of strontium-87 and strontium-86 showed ten out of twenty-five people had not lived locally in the last decade of their lives. Wherever they came from (the isotopes allow for parts of

Ireland, Scotland, Wales and much of England, as well as continental Europe, and some of the 'locals' could have come from the north of Britain), it's apparent that even before 3100 BC the site had more than a provincial draw. And when, finally, peak Stonehenge happened, the references – despite the novelty – were to native tradition and ancestral memories. The scale of work, however, was like nothing seen anywhere else in Europe.[10]

*

I could spend the rest of this chapter describing stones; it would be easy to devote an entire book to them. You would learn as much, however, and undoubtedly be more inspired, by going to look at them. For now, I ask you to imagine the sight of thirty huge sarsens, fresh from being pummelled and polished into shape and each weighing between fifteen and thirty tonnes, standing in a circle and supporting a gigantic, jointed ring-beam of thirty more slabs. If you had approached from the valley below, your back to the rising mid-summer sun, the wall of stone would have made it difficult to see what was happening inside. The tops of five independent trilithons (another term coined by Stukeley – Greek for 'three stones') tower above like titanic door frames. And all around, in the space between the sarsen ring and the trilithons, are gathered dozens of bluestones. Many are the size of human figures. The dark crowd seems to guard an invisible arena within, the stones turning and watching as they appear briefly in the gaps as you pass.

Over the following five centuries the bluestones were moved around. Encircling rings of pits were dug in the Early Bronze Age, though we don't know why, and the shapes of dozens of copper axe blades and a couple of daggers were carved into the sarsens. But the building of the great lintelled monument remains the most interesting moment. For around that time other things start to change. Very rare metal may be in circulation, and the earliest pots of an entirely new style, with new ways of commemorating the dead, are in the air. At first, there's no sign of any of this at Stonehenge, except for one thing: a handful of broken sherds. We call the pots they came from Beakers.

Unfortunately our dating of the first great Stonehenge is poor. I have said it began around 2500 BC, and this is the current favoured date. But it's a statistical estimate based on not enough good samples from a complex site. On that evidence alone we can't be certain who created Stonehenge: was it the makers of Grooved Ware, the native British pottery style (of which there is even less at the site than Beakers), or of Beakers, found across Europe? New aDNA research has made this a particularly poignant question. As I noted above, the evidence suggests that Beaker migrants substantially outnumbered the indigenous population after 2450 BC. So was peak Stonehenge the last glorious celebration of the ancestors of a doomed culture? Or did it signify the arrival of new people seeking land and power, and showing the world they meant it?

We might try to answer this question by asking who was buried at Stonehenge. Cremation cemeteries are found across Britain associated with the makers of Grooved Ware; they are a distinctive native trait. On the other hand, one of the markers of the users of Beaker pottery is that they practised a quite different form of rite: bodies were laid underground in large pits, on their side with legs bent. Distinctive artefacts – often including an actual Beaker pot – were placed in the grave. You know a Beaker burial when you find one.

The problem is that, on current evidence, burial largely ceased at Stonehenge around the time the great stones were erected. We know of only one later, significant prehistoric grave – tellingly, you might think, of a man accompanied by some of those distinctive Beaker artefacts. However, radiocarbon dates show he died well over two centuries after the stones went up. And there is a twist that raises a question only aDNA (not yet applied) might solve. The items with the body were an archer's wrist-guard and flint arrowheads, but the arrows were not gifts for his afterlife. They were the cause of his death.

More helpful is to look for the places where the people who built Stonehenge lived, and here recent excavation has triumphed. One of the great discoveries of the Riverside Project is a collection of houses at Durrington Walls, 2 miles (3 kilometres) to the north-east of Stonehenge on the west bank of the Avon. The Walls is a massive henge enclosure, distinguished by a deep quarry ditch on the inside of an encircling bank. Some 500 metres (1,600 feet) across, it's the largest of less than half a dozen examples that are all but unique to Wessex, another of which surrounds the great stone circle at Avebury.

A Neolithic house floor at Durrington Walls, with a hearth base in the centre on a compacted chalk floor and outer walls marked by stake holes.

In the 1960s the Walls was the site of a huge and controversial excavation (a road was about to be put through the henge), which discovered the remains of a great timber circle. Enormous pits had held several concentric rings of oak posts on a scale, and perhaps of appearance too, comparable to Stonehenge. A similar structure had been found on the hill just above in the 1920s, and dubbed Woodhenge. The oak rings in the Walls were littered with debris – animal bones, stone tools and broken pottery. The new excavations found that this debris derived from the feasting, living and working of people accommodated in small squarish houses. Extrapolating from the relatively small exposed area, Mike Parker Pearson, the project's director, thinks there was a village that may have housed as many as 4,000 people. It's the right scale, and more or less the right age, to be a temporary community gathered from a wide area to build Stonehenge. And they got through huge amounts of Grooved Ware.

Durrington Walls gives us the best evidence we might ever have that Stonehenge was built by people whose culture reached back to 3000 BC across the UK, and through them further back into the Middle Neolithic. Woodhenge and the great timber arrangement at the Walls, so like peak Stonehenge in plan, show that the megalithic concept did not appear from nowhere. It lay in a tradition of oak, represented at several sites across Britain. The engineering and design skills, even the carpentry jointing techniques, were co-opted at Stonehenge to make something unique: it drew partly on contemporary ritual architecture, and partly on the site's history, emphasizing, for example, the old alignment on the rising and setting sun, and incorporating the bluestone monument associated for centuries with the graves of ancestors.

Beaker pottery, the most common of a range of new artefacts that included barbed-and-tanged flint arrowheads, stone archers' wrist-guards, a particular style of button and, in the UK, the earliest metal, first appeared in Spain and Portugal around 2750 BC. Along with such traits as inhumation in large pits, these things were brought to Britain some three centuries later by migrants. Though their genome's closest parallels, as we currently know them, lie with Beaker-using groups from the Netherlands, it was distinguished by ancestry derived from further east on the Eurasian Steppe, from older movements of people that had stopped short at the English Channel. The Y-chromosome haplogroup and mitochondrial DNA are both continental, showing that the migrants included men (Y) and women (mtDNA). These people came to settle and make new lives.

Much the most spectacular Beaker grave identified in Britain – unusual even in a wider European context – was near Stonehenge, on the east bank of the Avon. The man buried there, dubbed the Amesbury Archer, died around 2335 BC. He could have had nothing to do with the creation of peak Stonehenge, which by then was two centuries old. But it would be hard to argue that the proximity of the two was coincidence.

The man had been buried in a pit, probably made for a plank-lined chamber. In the tomb was a collection of objects typical of Beaker graves, but conspicuously profligate. It's as if he'd taken the goods of several people with him: five Beaker pots, three copper knives and two stone wrist-guards, not just one of each (which alone would have been quite a boast); a tusk from each of four boars; no less than eighteen fine flint arrowheads, and dozens of other flint knives and flakes, including two possible dagger blades; a stone that might have been used in smithing gold or copper (both precious and very early metals); and two delicate gold ornaments.

A little further up the hill was another Beaker grave. This too was highly unusual: it had been badly disturbed, but what survived consisted of a communal burial pit holding the remains of nine or ten people, possibly all men, and their pots and other artefacts. They had been buried, not all at the same time, a century before the Archer.[11]

None of these men were locals. Isotope studies of their bones suggest that the Archer was born in central Europe (plus he had an antler pin whose design is best matched by one excavated in Switzerland), and the others might also have come from the continent. Their graves contain some of Britain's first Beakers, fitting a time of migration as painted by aDNA. By contrast, a man in a grave near the Archer's, buried with a similar pair of gold ornaments to his, could have been born locally. No aDNA has been retrieved from any of their remains, but the two men shared a rare inherited condition in the bones of their feet. Perhaps the second was the Archer's son, born to an immigrant within sight of Stonehenge.

Amesbury Down is not the only place where people shunned cremation and opted for inhumation with a Beaker pot. It happened across the Stonehenge landscape. Another very early example, from

A Beaker pot, buried with a man on Amesbury Down. Finer than the older, native Grooved Ware pottery, Beakers owed their shapes and decoration to traditions that evolved on the European continent. Height 16 cm (6¼ in.).

around 2375 BC, was revealed by excavation associated with A303 roadworks, just south of Stonehenge. Two graves were found, each with a Beaker: one was for an unusually tall man, the other a baby less than six months old. The burials lay on the edge of a known cemetery associated with a round barrow called Wilsford G1. First excavated in 1805, the site had already yielded several burials, at least seven of them accompanied by Beaker pots.

This was in effect a Beaker family vault. It established a tradition of round mound burial that continued on the site for generations, leading to one of the best-known barrow cemeteries at Stonehenge, strung out along Normanton Down. Here some of the wealthiest graves in the area – indeed in northern Europe – were excavated in the early 19th century. Burial continued for nearly a thousand years until at least 1500 BC. Many of the Early Bronze Age barrow groups around Stonehenge seem to have grown from a Beaker cemetery in this way, sited in what was then relatively empty downland, as if founding a dynasty's connection with the land.

More graves have been found in recent development work. The dead include three infants huddled together in a pit at Larkhill Garrison, a teenage girl laid to rest on Amesbury Down with a necklace of ninety amber beads, and another with an amber bracelet. Many of these burials were revisited by descendants, who dug into graves, removed and reburied bones, and on two occasions refilled the pits with flint nodules. Even the Amesbury Archer's grave was opened: bones had been disturbed and an entire rib was missing, and it's possible that objects had been added (perhaps men gave arrows: the eighteen arrowheads are of varied shapes and sizes, and were scattered through the burial pit). There is a physicality of ancestry here, a knowledge of individuals and tradition reinforced by the repeated memorialization of graves, reaching back through generations to the first Beaker people, the original colonists.[12]

The genome project mentioned earlier examined fourteen of these newly excavated people. Where sufficient aDNA could be characterized, all of them showed steppe-related ancestry – they were all descended from recent migrants, if they weren't immigrants themselves. A man buried on Amesbury Down was seen to be the father of a young woman in a grave on Porton Down 3 miles (5 kilometres) to the south. Two men buried side by side on Amesbury Down were identified as father and son. Genetics and archaeology seem to agree:

from at least 2400 BC there was a sweeping change, ushering in new technologies, values, beliefs and people.

Thinking just about the DNA, as the scientists were obliged to do, it's easy to imagine some kind of catastrophic population replacement: there's been talk of 'disruptive events' and plague. But archaeology also has an important role to play in unravelling the story. What does it tell us at Stonehenge? Early in 2018, shortly before the Beaker aDNA research was published, I met a group of archaeologists who should know. What did they think?

Alistair Barclay, Bob Clarke, Si Cleggett and Matt Leivers all work for Wessex Archaeology. They have been responsible for managing and directing some of the most important recent excavations near Stonehenge, at Larkhill, Bulford and Amesbury – and they collaborated with the aDNA study, supplying samples from their excavations. We sat round a table in their head office near Salisbury, a building that had been an operations centre for an airfield in the Second World War, with a flight room where model planes were moved around table maps.

It was too early to draw definitive conclusions: even these archaeologists were learning about new discoveries from each other, and I struggled to keep up with all the finds still being excavated and awaiting study. But there seemed to be agreement that there were no signs of abrupt change or conflict in the landscape, even if people and fashions had changed. Si, sporting a generous beard and ponytail, his hands and arms dark with tattoos, referred to the futuristic film *Avatar*: like the Na'vi, he said, the indigenous creatures whose world was singled out as a quarry by humans, prehistoric people understood every detail of their environment.

The causewayed enclosure at Larkhill was sited with care to acknowledge the shape of the land and the rivers: thousands of years later, Beaker graves in the same area reflected the same understanding. 'They are using the same hallowed ground,' said Si. 'Nothing to do with ancestral ownership, but the meaning of the landscape has remained special.' Among the archaeologists' discoveries are two ring ditches, each surrounded by a circle of pits. There was a hollow at the centre of one of the rings where the roots of a falling tree had ripped up the chalk, as if the earthwork had been built around an old, lone oak or ash – the Larkhill treehenge, perhaps. The Na'vi Hometree.

This is highly subjective, but it fits the little evidence we currently have on the issue. If Stonehenge and the oak rings at Durrington Walls were the creations of indigenous, Grooved Ware-making people, both sites also have very small amounts of Beaker pottery, apparently broken and lost before the first burials appear. It is common to find Beaker pottery at older Neolithic monuments across Britain with little apparent evidence of desecration. This suggests at least a toleration, and perhaps a sympathetic continuation, of native traditions by the earliest migrants. And if peak Stonehenge was built without the help of distant migrants, it didn't stand still for long. On at least two occasions, the bluestones were uprooted and rearranged, between around 2400 and 2100 BC – the prime Beaker era.

In 2009 the Riverside Project found the site of a small stone circle down by the Avon.[13] The pits are the right size and shape for bluestones, and the ring may have been created at the same time as the Aubrey circle at Stonehenge, out of sight $1\frac{1}{4}$ miles (2 kilometres) away. But what happened to the twenty-five stones? They are probably at Stonehenge: dug out, hauled up the Avenue – a wide path that connects the river to Stonehenge, marked by chalk banks – and joined with the other bluestones in a new arrangement. Exactly when that happened is unfortunately not certain, but it seems to have been when the first Beaker people were in the area – as if they might have been helping to re-enact, in a small way, the great original journey the stones took from Wales, in a grand gesture to ancestral memory. And it was their descendants in the Early Bronze Age who identified with Stonehenge by carving axe and dagger-blade shapes on the stones. They took ownership of the place: but they didn't knock it down.

We should also remember the 10 per cent of older indigenous ancestry that survives in the modern British genome. There was some intermarriage between people who made Beaker pottery and those who made Grooved Ware. From a longer perspective, they all had origins in a European pool descended from farmers with roots back east. They could hardly have known, by the time of Stonehenge, that, millennia before, there were other people in Europe to whom they bore little relationship. People whose lives were entirely different from their own, who knew landscapes and coastlines that would have been unrecognizable to the farmers. They were our last hunter-gatherers, the subject of the next chapter.

Chapter 7

# Deer Hunters

*Star Carr, 11,000 years ago*

The Mesolithic, when people lived entirely on their personal abilities to exploit what we think of as the wild, lasted more than two hundred generations. That's more or less the time that separates us from the end of their era, with everything that happened in between, from Stonehenge to St Paul's Cathedral, the first wheels to the industrial revolution, and the first fired technologies of pottery and metallurgy to the smartphone. In the greater scheme, you might imagine, Britain after the Ice Age has essentially belonged to red deer, wolves and hunters and gatherers; we technologists, we farmers, are insensitive, interfering interlopers, never happy with a particular way of life.

The hunter-gatherers lived lightly on the land, leaving few monuments and hard-to-find ephemeral houses where we might see them at work. Dependent on natural and seasonal resources, people probably routinely moved about more than settled farmers would ever do. In the north, they must have lived differently from those in the south; on the coasts, people would have known things that others far inland might never have seen. And however they managed it, consuming a wide range of wild plant and animal foods, and with refined making skills using all the materials available to them, they were very successful. The great irony is that while culturally we can see only small changes over more than five thousand years, they knew a Britain whose natural transformations were unlike anything experienced by anyone since.

Climate can be brutal. As long as there have been people in Britain, the Earth's climate has been more wayward than stable. Over those million years there were a couple of dozen major fluctuations, making frozen wastes out of Britain before thrusting it back into a world like ours or warmer, as animals and plants fled and returned and fled again.

The last major cold era – one of the most severe, with glacial ice burying everything from the north down to the English Midlands and South Wales – lasted fifteen millennia until some 15,000 years ago. Then, with fits and starts, the warmth returned – gradually at first, then dramatically and quite suddenly, followed after 2,000 years by a millennium of intense cold. Meanwhile, the climate warmed and cooled in brief jumps that would have made it hard to know where it was going, before finally, some 8,000 years ago – after a sudden cold reversal – settling down for good. Nature then gave us an exceptionally long era of stable climate: if only we'd left it like that.

People came and went as the Ice Age reluctantly gave up its grip, feeling their way north when times warmed, shrinking back when they chilled. It was thought that even the last major cold episode was severe enough to banish people, but in this as in so much else, Star Carr, the focus of this chapter, has forced archaeologists to look again. From 11,500 years ago, it now seems, people stayed, as woodland – at first dense stands of birch, poplar and pine in an otherwise open landscape of grasses and tall herbs, and later more widespread oak, elm and ash – recolonized the once icy ground. The forest would have been broken not just by rivers but also by the tracks of animals and people, and by the places where hunters made their homes and shaped environments favourable to their way of life. They had fire and efficient axes, and we know they used both to clear vegetation.

Over the millennia, they faced changes in climate, flora and the animal herds, fish and other creatures on which they depended. They also lived in a changing landscape. In the far north, new expanses of sand, mud and rock were exposed on the shore as ground now free of the overpowering weight of ice rebounded. A lethal tsunami devastated the east coast. At the start of the Mesolithic, a vast area of highly productive land, with a wealth of marsh, rivers and estuaries and, we

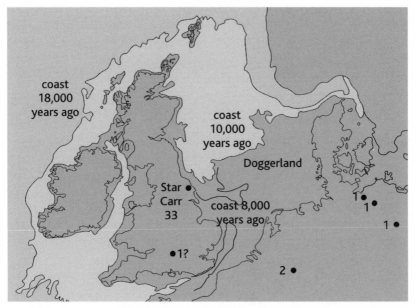

As the climate warmed during the Mesolithic era, sea levels rose, eventually separating Britain from the continent. Sites with worked deer frontlets are marked with the number found at each location.

have to assume, the homes of many people – sometimes referred to as Doggerland – reached without break from central England to southern Scandinavia. By 8,000 years ago it had disappeared, over-whelmed by the mounting waves that would become what we now know as the southern North Sea.

The rising water squeezed people together onto the remaining land, and divided Britain and the continent. With strong currents pouring through the Straits of Dover, people in the habit of moving freely between the Netherlands, Belgium and England were suddenly separated, friends and families cut off from ancestral hunting grounds. From that moment, their lives and cultures began to diverge.[1]

Given such dramatic changes, you might think the formation of a small lake in Yorkshire a minor sideshow. At the time, it clearly meant something to people: there is copious evidence that they camped and hunted and hung around its shore. But hunters and gatherers did such things all over Britain, on hills and in river valleys, on coasts and in mountains. What makes the lake matter to us is what it preserved, its peculiar deposits swallowing the works and debris of human lives like a great, tender museum, protecting them for over ten thousand years until archaeologists opened its doors and read its story. The old lake made Star Carr today the most significant hunter-gatherer site in Europe, and one of the most famous in the world.

\*

The landscape at Star Carr is striking. If you stand with your back to a small river tidied up into a canal two centuries ago, and look south, you see the chalk hills of the Yorkshire Wolds rising like a long bank on the horizon. The ground between is flat. Ditches marked by scrubby trees cut through green pasture. It's a featureless, wet place with an appealing, quiet atmosphere of its own, but not somewhere you'd think to look for landmark ancient monuments.

Yet these peaty fields have attracted almost as many archaeological excavations over the past seventy years as has Stonehenge. Star Carr has been argued over in lecture rooms and student seminars around the world, and its meaning dissected in books and articles. Artefacts are exhibited in four museums: up the road in York and Whitby, in the Museum of Archaeology and Anthropology in Cambridge, and in the British Museum in London. Others have been given to museums for research and teaching – in Scarborough, for example, in London (Natural History Museum), in Legon, Ghana (the university's Department of Archaeology), and who knows where else.[2] Star Carr was designated a site of national importance by the government in 2011, and it appeared on a Royal Mail postage stamp in 2017 (although at £1.05 it couldn't have graced many letters). Despite all this attention and industry, however, the great question remained: what was Star Carr?

None of this would have happened were it not for John Moore, a local archaeologist who went looking for ancient remains in the Vale of Pickering. In the late 1940s Moore started to find Mesolithic flint blades. He figured out that the peat had accumulated in what was once a lake, 3 miles long and, at its widest, 1 mile across (5 by 2 kilometres), around which early hunters had camped: he named it Lake Flixton, after a nearby village on the chalk. Even today, if you jump hard in the right place you can feel the ground tremor, sending a wobble deep below through waterlogged peat.

A Cambridge University archaeologist named Grahame Clark heard about Moore's finds and got in touch. Learning that the peat was throwing up not just flints but also remains of bone and antler, Clark set off for Yorkshire and met Moore at one of his sites, on Star Carr ('carr' is a local term, derived from the language spoken by Vikings, for swamp). Clark was hooked.

Socially awkward, with a lack of confidence that many mistook for self-centredness, Grahame Clark was profoundly humane and quite brilliant. Correctly predicting that the peat would have preserved Mesolithic wood, animal remains and ecological data that up to then had been found very rarely – and never in Britain – he embarked on a career-changing excavation, dragging his brightest students and a team of scientists up to the sulphurous swamp for three summers between 1949 and 1951.

Together, they painted a picture of a few families camped by the lake, cutting down trees, cooking meals, making their clothes and hunting kit, and setting out on long expeditions to follow herds of red deer. Among the wealth of artefacts was an extraordinary collection of stags' skull caps with antlers still attached, hollowed out and perforated with pairs of holes – worn to aid hunters stalk deer, wondered Clark, or made for ritual dancing?

Twenty years later, having promptly published a monograph on his dig that remains one of the best of its kind, Clark revisited his deer hunters, updating the research and throwing out some new ideas. It was just before his retirement, and soon his elegant writings and the exceptional site inspired a new generation of archaeologists. The journey to really understand Star Carr, with all the help of modern science and institutional funding, had begun.

Further sites were found along the old lake edge. At Star Carr itself, Clark thought that deer hunters had come to the water twice over twenty-five years, but radiocarbon dates from new excavations showed that the site had a longer history – more than two centuries – and was older than Clark could have guessed. Studies of ancient pollen and charcoal indicated that people had burnt the reed swamp and vegetation on dry land, perhaps to clear ground for their camps and to encourage new growth that would attract browsing game.

These small excavations also revealed a worrying twist. Bone and antler that would have been well preserved in Clark's day was now in poor condition. Away from the lake, flint tools in the ploughsoil

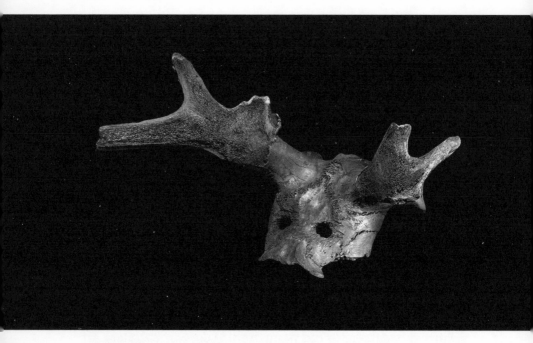

A red deer frontlet excavated at Star Carr around 1950, worked from the skull of a large stag. The antlers have been trimmed, the bone has been shaped and thinned, and two holes have been cut through the front.

showed that new farming was eating away at the evidence, cutting into remains that had lain safe underground for millennia and throwing them into the open like tiny smelt on a fishmonger's slab, torn from their habitat, silently mouthing.

Star Carr was still unique. There was nothing like it in Europe: even elsewhere around Lake Flixton, thirty years of work had turned up one antler harpoon point; Clark had found nearly two hundred at Star Carr. Archaeologists continued to write with undiminished disagreement about what people might have been doing there 11,000 years ago, but the Star's light was fading. Only intervention could rescue the site.

Three friends who had been taking part in the fieldwork since the 1990s decided it was time to act. On an autumn day in 2003, fresh from walking over ploughed fields looking for flints, Nicky Milner, Chantal Conneller and Barry Taylor sat in a pub near Flixton. 'We were all in our early thirties,' Nicky told me, 'super-enthusiastic about Star Carr, and we knew the site hadn't been finished.' It would be 2018 before their project was done.[3]

*

They started on a shoestring budget, based at the various universities at which they were then working – York (Nicky), Cambridge (Chantal) and Manchester (Barry), and at UCL (Tim Schadla-Hall, their mentor and a force of nature in the Vale of Pickering). That summer they talked to the farmers, who agreed to allow them to dig test pits across their land, and in early September – on Nicky's birthday – they learnt that they had permission to dig Star Carr itself. 'It was the best ever birthday present,' said Nicky. 'We were on site the next day. We had to be.'

Eleven thousand years ago Star Carr was on the end of a little finger of land that protruded into the lake's waters. Over the next two seasons the archaeologists walked intensively over the peninsula, bent double seeking flints, and dug small test trenches. They found artefacts for 150 metres (500 feet) along the little ridge. They dug two larger trenches across the lake edge, so they could see how the organic remains were faring. Scientists warned that the antler, bone and wood that was still there would probably be gone within five or ten years. 'Tim said that back in the seventies, you couldn't see the peninsula,' said Chantal. 'It was covered in peat. But now we could. The peat was shrinking.' And with it seemed to be going everything that made Star Carr special.

Peat – the living stuff, not the dry powder you can buy in garden centres (but really shouldn't: you are destroying antiquity) – is heavy and dark, textured by the compress of the half-decayed plants of which it is made. What is not solid is water, and the wetness and lack of oxygen slow or halt decomposition, just as streams preserved writing tablets in London and houses at Must Farm. Moss, seeds and twigs can look almost new, though they might be thousands of years old. At Star Carr, peat growing on the lake edge when the only people in Europe were hunters and gatherers preserved the branches they cut down and laid in the water. It preserved their antler harpoon tips, their worked timbers and their firewood, the fungi, reeds and rolls of birch bark they collected, and the many bones of animals they had hunted.

In normal conditions – that is to say, the places where archaeologists do almost all their work, in dirt, soil and rubble – bone or antler sometimes survives, but none of the rest does, unless fortuitously carbonized into shapeless burnt scraps. It's magic, this wet peat, offering a world we hardly ever see, its soft embrace halfway between earth and water shrinking the distance between present and past. It's also a tease. The timbers, antlers and bones are not all they seem.

They look solid, and preserve intricate details of their surfaces that make them so precious to archaeologists. But like the peat, they are soft. 'You could squash the wood in your fingers,' said Nicky. 'It was mainly just water masquerading as wood.' Archaeologists typically work with picks and steel trowels. At Star Carr they dug with their fingers and small wooden tools, feeling gently in the black for the subtle changes that said they'd found something. And new scientific studies revealed a further problem.

At its best, the antler was now soft and leathery. Otherwise it was just gelatine: 'We had quite a lot of jelly-bone,' said Nicky, 'and jelly-antler.' The sediments holding it all together were acidic, and the effects of this were being exaggerated by the lowering of the water table through drainage installed so farmers could plant crops. A natural reaction between sulphate and iron in the ground was generating sulphuric acid. At the level of the archaeological remains, typical peat had a pH of 3.0 – like vinegar or a rough wine. One wood sample clocked a pH of 1.7: stomach acid. Now they were really worried.[4]

In 2007 they opened their first – *the* first – large, dry-land trench at Star Carr. They found a house. That sounds grand, but all that was left was a shallow hollow, 3 metres (10 feet) across, ringed by small holes that would once have held posts. Mesolithic houses seem to have been rounded, tent-like structures, probably made of timber, reeds and earth, warmed by an open hearth on a floor raised over a hollow. Nicky had previously co-directed the excavation of the best-preserved example yet found in Britain, at Howick in Northumberland. At Star Carr, this was the first indication that hunter-gatherers might have slept there even for a night. Radiocarbon dates told them it had been built nearly 11,000 years ago: it was much the oldest house yet found in Britain.

Star Carr was disappearing, yet its importance seemed to be growing. The following year Nicky and her colleagues were back digging test pits, revealing Mesolithic occupation across an area of almost two hectares – the equivalent of two sports fields. Oddly, when they began in 2004 some archaeologists thought they should leave it alone. What more was there to learn: hadn't Clark found everything? Decades of argument about what it meant had got nowhere, and it was time to think about other sites. A few even questioned their abilities. But having spent years getting to know the place working with Tim Schadla-Hall, they believed in themselves and in Star Carr, and persevered. Now others were seeing it too.

Historic England, which was sponsoring the scientific studies, held a seminar in York, and there was another in Cambridge. The team got new funding for their largest dig yet, lasting all of three weeks, and opened three trenches, revisiting some dug by Clark himself (in one were two complete birch trees, lying flat on the ground: the same trees had been exposed in 1950). Encouraged by all of this, Nicky applied for a large European Research Council grant and, to the surprise of them all, won it.

Between 2013 and 2015 they had three eight-week seasons at the site. With dozens of students and specialists, they excavated the largest area to have been dug at Star Carr in sixty years. They had enough funds for on-site labs, where material could be examined as it came out of the ground – the dig was more like a *Silent Witness*

A birch tree on the edge of a Mesolithic platform at Star Carr, excavated in 1950.

TV crime drama than *Time Team*. It was an entirely new project, yet with the advantage that, having already spent so much time there, they knew exactly what to do and how to go about it. What they didn't know, however, was that what they would find would change everything. The hunters and gatherers of Starr Carr were about to come to life in the 21st century AD.

\*

People were in the area close to the end of the Ice Age, hunting horses as soon as there was sufficient vegetation in the warming climate to encourage herds to come this far north. Culturally these were the final representatives of the Upper Palaeolithic, the first era of modern humans in Europe, which we will explore in the next chapter.[5]

Then, for a brief century or so, there may have been no one. As the climate warmed enough for juniper scrub and birch to start breaking up the windswept grassland, the first to interfere with the

In the new excavations, dark peat marks the edge of the former Lake Flixton, preserving remains of timber platforms. The lighter area, where evidence for three houses was found, was dry ground 11,000 years ago.

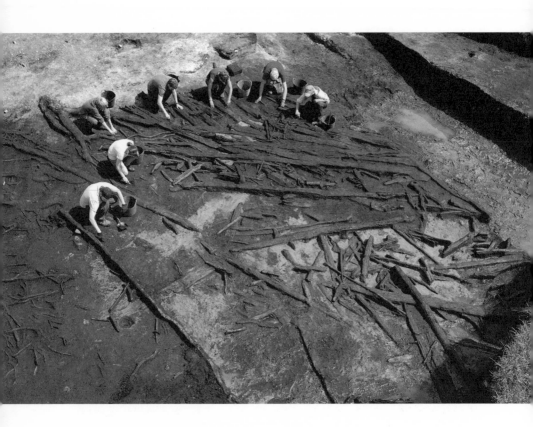

The central platform under excavation in 2013.

edge of the lake were beavers; a handful of gnawed pieces of wood are among the oldest things from the site. These large furry rodents, however, didn't have the place to themselves for long.

Mesolithic people were at Star Carr by 11,300 years ago. For as much as two and a half centuries they came down to the water's edge, living and working on the dry land and throwing the remains of butchered animals and other debris into the swamp. Nettles and ferns grew in the wet soil around willow, aspen and birch. Dense reedswamp reached at least 15 metres (50 feet) out into the lake, whose dark surface was decorated with water lily and pondweed.

The climate was not yet stable, however. During this time temperatures fell by as much as 10°C (nearly 20°F), and newly established birch clumps temporarily died back to let in the old grassland. It would have been impossible for people to have survived without fire and warm, protective clothes. And the challenge was not just the cold, but also the speed at which the climate changed – fast enough for people to see it happening. But somehow they knew how to cope.[6]

Loose brushwood was already beginning to accumulate at the western edge of the site, most of it probably washed up by the lapping water. People made their own wood scatter nearby, laying down trees and split timbers in the first of a succession of improvised platforms that may have helped them cross the swamp to reach open water and dugout canoes. Inland, away from the shore, they settled into a shelter (the Central house), fixing poles over a hollow in the ground to support a weatherproof cover. Other postholes in the area suggest further structures (the North house), but what it or they were for is not clear.

And then they left. The climate warmed and within decades birch woodland became more established. Reeds spread further into the lake as it slowly filled with peat and sediment, and at its edge the swamp ceded to sedge and then ferns as trees expanded onto the drying ground. On this part of the shore, at least, no people were to be seen for as many as half a dozen generations. The first signs of their return were flames and smoke. For perhaps two or three generations people off-stage set fires that periodically swept the vegetation. Then a little after 11,000 years ago they were there again, cutting down trees and dragging large timbers into the swamp to make the Central platform, perhaps having cleared the area with the last fire of this time. Making their mark, they dropped or discarded tools and debris among the half-submerged, glistening branches.

People stayed for two or three generations, and then left again. They were back after a further three or four generations, some 10,800 years ago, laying out another spread of split timbers and trees (the Eastern platform), as always just avoiding the areas used by their predecessors but clearly attracted to this particular part of the lake, where it started to narrow before flowing out as a river to the west. Episodic burning continued. They made two structures in the excavated area, one a house (the East house) and the other less certainly so (the West house). At the latter, where people fixed poles but excavated no hollow, they left quantities of animal bones, stone tools and working debris, much of it burnt. They used the tools to process plants, wood, animal hides and bone, to butcher meat and to make beads.

It was at this time that the deer hunters did something really odd. In the western part of the site they stashed a huge amount of bone, antler, wood and stone in the swamp, a mix of debris and tools, hunting weapons, precious beads and more. It sank rapidly down into the mud, and may have been put there in a single burst of determined effort.

A century later people laid down another walkway of split and unsplit timber leading out towards the water (the Western platform). A century after that, fire swept the area again, and within a few more generations, by around 10,500 years ago and eight centuries after people had first dipped their toes into the edge of the lake, they left, never to return. When, a thousand years later, someone dropped or discarded an arrow or light spear – only the five tiny, sharp flints that had armed its tip, known as microliths, had survived for the archaeologists to find – it's unlikely its owner knew anything about what had happened there before.[7]

Hunters and gatherers had the land to themselves for a further three and a half millennia before the first farmers started to swing their new-fangled axes in the old woods. By then, as significant as Star Carr had been to the families of early deer hunters, the place, the people and all that had happened there had been entirely forgotten. Nonetheless, thanks to the hunters' habit of filling the swamp with the material diaries of their lives, combined with the preservative power of the wet peat, this bald outline of events can be enlivened with insights into exactly what they were getting up to. Before I do that, however, I want to explain how extraordinary and important the narrative is. In some ways it is the Star Carr project's greatest find of all.

Today, as we have done for a century, we call the people of Star Carr hunter-gatherers: they made their way by hunting animals, and by gathering fruits, nuts, greens, grubs, eggs, shellfish and anything else edible that didn't demand too much risk or heavy lifting (and yes, in the traditional, male-dominated literature, hunters were thought of as men, gatherers as women, and hunting the bit that really mattered). The description would have meant nothing to them, as it makes sense only from our perspective as farmers (most of us of course are not farmers, but we all depend for our food on the few who are). 'Hunter-gatherer' is just a way of saying 'not farmer'. It would be like an alien coming to earth and telling us that what defines us is the fact that we don't live on Zorg.

For more than 85 per cent of the time that modern humans have been in Britain, they (we) have been hunter-gatherers. If you take in the years before, when earlier human species were here hunting rhinos, mammoths and giant deer (and, presumably, gathering nuts and greens), the figure rises to more than 99 per cent. Extend that to Africa, where earlier human evolution occurred, and the human lineage has effectively been happily living off the wild for ever.

Yet from our extremely narrow modern perspective, we judge hunter-gatherers as inferior. In children's books and the Home Office guide to British history, our hunter-gatherer past is dismissed as an episode of timeless savagery where nothing happened. In countries where there are hunter-gatherers today (often people pushed into marginal places where anyone else would find it hard to live at all), they can be treated as second-class citizens. They own little property, have no fixed address, and are difficult to pin down and control; not infrequently, they are also in the way of businesses wanting to mine or otherwise deplete their world. They don't fit. They are a blot on modernity.

The most telling assessment of hunter-gatherers is the idea that they have no history. You see this, for example, when a blogger or journalist (or worse, an academic) talks about our early existence on the African savannah. Here, it is said, millions of years ago our brains were wired to be sexist, shop in supermarkets and value waterfront property (apparently we like fewer trees and a bit of grass and water). Now, some early humans undoubtedly spent a lot of time in savannah. But Africa is a big place, and its landscapes are vast and extraordinarily varied – and they changed as humans evolved. Some human species close to us (Neanderthals, for example) did not evolve in Africa at all, but in more northern latitudes with climates that ranged from Mediterranean to subarctic. And as humans evolved and spread across the globe, they encountered new plants and animals – which changed not just as they occupied new worlds, but also as climate changed, forcing dramatic transformations in fauna and flora in the same place and to which people had to adjust. To call all of this 'African savannah' is crazy.[8]

The label still further conceals the people themselves: despite all that evolving, it seems, they had no agency – no ability to think on their own, to choose to do things that would have an impact on their lives and the lives of others. In Samuel Beckett's *Waiting for Godot*, four men and a boy occupy a stage empty except for a half-dead tree. They talk about themselves and about being human, expressing their apparent failure to understand or control anything (if you don't know the play and that sounds bleak, it's actually very funny). They might be a metaphor for how early humans have been depicted; a better image still, though, would be the tree.

Over twenty years ago I wrote about an archaeological excavation at Boxgrove, West Sussex, where evidence for pre-Neanderthal humans had been wonderfully preserved (we will encounter Boxgrove in Chapter 9). An issue then was how intelligent these early people had been – could they hunt and kill, for example, or did they have to wait for animals to die? To make a point, I described research on chimpanzees that revealed that these great apes, with whom we shared a common ancestor seven million years ago, were seen to behave in more sophisticated ways than archaeologists credited to humans a mere half a million years ago.

Something was wrong with the archaeological vision. And we can make the same point about history. The longest-running study of chimpanzees in the wild originated with Jane Goodall's fieldwork in Tanzania. A few chimp generations and much observation later, we can see that chimpanzees make history. Individuals rise and fall in power, plot against one another and shape communities and how they live. In the 1970s there was something known officially as the Gombe Chimpanzee War: a community split into two groups, and over four years all the adult males in one group were killed by the other. The victorious chimps took over the seized territory, only to have to backtrack when they came up against new and stronger neighbours.[9]

If chimpanzees can have history, so can early humans. So too could a succession of anatomically modern human communities beside a lake in Yorkshire 11,000 years ago. And that is what Nicky, Chantal, Barry and their team found. Star Carr reveals the lives of early hunter-gatherers in a changing world, in which history was also being made by them, no one generation doing exactly the same on the edge of the lake as another. Houses and platforms were built and abandoned. Fires were lit, animals hunted and eaten, tools made and discarded. People would have told stories about events there and elsewhere. They were never written down, and we can never recover them, but that makes them no less important, as forms of entertainment and bonding, and as ways of affirming – and doubtless also inventing – history. What we can do, however, is look at some of the things they were getting up to. They knew what they were doing. And in this, as we shall see, the mark of history is everywhere.[10]

When Grahame Clark dug at what is now the western end of the site ('the site' is defined by archaeologists' trenches, and were these to be yet further extended, indications are that more remains would be uncovered) he found everything he hoped a small Mesolithic community would leave behind. There were bones of animals that had been hunted for meat and furs, burnt stone and charcoal from hearths, flint tools and debris from making them, hide scrapers made from cattle bones and bodkins from elk bones, a broken wooden paddle, little stone beads and so on. But what most impressed everyone was the antler. Nothing like it had been seen before.

First there were barbed points. These are aerodynamic pencil-like rods typically around 20 centimetres (8 inches) long but with quite a range in size, carved out of red deer antler. One end, usually the shorter part, is plain and flattened for fixing to a wooden arrow, javelin or thrusting spear (no such hafts have been found at Star Carr, so we're guessing a bit here). The rest of the point has a neat row of barbs down one side, and it comes to a narrow tip.

Clark found 191, and with the other excavations the total has risen to 227. Even now, with all the archaeology that has been happening in recent decades across the country, there are only seventeen more from the rest of Britain. And we don't have just the points from

Star Carr; we have the debris from making them too. Not only does this look impressive – Clark found 104 antlers from mature stags, and these deer were larger than modern specimens – but also it tells us how the points were made. That evidence has been backed up by experiments making replicas with fresh antler.

A barbed point may have started as a cooperative project, with one person holding an antler – with part of the skull attached if it had come from an animal they'd killed, or not if they had collected shed antler – and another working at the hard surface with a flint blade. Two long parallel grooves would be cut down into the soft, spongey tissue, the ends cut across and a thin rectangular strip levered out. This would be trimmed to shape by cutting and rubbing on a stone, and finally the barbs would be sawn and scraped out.

This precise and distinctive technology is known as groove-and-splinter, and it was practised elsewhere in Europe at the time of Star Carr. It was not invented then, however. It was also used back in the Ice Age, by people who created some of the most spectacular cave art, to arm weapons for hunting giant cattle, horses and reindeer, and perhaps rhino and mammoth. The first signs of the technique date from 20,000 years ago, before which antler was worked with a more hit-and-miss process of hammering and chipping.[11]

At Star Carr groove-and-splinter was applied to red deer antler, but in the Ice Age reindeer antler was used. So when two people sat down to make a barbed point at Star Carr, they were drawing on a craft tradition that had been developed for a different material (to say nothing of the process of obtaining it), that had been applied to the hunting of different beasts in a different world, and that had been passed on from one person to another for 10,000 years. That's a long time – around twice as long as the time between the first wheel and today. But it seems reasonable to imagine that a memory of some of that ancestry, if in the vaguest sense of older times and different worlds, might have accompanied the learnt technology.

Modern humans, our most immediate ancestors in Europe, experienced 40,000 years of dramatic changes in climate, landscape, fauna and flora, as sea levels rose and fell and glaciers consumed great areas only to release them again. The people at Star Carr had been that far north for only a few generations, if that. With their experiences and their history, they must have known Europe and its ways of the wild like nobody since. As they moved across estuary-riven grasslands where the southern North Sea now is, they entered a land where there were no people; and they never left. In that sense they were Britain's first immigrants, discovering shores and hills, naming rivers and watching sunsets for the first time at the start of continuous human occupation. Other people followed, as we saw in the last chapter, on current evidence most significantly around 6,000 years ago – the first farmers – and again 1,500 years later, bringing Beaker culture. We don't know what happened to the hunter-gatherers. But their European world, and all the mixing and changes that happened in subsequent millennia, seem more relevant to our deeper British psyche than a mythical 'African savannah' – though, as we shall see in Chapter 10, there is a twist to this tale.

\*

At Star Carr people are making hunting kit from deer antler. Removing a strip from the beam is made easier if the antler is soaked in water for a couple of days, and kept wet while working it. This might be one reason why people were on the lakeshore, using the platforms as places to work; the same water preserved the discarded debris for archaeologists to find. Finishing the point, however, is better done dry, and like most things, this would have been achieved on land.[12]

Grahame Clark sited his trenches almost entirely over the lake edge – he was after organic remains preserved in the peat. One of the great achievements of Nicky, Chantal and Barry's project was to excavate a great swathe of dry land as well. Eleven thousand years ago the lake offered birds and fish, attracted game, and was a place to splash about, doing things that needed water, and – why not? – occasionally to gaze across, sitting on the end of a wooden platform, lost in thought. But humans have never had webbed feet, and the hunter-gatherers would undoubtedly have spent more time on dry ground. The archaeologists' new excavation backs this up.

They plotted everything they found, every last tiny piece of flint and bone, onto the site plan – the sort of thing it's difficult to do without a large grant and enthusiastic student labour (there were nearly twenty thousand flints on land). Chantal spent much time trying to fit waste flints back together, to see what was being made where. The result made it all worth while.

We have seen how four or five timber platforms were laid across the lake-edge swamp over eight centuries, and three or four houses raised inland. The flints show there was more going on than this. There were a lot at the houses, especially the West and the East ones, as we'd expect. There were nearly seven thousand flints in the East structure, one in five of them burnt; most were not on the bottom of the hollow, but in its upper fill, indicative of a raised floor. But there were many other places that flints told of people where otherwise there was little left to see.

There were suggestions of several hearths, apparently out in the open, a handful of burnt flints and nearby a few tools and perhaps a strike-a-light, a flint battered from making sparks. Occasionally, lumps of good flint had been cached underground, as if someone had meant to use them at a later date. In one place were over a thousand pieces, many of which Chantal was able to fit back together, where wood-cutting axes had been made and re-sharpened. Out on the platforms above the swamp were relatively very few flints, and virtually none that had been burnt. They were mostly tools. No one sat over

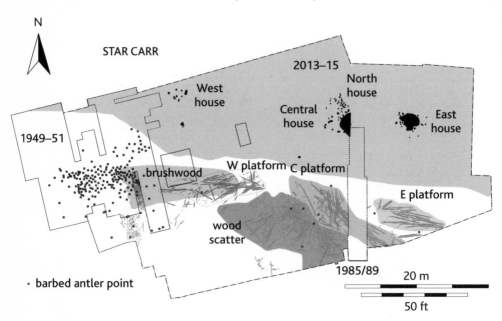

Main excavation areas at Star Carr. Darker zone to north was dry land, where post holes and hollows mark the UK's oldest houses. To south, peat on the edge of the former lake has preserved timber platforms and antler points.

Shaping and sharpening flakes refitted to a flint axe blade. Length: 7.5 cm (3 in.).

the lake knapping flint or making fires, but they worked on tasks requiring knives or scrapers and occasionally left or dropped them.

The working edges of flint tools take a fine polish whose appearance, seen under high-power magnificaton, differs depending on what materials they have been in contact with. If very well preserved, as at Star Carr, ancient polish can reveal distinct activities. On land there seems to be little the hunter-gatherers didn't do, from cutting meat, scraping and boring hides, and processing fish to cutting up and shaping bone, antler, plants and wood. Over the swamp, again, we can see more restricted work, mainly processing plants and wood on the wetland edge and butchering animals further out.

Other finds tell their own stories. The main meat animals, in popularity order as indicated by the bones, were red deer, roe deer, elk, aurochs and boar (interestingly, at contemporary sites in the south of England, this order is often reversed, possibly because of the warmer climate there and its effect on vegetation). Bones were systematically broken to extract marrow. A few were gnawed by wolves or dogs, both of which were present – a nearly complete dog skeleton lay in the swamp.

A willow bow, too small for big game at 1.4 metres (4½ feet) long and perhaps used in fishing, is one of the oldest bows known in Europe. There are three or four knob-ended digging sticks, a willow platter and a bit of withy made from two willow coppice stems (a very early case of plying, in which two stems were twisted in one direction and then plied together in the opposite). There is a scrap of shaped board, a bit of mat made from layers of birch bark, and a small bark cup or bowl. Somewhat enigmatic are nearly two hundred rolls of birch bark, most no more than 5 centimetres (2 inches) long. It seems some of these were destined to be heated to extract tar, useful for mounting flint microliths and blades to hafts, and some to be fixed to the ends of canes as flaming torches. Perhaps these were stuck on the water's edge as people bedded down, hearing the night come to life, knowing the dangerous creatures out there – bears and wolves, giant oxen and boars – comforted by the flames flickering in the dark ripples of the lake.

Not everything was about survival. Clark found some forty beads, mostly small, disc-like pebbles of local grey shale, perforated with a flint awl. Several were gathered in little heaps as if there had been necklaces or, perhaps, lost items of clothing to which they had been attached. There were more in the new excavations, most notably a larger, triangular piece 3.5 centimetres (1½ inches) across, with a hole in one corner. One side is covered with short lines scratched into the surface, looking tantalizingly like a map or some kind of tally, but of course impossible to read.

And so we come back to red deer antler. The one thing that distinguishes Star Carr from every other site of its kind and raises the most unanswerable questions is the collection of hollowed-out deer skulls I noted briefly above. Whatever they were, they are fascinating, and take us, perhaps, closer to the people who made them – in a distant, uncomprehending way – than anything else.

Red deer were important to the people at Star Carr – though by no means the only important animal – for their meat, their hides, their bones and their antlers (a type of fast-growing, seasonally renewed bone). The bones are scattered and there are no complete skeletons, so it's difficult to know how many individual deer are represented. But there were at least thirty. If that sounds low for eight centuries, it's a reminder that what survives at Star Carr – what we see at almost any archaeological site – is a tiny sample of what would have been there.

Animals have heads. Deer were hunted, and we would expect to see skulls at the site, but there are more skulls and antlers – from around a hundred deer – than there are animals as represented by other body parts. Partly this is because antler was such a precious material, and would have been collected and stored. But it's also because people treated deer heads in special ways. Skulls, commonly with antlers attached, were trimmed and hollowed. Around a third of these treated skulls have a pair of holes gouged out of the bone, as if for tying or suspension. Such skulls have been found at Mesolithic sites elsewhere in northern Europe. There is one from Thatcham, near Newbury in Berkshire. Five have been found in Germany (two at one site, one each at three others).

There are thirty-three from Star Carr.

They were made over many generations: the oldest were among the wood scatter of the first platform (over 11,000 years ago), and there were many in the dump of stuff at the site's west end (8,800 years ago); others may be younger. Experiments suggested to Ben Elliott, a research student of Nicky's who examined all the excavated skulls, that heads were first cooked in a fire, making it easier to remove unwanted matter. Antlers were reduced using the groove-and-splinter technique, but spongey tissue was cut out as well as bone that might have been made into points, and the effect was to substantially lighten the weight of skulls that were significantly larger than those of modern stags. This would have been done on dry land, and as little of the discarded parts – jaws and the fronts of the heads – were found at Star Carr, it seems that most of the skulls, at least, were worked elsewhere.[13]

Of Clark's two proposed uses for the treated skulls (they were then the only ones known) – as a hunting disguise or a shamanic headdress – the former now seems less likely. The idea is that hunters would have worn the antlers on their heads as they stalked deer; early European settlers recorded Native North Americans doing just this. However, we now know that, at Star Carr, a certain number of deer were hunted in the summer, when they didn't bear antlers themselves, and that some of the carved skulls had no antlers – they were made after antlers had been shed, or from the heads of does that didn't have any in the first place. Consequently, the skulls would have done as much to draw the attention of puzzled deer as to obscure the hunters.

Smaller antlers of a roe deer skull (bottom right) lie over a larger carved red deer frontlet, among other artefacts and bones, all some 11,000 years old, in the new excavations at Star Carr.

Instead, archaeologists have turned for inspiration to 18th-century records of people in Siberia – geographically closer to Star Carr than North America, and where the material culture has more in common with Mesolithic Europe. Deer headdresses, looking remarkably like some of the hollowed skulls from Star Carr, were worn exclusively for dancing. Clark noted a British tradition said to date back to at least late medieval times, in Abbots Bromley, Staffordshire: men carry reindeer 'horns' around the village, accompanied by a melodeon player and other dancers in fancy dress.

Though the bone itself is from the back of the stag's head, where the antlers grow, archaeologists have called the shaped skulls 'frontlets' – forehead ornaments. Conjuring Morris dancers with jingling bells and an eye on the next pint, this begins to sound a bit twee and Merrie England. But Siberian shamans are not twee. Neither are freshly carved deer skulls, taken from hunted animals and reeking of putrefying brains and blood. These were not ornaments, but masks. We are in the dark side of Star Carr, and perhaps the nearest we can be to the reality of the time.

Behind a mask, says Chantal, lies someone hiding not from deer but from other people. The bone speaks of deer, perhaps a specific beast that had been followed and watched for years, making the wearer half human, half animal. The mask's expressionless gaze blurs life and death. The performance wells from a view of the world that draws no distinction between human and nature. The mask is not a disguise, but an expression of continuity, between the hunter and the hunted, their daily lives entwined, their souls exchanging stories.

In such a vision (wider than the specific practice of shamanism), artefacts made from the bodies of deer would also have had that power of communion. And perhaps this was true not just of the red deer. Neil Overton, one of Chantal's research students, noticed that of six roe deer skulls at Star Carr, five are broken up in the same way as the red deer masks. These skulls are poorly preserved, so it's difficult to prove they had been worked, but their very presence – there are no equivalent female roe skulls – suggests they had been collected and saved.[14]

The idea could have had considerable antiquity. Among the many thousands of animals painted in Ice Age caves across Europe, recognizable depictions of people are extremely rare. The most famous are two in a cave in the south of France known as Les Trois

Frères, created perhaps only a few thousand years before the head-dresses at Star Carr.[15] In one, a human sports antlers – probably reindeer – and a tail, in the other horns and a bison snout and again a tail. Both seem to be male, and the message of the headdresses is reinforced by other elements that merge human and beast.

So in that heap of material that Clark found, and that Nicky, Chantal and Barry were able to excavate yet more of, we might imagine that everything – not just the two dozen deer masks, but also the barbed points, the antler debris, the bones, the flint tools and so on – was alive. That it was not just Vladimir and Estragon who were waiting for Godot, but the tree too. This was no mere rubbish, but a celebration of existence, of memory and respect, of everything people depended on, and of the families and their world beside the lake.

What inspired the great disposal? Radiocarbon dates suggest it could have been a single event. Nothing like it has been seen else-where on the shore of Lake Flixton, or anywhere in Europe. It is as if an entire community – or more than one, even – had swept up their things and carried them to the water. There must have been specific, historical explanations that we can never recover. Someone died; everyone died. The rain stopped; the rain never stopped (Lake Flixton is at the source of a significant local river – the Derwent – that flows west and then south, joining the North Sea). Perhaps, as might have happened at Must Farm, and as did with the Gombe chimpanzees, one community rounded on another.

During Ben Elliott's experiments, something astonishing happened. His antler had dried for three years. To make it easier to work, he soaked it in water. The spongey core contained dried blood, and when Ben opened it up with his flint blades and wetted it again, the water flowed out blood-red. The antler seemed to pump blood. So, for thousands of years, the lives of the people of Star Carr lay at the edge of the lake, preserved by peat, seeping into the earth, preparing the ground for those who would follow.

In the next chapter we will encounter more hunters, thousands of years older but modern humans still, for whom shaping skulls was also a defining practice. Only in their case, the heads were human.

# Chapter 8

# Cannibals

*Gough's Cave, 15,000 years ago*

Worthington G. Smith, an eccentric Victorian who earned his money as an illustrator and journalist, once described an ancient scene that might have inspired the opening sequence in Stanley Kubrick's *2001: A Space Odyssey*.

'Let us suppose', he wrote in 1894, elaborating on his archaeological discoveries in Bedfordshire, 'that it is night, and that we have reached, under the cover of darkness, a haunt of primeval savages. The nocturnal sounds are strange and startling; we hear the roar of the lion and the chattering of the ape. But of all the sounds, none equals in interest and importance the voice of man himself. A shriek or groan of pain is heard, and quick, jabbering, threatening sounds of quarrelling. If we imagine the darkness to have lifted, we see the men and women standing about or crouching. Bones are strewn about in all directions.'[1]

Smith's primeval humans have pointed ears – he illustrates with 'a sketch of an ear, possessed by one of my neighbours at Dunstable'. They eat not only mammoth, horse and deer, but also snails and frogs – 'still highly esteemed in Normandy and Brittany'. Then, to show how remote these savage lives were, he says this: 'If other animals were not to hand, the brains, marrow, and blood of other human beings would doubtlessly be used as food. Human skulls, with the face and occipital bones broken off, would make good drinking-bowls. From such vessels water, blood, or blood and water, would be quaffed.'

This chapter is about the discovery of cannibalism at the root of the modern human story in Britain. It's a difficult subject. There is an old tradition of sensationalizing the practice. Worthington Smith (who had no evidence for his vivid images) is unusual in not judging the people he wrote about. He was an observant pioneer collector of Ice Age flint artefacts, and he respected those who had made them. For him, 'Man...was not a degraded animal' but, up to that now ancient moment, at the pinnacle of achievement.

Writers more commonly linked cannibalism with condescending notions of modern savagery. Early Spanish explorers in the Caribbean exaggerated, at the very least, instances of cannibalism to justify their killings and land seizures (the word 'cannibal' derives from Spaniards' stories about the Carib people). Eighteenth- and 19th-century writers promoted books telling of their heroic escapes from cannibals in remote locations: the first title from Herman Melville, better known for his novel *Moby-Dick*, was *Typee* (1846), a supposedly true account of being captured by cannibals on a South Pacific island.

William Sollas, a respected English geologist and anthropologist, wrote in 1911 that cannibalism 'is chiefly confined...to black races', and is most commonly practised because 'human flesh is a great dainty'. Cannibals encountered on exotic travels featured in early ethnographic films. In such features as *Cannibals of the South Seas* (1912), the practice was portrayed as real (though never documented) and used as a box-office draw. The theme became a staple of fantasy movies, from *Night of the Living Dead* to *The Silence of the Lambs*, and underlies endless Dracula plots.

The perhaps inevitable modern reaction to this mix of fairground melodrama and cultural offence was denial. Late in the 20th century several archaeologists and anthropologists came almost entirely to reject the idea that in the real world people had ever, at any time or place, eaten other people. Only extreme cases were admitted, such as a famous plane crash in the Andes in 1972, when starving survivors ate from the frozen corpses of fellow passengers.

Nonetheless, dispassionate studies have shown that what is known as cultural cannibalism – people eating parts of people in particular approved situations – has occurred around the world.

There are many reasons, the commonest being linked to funerary ceremonies, or to warfare and aggression. The result of heated debate, however, and you might think quite reasonably so in the circumstances, is that any case for historic cannibalism has to be supported with particularly strong evidence. Which for archaeologists is a problem: proving cannibalism from excavated remains is surprisingly hard. Explaining it is even harder.[2]

While academics argued about cannibalism and movies revelled in it, supposed early evidence emerged in Somerset in the 1930s, from Gough's Cave, a deep tunnel in the side of Cheddar Gorge. Together with cheese, spectacular cave formations and a Cave Man Restaurant (where the eponymous skeleton was a welcoming host rather than on the menu), cannibalism happily took its place in a package of tourist attractions.

The first recorded archaeological discoveries at Gough's Cave were made in the 19th century. The most important excavations occurred between the two world wars, and ancient remains continued to turn up for decades. All this work and more is part of this chapter's story: but its focus is a modern project, which began in the 1980s with another excavation, and worked with the best of archaeological sciences until the final, striking conclusions made headlines in 2017. We will meet Silvia Bello. She is convinced that remains from Gough's Cave are among the oldest dated examples of cannibalism anywhere in the world. What's more, she argues that the people who consumed adults and children, and who lived nearly 15,000 years ago in a cold, challenging world alive with reindeer, bear and mammoth, didn't just look like modern humans. In some deeper sense they thought like us as modern humans. And she knows that, she says, because they ate each other.

'Ice Age' is a colloquial term. It can mean the last time when glaciers covered much of Europe, known in Britain as the Devensian (80,000–11,500 years ago). Or we might be referring to the whole 2.5 million years of the Pleistocene glaciation, a long succession of climatic periods that were alternately cold (glacial) and warm (interglacial). We are still in this Ice Age, enjoying the balmy days of a long, unusually stable interglacial. How and when it will end is now much debated. For the first time, we have ourselves become a significant factor driving climate change.

In the next chapter we will move far back into this long Ice Age, to an interglacial some 400,000 years ago. For now we are reaching only into the last glacial period, the Devensian. It was not a continuous long freeze. There were several occasions when the climate warmed, for a few centuries or even less, enough for people to come as far north as Britain, following the herds of reindeer, mammoth, horse and bison on which they depended. At other times the whole of the UK would have been uninhabitable, with dense sheets of ice covering all of Scandinavia and the far north of Europe, including most of the British Isles.

Earlier in the Devensian the people who knew how to survive in this world, hunting great beasts and stitching skins and furs into warm, dry clothing, were Neanderthals. We see their presence in a quarry at Lynford, Norfolk. Here, forty-five beautifully preserved flint handaxes, all-purpose cutting and chopping tools the size of an outstretched hand, lay among the bones of a dozen mammoths where they had been dropped 60,000 years ago.[3]

Britain's earliest remains of *Homo sapiens*, part of a jawbone and some teeth from Kent's Cavern in Devon, were identified in 2011 and date from some 43,000 years ago. By then Neanderthals were becoming scarcer. While the two populations lived side by side in Europe for thousands of years and occasionally interbred, only one survived: by 39,000 years ago Neanderthals were extinct. In France and Spain modern humans created astonishing wall paintings in deep caves, portraying the large game they knew so well with anatomical precision and artistic flair. Nothing survives in Britain to match the quality and grandeur of the best Palaeolithic art on the continent, but we know there were artists here too. Archaeologists have found fragmentary engravings of deer, horse and other creatures in limestone caves at Creswell Crags, on the border between Derbyshire and Nottinghamshire.[4]

As the Devensian drew to a close, between 15,000 and 11,500 years ago, there were three brief periods of extreme cold. People were forced south across a great plain where now is the southern North Sea and which made Britain part of the northwestern tip of the continent. Each time the climate warmed, a different group of people returned, until the last stayed – as represented at Star Carr – and the Mesolithic era began. Before the first of these three great freezes, people we know as Magdalenians (after a cave in France, in an era we know as the Upper Palaeolithic) used Gough's Cave for shelter and ceremonies. They left behind by far the largest and best-preserved collection of artefacts and bones – animal and human – yet found in Britain of this age. They also bequeathed a conundrum that has challenged generations of archaeologists.[5]

\*

'I can't imagine working in any other place, because of the people here,' says Silvia Bello. She is sitting in her office in the Natural History Museum, on the busy Cromwell Road in London. 'We work very well together, we are a good team.' A front page from *L'Eco del Chisone*, a Turin newspaper, is pinned to a board. It features a photo of Silvia smiling down at a human skull; she is famous, it says, for confirming cannibalism 'among the primitive British'.

A European Commission grant brought Silvia to London, after studying for degrees in Turin and Marseille. The Natural History Museum, she says, has 'fantastic facilities', and, she adds, lowering her voice to an awed whisper, 'they have Chris Stringer'. Chris, who has only ever worked at the museum after growing up in a poorer part of London's East End and taking degrees in London and Bristol, leads research into human origins. In his career studying human evolution, he helped to build the now standard theory that modern humans evolved in Africa. He directed a decade-long project to research Britain's earliest people, achieving an astonishing number of discoveries and breakthroughs, drawing in over sixty scientists and publishing hundreds of scientific papers.[6]

Silvia joined Chris's project as a research assistant. The museum had acquired a new machine called an Alicona 3D InfiniteFocus. It's a sort of electronic microscope that projects 3D images onto a screen at very high levels of magnification. It can take precise digital measurements of distances and angles on the surface of objects, making it popular in precision engineering. Chris's colleagues had been finding butchery marks on ancient bones, and they thought the Alicona might help with their research.

Silvia began her study with a bag of pork ribs from Tesco. A colleague made her a flint knife, she cut up the ribs in her kitchen, and then put the bones under the Alicona. It was the first time anyone had measured such cutmarks in 3D. She could read how the knife had been held and distinguish marks from those made with a steel knife. Next she cut up a roe deer with a more sophisticated flint tool, and compared the marks this made with supposed butchery marks on ancient bones, again with positive results. Then one day Chris said, why don't you look at Gough's Cave?

Gough's Cave had been a powerful presence for archaeologists at the Natural History Museum long before Chris's early humans project came along. This was partly because of the site's significance, but there was another reason. The cave is private, with its own museum where many of the finds that have been saved over the years were stored or displayed. Their owner is the 7th Marquess of Bath, better known as the occupant of Longleat House, a stately home with lions and a safari park. In the early 1980s, when Chris and his colleagues had taken a new interest in the remains, the estate loaned the Gough's Cave finds to the museum in London. At once they became a focus of intensive new research.

Cheddar Gorge is a great, meandering gash carved out of the Mendip Hills during cold periods of the Pleistocene, when freezing ground and sparse or no vegetation made the soft limestone vulnerable to the surging waters of spring melts. In warmer times, as now, water flowed underground, feeling its way through the fractured rock, eroding fissures and tunnels, and dripping mineral-rich trickles that grew fantastic shapes in stalactites and stalagmites.

By the 18th century visitors were coming to the gorge to witness its steep, winding road trapped between towering cliffs and its candlelit caves of 'grotesque forms'. Near the bottom was the village of Cheddar, which provided a home, in 1868, to Richard Gough. He was already showing a nearby tunnel to the public when in 1890, seeking to grow his business and outdo the competition, he started excavating a path in the floor of the cave he would make his own. He was in luck. Over the following decade, Gough's Cave became Cheddar's main sell, its huge chambers festooned with spectacular calcite formations, each breakthrough announced in the local press with mounting excitement; an early discovery was marked with a concert, lit by 'fairy lamps, Chinese Lanterns, gas and candles', attended by a crowd of 600.[7]

Human metatarsal (from a left foot) from Gough's Cave, with damage that closely matches that on a modern pig bone that had been smashed and heavily chewed by a student in an experiment. Length 45 mm (1¾ in.).

Thousands of tonnes of rock, clay and sand were shovelled out and spread on the ground outside the cave entrance. It soon became apparent that people had been in the cave long before, as workmen found bones and teeth of extinct animals, and 'flint knives and bone instruments'. In 1903 they discovered a complete human skeleton. Cheddar Man, as they called it, became a valuable asset in the Gough family's quest to outdo rival caves, and all kinds of things from the gorge and beyond were displayed in an impromptu museum near the tea room.

Archaeologists and anthropologists descended with their expert opinions, published scientific papers in national journals and agreed that most of the finds were late Ice Age in date, making them of international importance. Unfortunately, however, while the cave's proprietors were often helpful in allowing study of the remains, archaeologists had no say in the excavations, which continued with gusto. Growing numbers of visitors had to be accommodated.

The largest clearance occurred between 1927 and 1931. Over the winters, with the caves closed for business, several thousands of tonnes of deposit were removed, scraped from the floors and shaved back from the walls to bare rock. The work was supervised by Fred Parry, the Marquess's local estate bailiff. Interested in archaeology, Parry did a remarkably good job of recording progress. He labelled many of the bones and artefacts in pencil, making it possible to say roughly where and at what depth they had been found. But his detailed records are lost. Someone who took part in the excavations later recalled that tea-chests of bones were thrown out, considered 'unidentifiable or duplicates' (as you might discard a spare Rembrandt).

And so it went on. Further material was dug out when new offices and the Cave Man Restaurant were built in 1934. By then the cave lease had reverted to the Longleat estate, which employed fifty-four staff in Cheddar, and annual visitors had passed a quarter of a million (they have since doubled). It seems remarkable that anything still remained, yet more deposits were found whose removal enlarged the caves throughout the following decades.

By 1980, the obvious significance of Gough's Cave for Britain's ancient story had been rather left behind by science. Chris Stringer had been working with colleagues nearby, and they had visited the site and decided to see what could be made of it all. He produced the first modern study of the human remains, and others looked at various aspects of the cave's history and discoveries. A particularly important project was conducted by Roger Jacobi. With an unmatched knowledge of Ice Age material across the UK, having examined first-hand almost everything that was known at least once, Roger set out to track down all the surviving flint artefacts from the cave.

It took him several years, identifying pieces in museums and private hands beyond Cheddar; his photographic memory allowed him to spot broken flint artefacts whose two parts had ended up in different collections. His meticulous and wise report, published in 2004, was a landmark for the site. His unique insights, aided by all the other work done at this time, allowed him to place the cave's occupation at a particular moment in the Ice Age, and relate it to what was happening then across northern Europe. He could see families gathering in summer and winter, possibly around fires, in a dry space with room to stand and a fresh spring nearby. With awls and needles made from hare and swan bones, they worked the hides of horses and red deer they had hunted in the gorge, stitched with sinews skilfully cut from these animals' lower legs. Outside in the dry, open landscape with scattered trees were ptarmigan, arctic hare and arctic fox, lemming, reindeer, saiga antelope, wolf, lynx, brown bear and mammoth. Later research would confirm that small grey wolves owed their unusual size to having been partly domesticated, valuable as accomplices in the hunt and at night as guardians.[8]

A key outcome of Roger's analysis was the realization that, despite the uncontrolled excavations and the poor survival of finds and records, with skill and patience it was still possible to piece a story together with some confidence. Gough's Cave had more to offer. Then, on one of his many visits, Roger noticed human teeth and ribs sticking out of the wall not far from the cash till at the cave entrance. It seemed almost incredible that after all that time there should still be anything left to excavate. But there was, and with the support of the Longleat estate, Roger, Chris and Andy Currant, a museum colleague specializing in animal history, carefully took apart a slab of deposit the size of a table top that had been hiding behind a large fallen rock.

This changed everything. Now, for the first time, archaeologists had fully contexted fresh remains, including more human bones.

# Chapter 8

Longleat and the Cheddar Caves agreed to lend artefacts and bones to the Natural History Museum (then formally part of the British Museum), where they could all be examined, and Chris led a large international team of experts to look at every last detail. Before long, the new study came to focus especially on the people themselves. It was time to pin down exactly what had happened to the hunters in Cheddar Gorge.

*

Among the ancient residents of Gough's Cave, Cheddar Man has always drawn the limelight, and as I was writing this chapter, an aDNA study was underway that would make new headlines. His is an interesting story, as we will see in the last chapter; but he was not part of the Ice Age world to which most of the cave's remains belong. Radiocarbon-dated to 10,250 years ago, he died early in the Mesolithic. The Britain he knew was nearer to ours than the land of reindeer, mammoths and the last Magdalenians.

The first scientific study of human remains from the cave was of other fragments, among which, in 1929, were identified limb bones that had been split in the same way as bones from animals that had been eaten. The implication was soon picked up by local writers, who noted that these early cave people seemed to have been occasional cannibals. And no one thought much more about it, until the bones arrived in London.

When he catalogued them, Chris confirmed that several had possible cutmarks, leaving their study to Jill Cook, an archaeologist at the British Museum who had already been experimenting with such marks under a scanning electron microscope. She described grooves and scratches, but none, it seemed to her, were likely to have been made with knives. The culprit, she thought, was natural erosion, as stones pressed against the bones underground. There was just one exception: marks on a lower jaw could, perhaps, have been made when someone's tongue was cut out. That might have been it for the cannibalism theory. But even as she wrote, Chris, Roger and Andy were carefully excavating under the floor near the cave entrance, and finding fresh human remains. Their message would be anything but equivocal.

Remarkably for such a small dig, as well as animal bones and flint tools, they found the remains of at least three people – two adults and a child. The adults featured as parts of skullcaps, some of which could be fitted to fragments of a skull found nearby some sixty years before. The new bones, fresh out of the ground and untouched by modern handling and preservatives, had unmistakable knife damage. Ribs had been sliced from spines and jaws from crania, and one of the skulls was covered in cuts.[9]

Cheddar Caves naturally wanted to tell the world of their latest revelation – Richard Gough would have expected no less. At a press conference, archaeologists reported that there were clear signs that human bodies had been dissected, but emphasized that it was too early to say why. Perhaps they had been defleshed during burial rituals. If human parts had been eaten, that needn't mean routine cannibalism. It would probably have been for unusual reasons – people were starving, for example, or caught up in a violent attack.

They might as well have been talking to a stalagmite. While papers the next day acknowledged the great significance of the dig ('the most important find for its age in northern Europe', said the *Daily Telegraph*), headlines were sensational: 'Ancient Brits Ate Children' and 'Stone Age Brits Ate Kids' led into stories of 'a canni-bal's feast' at which 'victims' tongues and eyes had been cut out' and 'bones were cooked'. The media had found their inner Worthington Smith. Whatever the truth (there is no evidence for cooking), can-nibalism was not going to go away now. The issue had to be tackled.

The excavators' view was that there was no doubt that human bodies had been processed near time of death, but that it was too early to say why this had been done. The task, once again, fell to Jill Cook. She had joined the British Museum as a prehistoric specialist in 1986, the year the new excavation at the entrance to Gough's Cave began. Now a deputy keeper, she has a special empathy for the people who made Ice Age art. The Magdalenians were creators of some of the world's greatest early paintings and sculptures, works that have impressed generations of connoisseurs and tourists. Was it possible they had been cannibals?

Jill agreed that the fresh condition of the new bones made it obvious that they were covered in ancient cutmarks. Incisions showed features characteristic of sharp stone knives she'd seen in her own experiments. The marks were in the right places if people had been cutting particular muscles, chopping at ribs, decapitating, detaching jaws from skulls, removing tongues, and freeing the tops of heads from their flesh and scalps. In every case, such incisions 'must have been made deliberately by a human'. The bodies had been butchered.

Why this happened was another question, and, Jill said, one that would have to wait for an answer. Corpses may be dismembered after death as a way of disposing of the remains, but that didn't seem to explain Gough's Cave: human bones had been thrown away with butchered animal bones, with no signs of careful burial or ritual. Speculation about cannibalism was 'difficult to confirm or refute'. At the very least, she added, if cannibalism had been practised, it couldn't have been because anyone was starving. The animal remains made it plain there was plenty of other food to enjoy. Research was continuing, and whatever she might find it would be impossible to prove anything.

In the event, the more complete study fell to Yolanda Fernández-Jalvo, a Spanish post-doc – who, like Silvia, had come to the Natural History Museum to research human remains – and the museum's then head of human origins, Peter Andrews. Both were experienced in looking at how fossils came to be in the ground and how they might be affected by the burial processes (a field known as taphonomy). Yolanda was researching human remains from an excavation in Spain, at Sierra de Atapuerca, where she was identifying much older evidence for cannibalism, on bones of what may be Europe's first early human species, *Homo antecessor*, from 800,000 years ago – still the oldest convincing case in the world. Cannibalism at Atapuerca appears to be devoid of ritual, and may have been a matter of food – 'nutritional cannibalism'. Another theory, proposed by the site's excavators, assumes people were killing each other and draws on chimpanzee behaviour to suggest this occurred between neighbouring groups competing for food.

With such a background, Yolanda and Peter powered through the Gough's Cave remains as part of Chris Stringer's early humans project. They covered the lot, looking at all the available human and animal remains, especially horse and red deer; which parts had been found and which were missing; how they had been damaged; and whatever marks there were from human processing or chewing by people or carnivores. They found Jill's cutmarks and more, and also the same incisions in animal bones, including, for example, signs that a horse had had its tongue cut out.

They decided that the only differences between how people and animals had been butchered was down to body weight. A type of fracture known as 'peeling', similar to the way a fresh twig splinters when bent between two hands, was unique to human bone, but only because of the body's lighter frame. Otherwise, both humans and animals had been dismembered, skinned, filleted and eviscerated in the same way, and tongues had been extracted and bones crushed to release marrow. Such very similar butchery practices and identical waste disposal for animals and people could mean only one thing, said Yolanda and Peter: people were eating people as they were also eating deer and horse, for food. This was a spectacular case of nutritional cannibalism.[10]

Nonetheless, that evidence on its own need not mean that people were eaten. At Atapuerca, our understanding of early humans makes nutritional or aggressive cannibalism the most likely explanation for the bone damage seen there. A million years ago, there are no indications of formal rituals. There is nothing to suggest an imagination that created worlds in the minds of people beyond what they could see. In Somerset at the end of the Ice Age, however, things are different. Across Europe there is a history of nearly 30,000 years of art, in which things that matter to people – the animals they hunt and live off, and themselves, especially women and fertility – are realistically depicted beside symbols we cannot read. Sometimes when people die, bodies appear to be buried with care, though this is rare. We don't know what they were thinking, but we can easily imagine that these were people experiencing and expressing emotions we can identify with: hope and fear, in hunting, feeding and giving birth; anxiety and loss, perhaps, in the face of death.

For some, the similarities between the way people at Gough's Cave treated the animals they ate and their own dead suggested cannibalism; to Yolanda and Peter this meant nutritional cannibalism, to another archaeologist, 'aggressive warfare-cannibalism, in which enemies are treated as animals and eaten'.[11] But other interpretations were possible. Perhaps the hunters' intimate understanding of animals imbued skilled butchery with an element of respectful ritual. And perhaps, faced with the death of people in their group, they extended that practice into a funerary rite born of reverence.

It was thus that Roger Jacobi suggested an alternative explanation. Like Jill, he wasn't convinced the people in Gough's Cave actually needed to eat each other. There was copious evidence for meat consumption and the herds of animals they were accustomed to hunt, attracted to the gorge by springs and easily corralled and killed. If they were eating human flesh, it might have been during funeral rituals, or after feuding – though, he noted, no wounds had been seen. But need there have been cannibalism at all?

The finds from the cave suggest that while people might have been there in both winter and summer, not all of them were in the area all of the time. A search by archaeologists for the nearest source of the quality flint the Magdalenians might have used led them to Salisbury Plain, 40 miles (70 kilometres) to the east. Winkle, whelk and cockle shells, said Roger, could have travelled to Gough's from a beach somewhere, 'in a child's pocket'. The nearest direct source for two amber pebbles, one of them found in the new excavations, would have been the shore of the North Sea, then some 350 miles (550 kilometres) to the northeast. Climatic warming had made life in southern Britain possible, but it was still cold enough for there to have been substantial amounts of water trapped in glaciers that no longer exist. This drove down the sea level and exposed an unbroken landscape east from Gough's Cave to Denmark and beyond.

Flint and amber were not the only artefacts carried to Cheddar. There were mammoths at this time in England, a species called *Mammuthus primigenius*. The bones of a number of these beasts, the largest a bull the size of a modern African elephant, have been recovered from a gravel pit at Condover, Shropshire; the animals are thought to have become mired in a pond over several years. The bull's bones were so well preserved that a scientist, boiling some up in preparation for radiocarbon dating, inadvertently made a soup which he described as smelling of Bovril (he claimed not to have tasted it).

There is a piece of mammoth ivory at Gough's, about 25 centimetres (10 inches) long and shaped into a point, perhaps for a spear tip or something more decorative. There are also several tiny fragments, all of which may originally have been part of a single rod, with short parallel incisions engraved along their sides. These came from the recent excavations, and further shaped pieces were found in the earlier work. But they are the only sign of mammoth in the cave, so the ivory (or the finished artefacts) had probably been collected elsewhere. The same applies to reindeer. There are some important artefacts carved out of reindeer antler, consisting of three more or less complete 'batons', distinctive Magdalenian objects that look from a distance like some strange type of spanner: they have at least one hole at the wider end, and the 'handles' often display engraved lines or the forms of animals. What they were for has long been a topic of debate, a popular idea being that they were used to shape wooden spears, and perhaps also to help throw them. Whatever the case, these were clearly treasured items, like the ivory, and again are the only representation in the cave of the animals that supplied them.

The indications of travel given by the flint, amber, ivory and reindeer antler, and perhaps of different groups of people meeting and exchanging things, fit how we imagine the Gough's hunters to have lived. With summers a little warmer than today and winters that appealed to creatures that now live in the colder parts of Siberia, people and the animals they hunted are likely to have moved seasonally to make the best of what the landscape had to offer. Gough's Cave, argued Roger, might have been a chosen place for laying down the dead. If someone died far away, at a time when the ground was frozen solid, their group might have wanted to carry the body home. Dismembering and cleaning it would have made it less of an attraction to flies and carnivores, and easier to transport in a neatly tied package.

And then Yolanda and Peter had another go. This time they looked at what happened when people chewed bones, and whether it was possible to tell if teeth marks had been made by humans or 'other animals'. They studied bones experimentally chomped by students and by a group of hunter-gatherers in South Africa, and compared the results with fossils – from Atapuerca and Gough's Cave. They found that a particular series of marks and splits made it possible to distinguish the actions of human teeth. And sure enough, those features could be seen in the human bones from the cave. 'Think that a member of your group dies,' Yolanda told Discovery News. 'Hunting was always dangerous at that time. What to do with the dead body, that may attract other dangerous carnivores that may attack the group? Cannibalism could be a good solution.'[12]

Any notion that some form of cannibalism had not been practised was beginning to look like very special pleading.

Meanwhile, Silvia Bello had finished her own experiments, buying ribs, cutting up meat and putting the bones under the Alicona, and was ready to examine the remains from Gough's Cave. She agreed with Peter and Yolanda's original analysis, she told me, but 'I just found that it is a short paper describing the whole collection, human and animal in one go.' This was not how she had been taught. 'Coming from the French tradition,' she said, 'and still almost on the edge between PhD and post-doc where you have to describe everything in massive detail, I thought, that's what I wanted to do with Gough's Cave – every specimen draw, and describe what is on it.'

And that is what she did.

*

Silvia started on the heads. She had some forty fragments of skull and jaw to look at, a few saved from excavations in the 1920s, but most from the small 1980s dig. She had the museum's new electronic microscope. She had help from Simon Parfitt, a leading specialist in Ice Age mammals and their exploitation – and butchery – by early humans, who was working just down the corridor (and whom we will meet again in the next chapter). And she had time in Chris Stringer's early humans project, and her attention to massive amounts of detail. Silvia pored over the pieces one by one, and she found things that nobody had seen before.[13]

Earlier work by Chris and others had established that the bones came from at least five people – I say at least, because the scattered and disarticulated remains do not make that calculation easy, and academic custom is to see how few individuals can account for any collection. They narrowed it down to a three-year-old child, two adolescents (between twelve and fourteen, and fourteen and sixteen, respectively) and a younger and an older adult. Three of these (the two adults and the child) were represented by remarkably well-preserved skull fragments.

Almost every scrap bore fine cutting marks left by sharp flint knives. A little under half had also been damaged where the bone had been struck with a stone. These were not signs that might have been expected if the butchers had been starving: other studies have found that in such circumstances skulls are invariably more

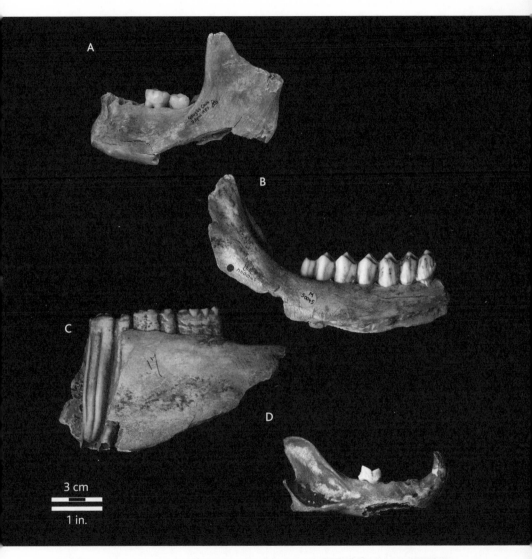

Human and animal mandibles (lower jaws) from Gough's Cave show the same breakage patterns you would expect to see after the extraction of bone marrow: human (A), red deer (B), wild horse (C) and lynx (D).

fractured, by people striving to extract the brain through the top of the head. By contrast, all indications at Gough's Cave point to skilled, delicate dissection – we might call it surgery – conducted shorty after death, before any desiccation or decomposition. The three heads each revealed exactly the same pattern, adult and child alike. Whoever did this had a keen understanding of human anatomy. They had done it before. They might, in fact, have taken pride in their accomplishment.

The forensic trail of precise deconstruction allowed Silvia to read what had happened. The task begins with the separation of the head from the body, by slicing through the neck muscles close to the base of the skull. Next, the lower jaw is removed, cutting the muscles and, in at least one case, using a lever inserted between the front teeth. The scalp is peeled off after delicately cutting through the skin around the head. Soft tissues are taken out, one by one – the tongue, the lips, the cheeks, the nose and the ears. The eye muscles are severed and the eyeballs squeezed out of their sockets.

The next procedure is so well done that perhaps now the bloody and greasy head, weighed by the brain within, is washed down with water. With a stone, such as in different circumstances the man or woman might have used to make the flint blades with the razor-sharp edges, the bone is shaped. The face and the bottom of the skull are carefully hammered away, without damaging the vault or skullcap, up to a level between the top of the nose and the back of the head. There are no cutmarks at all inside the skulls, so it would seem that at this stage the brain is gently encouraged to fall out. Then with a controlled, steady rhythm, with the occasional help of a stone anvil, small flakes of bone are chipped off the skull to smooth out the irregularities where the face and base were removed. All that remains is the dome of the head, looking, turned upside down, like a bowl.

Meanwhile, there is a headless corpse. What to do with that?

Answering that question, with the many more bone fragments deriving from more body parts, was a greater challenge still. As well as Simon Parfitt, this time Silvia had three Spanish colleagues to help her. Their study of the post-cranial remains – everything but the heads – took three years. They had over a hundred and sixty pieces to look at. As before, the great majority had come from the recent dig, and again there was more to tell. The first thing to happen was that they found another person.[14]

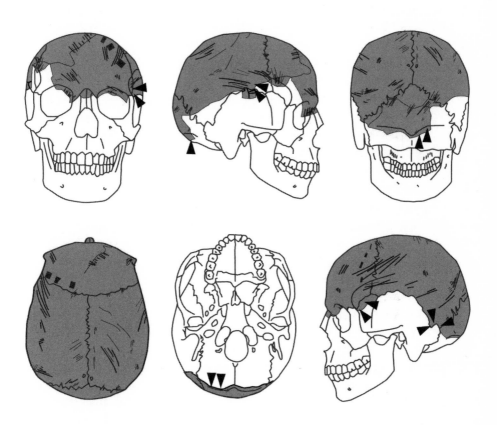

Marks from cutting (fine short lines) and striking (arrows) on the same skullcup.

## Chapter 8

The accepted judgment, as we saw, was that five people were represented by the bones. Now Silvia and her team found five people among the post-cranial remains. However, there was no child there, who it appeared was present only in the form of a skullcap, which meant there was now a minimum of six people. All five of the bodies had been eaten.

As with the cleaning and shaping of the skulls, the work on the bodies is methodical, skilled and comprehensive, and conducted shortly after death. We don't know what happens to the infant: perhaps the immature bones do not survive or are not found, or perhaps they never make their way into the cave. But the others, juveniles and adults alike, are butchered and devoured beyond recognition.

Arms and legs are removed, separated at the joints, skinned and filleted. Hands and feet are disarticulated. The rib cage is opened up, the body skinned and eviscerated, muscles cut away from the shoulders, back and hips, the bones separated and every last piece of flesh removed. Up to this point the treatment parallels that of the head. But then it moves in a new direction. Bones are chewed.

Silvia found far more chew-marks than anyone had seen before. They are everywhere, on vertebrae, ribs – which, judging by the sheer number and variety of marks, were particularly attended to – shoulders, hips, arms and legs, hands and feet. These marks are all human. Remarkably, given the range of carnivores at the time, including fox, wolf, wolverine, lynx and bear, there is only one animal tooth-mark in the entire collection.

There is a limit to what the human jaw can achieve, and the final step is to break up bones to get at the marrow. Arm and leg bones, even the dry, rod-like ulnas from the lower arms and fibulas from the lower legs, are smashed on an anvil with a stone hammer, as is the lower jaw. Foot bones are broken to extract grease. Epiphyses, the articular ends of longbones that fuse to the bones only when growth stops, are crushed and chewed.

We cannot know what happens to the soft tissues, as only bone survives. But we might guess, given the treatment of the bones and the intensive butchery that exactly matches the process seen with other large mammals at the site, that they were not wasted. Even if we imagine, however, that only the bone fat and grease was consumed, this is still more than one person could get through in a sitting. The processing and consumption of a body, of which of course we are seeing only a particular, narrow aspect, must have been a communal affair.

So why did they do it?

There are clues. We might focus on the chewing and smashing, and the high nutritious value of fat, especially for people living in subarctic conditions. That cannot be denied, and who's to say how they felt as they ate? But the skulls, which were not chewed, were turned into artefacts, something not seen with any animal butchery at the site. The skills displayed in making the cups suggest the practice was routine, not something that happened in rare, extreme moments. That impression is reinforced by two things.

Not long after Silvia had started her research, a new radiocarbon-dating study was conducted on remains from the cave. The latest technologies enabled a much more precise assessment of age than had been possible before. It had been thought that people had used the cave for a good millennium. Now it could be seen that they were there for probably no more than two or three generations, and possibly even fewer, around 14,500 years ago. We have only a small sample of what has been dug out of the cave, still less what was put into it. It's likely that anyone of a reasonable age witnessed the dissection and eating of members of their group, even if they didn't partake.[15]

Furthermore, Silvia found that the practice was not unique to Gough's Cave. Across Europe during Magdalenian times, while burial of complete bodies was extremely rare, scattered fragmentary human bones were commonly left behind. In several cases archaeologists have described cutmarks, and, at two sites in southern France, skull-cups very much like those from Somerset. Nine were excavated in the 19th century in La Grotte du Placard, a large cave with many other pieces of carved bone and antler and engravings on the walls. Early in the last century fragments of four were found in La Grotte d'Isturitz; remarkably, one of these has a shallow engraving that appears to represent an animal, and on another is the outline of a possible person.

There are no such figures from Gough's Cave, but it had one more secret to reveal. Silvia's next project was to address a bone marked like no others. It's part of a radius, one of the two bones in the lower arm, from an adult. Excavated in 1987, it's in fresh condition and in two pieces, cracked open to extract the marrow. There are human teeth marks at one end. So far, so same. But what makes it unique is a set of eighty-seven short vertical scratches grouped in a wavy line, giving the effect of a long jagged mountain range, extending for 63 millimetres (about 2½ inches). It was clear to Silvia, after intensive study under the Alicona and comparisons with a variety of other incised and engraved objects, that they were different from all the cutmarks on the Gough's Cave human bones. These were deliberately engraved. They were art.

This was a controversial claim; the first scientific journal Silvia and her colleagues hoped would publish their article rejected it. But as well as the microscopic evidence, the form of the design supports the case. The wavy line of short incisions is a common motif seen on decorated animal bones of the same age excavated in France. The bone was engraved with the same tool used to fillet it, and before it was broken. So the process of creating art, a brief pause in the dissection of a body, was an intimate part of butchery and consumption. For Silvia, this was the final confirmation of what she had been seeing over the previous decade. The people of Gough's Cave had enacted human cannibalism as part of rituals that embraced the moment of death and loss.[16]

And this, she told me, was what made them human, like us.

'Everything is filtered by our perception,' she said, 'and not their perception. Cannibalism is actually very human. With modern humans you have the first graves, and then you have jewellery, and painting and art. Cannibalism is just another complexity feature of modern humans, is treating a dead body in a different way, with respect. They're not that different from us.'

We look at the astonishing art in Ice Age caves, and we imagine sentient minds responding to the world around them with creativity and vision, and a sense of awe and drama. This art, we say, is a sign that these were people like us, endowed with inventiveness unique to modern humans. Our immediate instinct when confronted with evidence for cannibalism, however, is to conjure an inhumanity that separates Magdalenians from us. And we struggle to reconcile the two points of view.

It becomes even harder, perhaps, when we are faced with Silvia's evidence from Gough's Cave that making 'art' could be an integral part of cutting up and eating people. But step back, and accept that

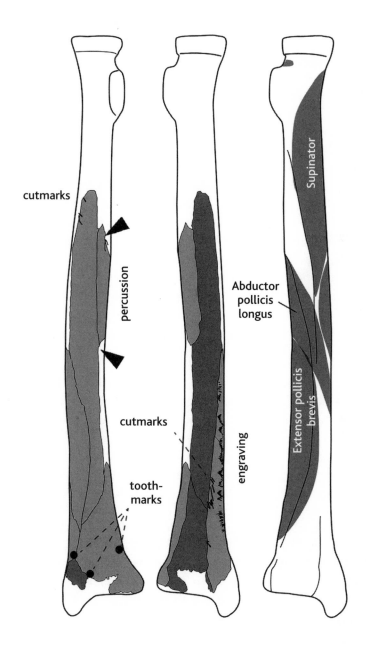

Engraved human radius from Gough's Cave, with surviving bone shaded (left and centre). On the right, muscle locations show how engraving is not in an area where filleting would have occurred (after Bello *et al.* 2017).

the surgery and consumption were a form of funerary ritual, and the behaviour takes on a different light. We know that people around the world today cope with death in any manner of ways, treating bodies differently, enacting different ceremonies and expressing different beliefs. These strategies have histories reaching back thousands of years, and all are framed by agreed conventions. Like art, the beliefs and rituals are formalized expressions of human imagination and creativity.

In the Ice Age, specifically in the Upper Palaeolithic, we might suggest that the art and cannibalism were both socialized ways of dealing with death – the paintings commemorate and bring to life hunted animals, the delicate butchery, even, doing the same for deceased people. This is what Silvia means when she calls cannibalism 'very human'. The great Ice Age art, the human butchery and everything else that people got up to in a world so very far from our own were things they had imagined and brought into being. Eating each other was the most personal and profound way they knew of saying, this is us. Us humans.

*

When Worthington Smith wrote about drinking-bowls chipped out of skulls, no human bones had been reported from Gough's Cave, and no ancient skull-cups had been recognized. So where did the idea come from?

Here's a possibility. In 1887 Constance Gordon Cumming sent an article to the *Popular Science Monthly*. Gordon Cumming was a travel writer and artist who would have appealed to Smith, and her theme was the loss of traditional medical practices around the world in the face of 'foreign influence'. 'Drinking-cups', she wrote, fashioned from 'a wise man's skull' and mounted in gold, silver or copper, were 'greatly esteemed in Thibet'. She then explained how such strange practices can be 'exactly descriptive...of the medicine-lore of our own ancestors'.[17]

Tibet, in fact, was far from the only place where human cranial vaults were then being shaped into cups. Where the bone was left unadulterated by metal and other decorations – by some Australian Aborigines, for example – the cups could look almost identical to those from Gough's. Gordon Cumming would doubtless be pleased to hear that human skull-cups can still be found today in the Himalayas, where they are used in Buddhist ceremonies. Silvia went there for a holiday, and in a street market somebody tried to sell her one.

It was very cheap – a fraction of the price for prayer bowls that were the stall's main stock. She was tempted, but knew she would never get it past customs.

'It's human,' said the vendor, hopefully.

'I know,' said Silvia. 'I can tell.'

Chapter 9

# Elephant Hunters

*Barnham, 400,000 years ago*

Four hundred thousand years ago there were no *Homo sapiens* on the planet; the first signs of Neanderthals, who evolved in Europe and Asia, were beginning to show, but they hadn't yet reached the far north. Nonetheless, there were people in Britain. Who were they? What were they capable of, and how might they relate to us? In recent years archaeologists have been trying to answer these questions at an excavation in Suffolk. It takes us to the heart of how early humans colonized and evolved in Europe.

The site was discovered after a fire. In 1902 flames consumed part of Euston Hall, a country house built in the reign of Charles II near Barnham. To make bricks for repairs, a clay pit on the estate was opened up, and labourers found ancient remains. There were two different types of flint artefact: simple ones that anyone could make (or so it seemed), and others – termed handaxes – whose manufacture and design required an intelligent and logical mind. The former lay deeper in the clays and gravels, and by implication were older.

Archaeologists couldn't agree what the two technologies at Barnham meant. Were they signatures of two species? Or were they made by the same species, but at different times or for different purposes? (There were no human remains from the site.) Perhaps the tool-makers sometimes found high-quality flint, with which they could make handaxes, and were at other times frustrated by rubbish flint, bashing out rubbish tools. Behind that debate lay another one, about the intelligence and capabilities of early humans, and about how many varieties there might have been.

A British Museum-led team returned to the pit in 1989, hoping to untangle its story. By then it was possible to place the remains in the Hoxnian period, a long, warm interglacial that began around 420,000 years ago and lasted thirty millennia. The Hoxnian had similar climatic and solar conditions to Britain today. At Barnham, animals had gathered around a small water channel while people, probably one of the rarest creatures, collected lumps of flint from gravel exposed around the channel's edge, to make tools with which they could butcher meat, and perhaps hunt.

These are things the archaeologists found out over six summers of excavation. They felt confident they had solved the stone-tool issue: both types occurred in the same place, with debris from their manufacture, on the southern bank of the ancient river, implying they were contemporary and made by the same people. This pleased many archaeologists, who felt their theories had finally been proved correct: inferior tools didn't have to mean different (stupid) people.

The excavation was important for another reason. It brought together three men who have since worked with one another on a succession of groundbreaking projects, creating an entirely new picture of early humans in northwest Europe: Nick Ashton, Simon Lewis and Simon Parfitt. Ashton is an archaeologist who has dedicated his career to the Lower and Middle Palaeolithic – the era of early humans – with a particular interest in stone technologies. Lewis is a geologist concerned with how landscapes form, and with global environmental change. And Parfitt, as we saw in the previous chapter, is a specialist in animal remains.

They have jobs in London to match: Ashton at the British Museum, Lewis in the School of Geography at Queen Mary University of London, and Parfitt at UCL Institute of Archaeology on secondment to the Natural History Museum. They and their many friends and specialist colleagues from across Europe have a common fascination with the story of early humans and their worlds. They bring their particular skills and knowledge to the same questions, which they seek to solve in carefully planned and well-resourced research projects, which they discuss in their trenches and over beers (no rural excavation, it seems, is far from a good pint), and which they consider in their separate labs and in books and academic papers.

They returned again to Barnham in 2013, with three goals. They would revisit the different stone technologies: after twenty years, some of them were beginning to wonder about the pat answers of the earlier project. They would explain sparse scatters of burnt flint and charcoal: if these were truly signs that early humans had used fire, they could be the most convincing instance of this age in Europe. And perhaps they would find human remains. The chances of turning up a human bone seemed good: who were these ancient people?[1]

*

It is June 2017. The Barnham team is on site, with thirty staff, students and volunteers. I approach through flat fields of ripening wheat, passing a few parked cars and container-like huts, and arrive at the quarry, which looks like a small sunken copse. Three inches of rain fell just before my visit – a month's worth in twelve hours. This is not good news for a forensic project in the bottom of a clay pit, which fills like a pond. Nick Ashton leads me down a short path through the trees.

Two trenches, about 100 metres (330 feet) apart, are in clearings cut from dense undergrowth of blackthorn, dog rose and nettles under a closed canopy of tall oaks. Archaeologists have pumped out the muddy water, and mop and clean. There is a smell of warm, wet earth. A robin pecks at the mud, and pauses on the handle of a shovel leaning against the pit edge. Students kneel in openings into the 400,000-year-old landscape. Steel tools scrape against flint.

Nick shows me a place where there have been excavations before, hidden beneath backfill and leaf litter. A ragged cliff rises behind, no taller than us, showing dark, almost black layers snaking through brown flinty clay; trees stand on the edge above, their roots hanging loose. Earlier archaeologists dug here, and so did the British Museum project (naming their trench Area I), all finding the same thing:

Excavating at Barnham in 2017. The rectangular pits were dug early in the last century to extract the grey clay for brick-making. What survives has preserved animal remains unusually well, offering a rich picture of a riverside ecology 400,000 years ago, which supported rhinos, elephants and early humans.

simple, sharp-edged flint flakes and cores (the lumps from which flakes had been struck) at one level, and, separately and higher up and so not quite as old, handaxes, or evidence for their manufacture.

Despite the grey in his hair and short beard, Nick has a boyish, impish look, with a simple haircut, a fading purple sports shirt and weathered jeans. He walks with his hands in his pockets. What they had most wanted to find in the 1990s, he says, were animal remains. After three years, they found some snails.

I am amused that from that ancient Eden of wondrous beasts, the first sign of life was so banal. But it was an exciting moment. Snail shells are thin and fragile, and dissolve easily in acidic water. If they were there, bones should be too. It turned out that around the edge of the old river channel, where archaeologists had found only artefacts, conditions were not good for bones. They survived only nearer the middle, in grey chalk-rich clays. During the course of the British Museum dig they wet-sieved 9 tonnes of sediment, washing the dried, crumbled clay by hand through a half-millimetre mesh to recover minute pieces of bone and shell, and teeth as small as a small bat's. The remains revealed a fabulous ancient world.

They identified fourteen different types of snail. A few years after their first dig, a couple of scientists analysed more of the stored samples, totalling a third of a tonne of clay. They found a good fifty species, half of them water snails, half terrestrial. Molluscs are fussy about where they live, so the different species offer a detailed guide to how the place looked 400,000 years ago. In the centre of the channel was shallow, standing water rich in aquatic plants. Lake limpets, for example, would have been clinging to the leaves of water weeds, and other species, now extremely rare in Britain, would only have been there if the water was very quiet, with little or no flow.

This was nonetheless a river, and the many land snails can be explained by imagining occasional storms and floods, eroding the banks and washing in more distant debris. Most of these land snails would have lived in marsh, but some came from forest or grassland. As what is now 2 or 3 metres (6 to 10 feet) of clay accumulated in the channel, the snails changed from being almost entirely aquatic to about a third terrestrial. Over the centuries, marsh and forest were closing in.[2]

Fish bones reflect the same changes, as species like gudgeon, roach, trout and eel gave way to tench, three-spine stickleback, pike and rudd, suggesting still or slow-flowing water, signified also by dabbling duck. As the basin became choked with mud and marsh, however, it teemed with what Nick calls an 'astonishing array of amphibians and reptiles'. There were seventeen species, mostly newts, frogs, toads and snakes – five more than are native to the UK today. Those five include the Aesculapian snake (a modern colony of this six-footer in London's Camden Lock is thought to have descended from zoo escapees), the common tree frog and the European pond terrapin. These are more typical now of regions of Europe with warmer summers; the terrapins lay their eggs in mud, requiring July temperatures no lower than 18°C (64°F) – six or seven degrees higher than today's 'normal' July lows.

The steady shrinkage of open water was a local development, but it occurred in the context of longer-term change driven by climate. Ancient plants themselves do not survive at Barnham, and are rare anywhere. But pollen is made of tougher stuff. As distinctive – when viewed down a microscope – as the plants it comes from, pollen has been found at Barnham and many of the other Hoxnian sites in Britain. It tells a consistent story: the spread, dominance and decline of deciduous forest.

The preceding cold period, known as the Anglian, was the coldest glacial people have ever known. At its most severe, the whole of Ireland, Scotland, Wales and England down to Bristol and London disappeared beneath a continent of ice that extended across the North Sea, Scandinavia and beyond. What little land was exposed would have been uninhabitable, permanently frozen at depth and crossed by seasonal streams in the brief springs and summers.

Britain was then at the tip of a continent. As the cold set in, animals and people would have been able to migrate, and to survive with warmth-loving plants in more congenial places to the south and east. When, 50,000 years later, the climate improved – which it did fast enough for people to have noticed it happening – and the ice retreated, flora and fauna would have spread back from their refuges. Reaching northwest France, they would have found a new topography: a river now flowed between France and England. With relatively minor rises in sea levels it would widen into a marine barrier. During this interglacial, there could have been a new inward migration to Britain, of plants, animals and people, whenever the sea fell enough to reconnect the land masses.

The systematic return of vegetation shows clearly in pollen diagrams and can be seen across Europe. In Britain the first sounds of
life are the wind in grasses, sedges, sea buckthorn and scattered birch
trees, and, presumably, the cries of birds (whose fragile remains are
less commonly found); a succession of beetle species, especially
sensitive to temperature, shows the climate warming. We enter
the Hoxnian, at Barnham as elsewhere, as birch spreads and pine
arrives. Then comes oak; alder and hazel increase; and finally yew
and elm appear, to complete the rich deciduous forest, broken by
patches of grassland.

The river at Barnham begins to clog. The climate cools. Hazel
and alder come to dominate woodland, and two species distinctive of
the Hoxnian arrive, hornbeam and wingnut trees. Then fir rises dramatically, while hazel, oak and other deciduous trees fall back, and
the landscape regains its hardy cover of pine, fir, birch and grasses.[3]

Down with the amphibians were a range of small mammals,
including several species of voles, shrews and mice, long-eared and
pipistrelle bats (the latter the only known example from Britain at this
time), a small extinct mole, a species of squirrel and a type of polecat.
There was the Russian desman, a curious furry mole with webbed
feet that would have swum for insects and frogs. And there were
rabbits – the last time they would be seen in Britain until, on current
archaeological evidence, they were introduced in Roman times.[4]

Further up the scale were badgers, beavers – whose effect on the
river valley would have been out of all proportion to their size – and
barbary macaques, monkeys that in Europe are today found wild
only in Gibraltar. There were wild boar, red and fallow deer, wild
cattle (aurochs) or bison, a rhino species and a type of elephant with
long, straight tusks. To a greater or lesser extent these last animals all
herd, and would have had a strong presence. There might seem to be
a contradiction between the evidence for forest, from pollen, and for
more open landscapes with extensive grassland, which is what herds
of browsing, grazing and trampling mammals imply. However, as
Simon Parfitt argues, there is no difficulty in imagining a patchwork:
dense woodland with grassy glades opening into wider areas of open
grassland, or closing in on marsh and riversides. Indeed, the animals
would have helped shaped this mosaic, allowing forest to expand if
they moved away or opening up areas they favoured, whether for
feeding or access to water.

Finally, there were two animals whose impact would have been greater than their number: bear and lion, the latter a monstrous beast, significantly larger than today's African lion. This is an extraordinary roll-call of wildlife for such a small area. It evokes for us an over-stocked nature park rather than our experience of a river through a wood, a scene concocted for a child's book, perhaps, with every beast and flower brought onto one page by the illustrator.

Yet there will also have been animals there – especially birds – whose remains have not yet been found. A couple of weeks after my visit to Barnham, Simon told me he had identified the site's first horse bone. And we need to imagine this rich world extending across the whole of southern England, at least; changing its appearance through the seasons, and from one year to the next with the vagaries of weather; and not just looking extravagant but also echoing to a great orchestra of noise, from the trumpeting and thunder of elephants, the roar of lions and the bellow of rutting deer to the cooing of pigeons and the quick splash of a diving water vole.

There is one significant creature missing among the shells and teeth and bones we nonetheless know also to have been there: us. Without the bones, we can only guess the species or subspecies, though we know it wasn't Neanderthal, and certainly wasn't *sapiens*. But it made its mark at Barnham in a way only people could have done. It filled the place with hazardous waste, which is still there.

For most of the past million years in Britain, and in Africa for more than the past two and a half million years, there has been one thing people have shared that now makes them seem overly common. They liked breaking up rocks. Freshly split stone, of the right type, gave them tools that greatly increased their capacity to feed and to survive. Often, these took the form of a sharp cutting edge. As people became more skilled and demanding, they developed a variety of specialist devices. Good flint, one of the best stones for tool-making in the world, can be found across south and east England. To make a tool involves skilled hammering – knapping – in the course of which most of the outcome is waste, flakes and chunks left to fall to the ground. Stone is all but indestructible. Every stone tool, every splinter of waste hammered out over millions of years, is still with us, mostly beneath the ground like a great cultural memory seasoning the Earth.

It is flints that Nick and I discuss as we look at the site of the old excavations. His dig with the British Museum had seemed to dispel the notion that the two types of tool in the pit were of different ages, settling one of the longest-running arguments in British archaeology. The two types were originally distinguished in the 1930s by a plus fours-wearing collector called Hazzledine Warren. Warren found great numbers of flint artefacts in the foreshore muds at Clacton-on-Sea in Essex (his love of old stones was such that, when he died, flint flakes were cemented onto his grave). He realized correctly that the Clacton flints were Palaeolithic, yet there were no handaxes – the fine, teardrop or petal-shaped flint tools known as Acheulean after 19th-century finds in France. Warren's cores and flakes were cruder and less regular, and thus, he said, were made by an older and more primitive form of human. He called his flints Clactonian. Soon, Clactonian flakes and cores were being found all over southeast England. I like to imagine archaeologists looking down their noses at the Clactonian day trippers, and welcoming French travellers: Clactonian flints, and their makers, were inferior.

In the 1930s no one knew that we had first evolved in Africa, that there were many early species, that often more than one was alive at the same time, and that our human-like origins reach back well over five million years. Instead, it was possible to imagine people emerging in Europe (the Piltdown Man fraud, which claimed to prove the first humans were British, would not be exposed for two decades). Now we know there were early humans in Britain nearly a million years ago, and that these must already have been a well-evolved species. A century ago, with less evidence and no scientific ways of dating remains, it was thought that the earliest Britons were both less evolved and much younger – even in the 1970s, the Hoxnian was believed to date to around 200,000 years ago, not 400,000.

Nick and a colleague, John 'Mac' McNabb, went on a mission to prove Warren wrong. Mac argued that Warren and his contemporaries were overly influenced by the times in which they worked. A Victorian vision of the history of civilization as a steady rise from savage obscurity to gentlemen reading *The Times* still influenced ideas about British antiquity. The discovery that old, primitive flint tools later evolved into sophisticated ones confirmed this prejudice – the Clactonian was the most ancient discernible manifestation of the primeval mud from which Britain had risen by its bootstraps.

Mac decided that the Clactonian didn't exist – at least, not in the sense of an era or culture. It was, he said, no more than collections without handaxes: it was just what early humans left behind when they made simple tools, even if sometimes they also made better ones. There was no link between the Clactonian and particular ancient people.[5]

Nick leads me on past the old dig site towards the east end of the clay pit. It's brighter here, where they've cleared vegetation and cut back the quarry edge to reveal fresher, lighter-coloured sands and clays. A small blue marquee provides shelter from the rain. Students and staff are delicately busy at a line of small trenches. Nick and his team again first excavated here in the 1990s. Behind us in Area I, they confirmed that Clactonian flakes could be found at a deeper level than Acheulean handaxes. But here they found the two types lying together on the same ground surface, confirming Mac's hunch. And now they are expanding on their original investigations, here and across the quarry where animal remains are so well preserved.

\*

To help explain what makes Barnham so interesting, I'm going to introduce three other excavations. They are all the work of the current generation of archaeologists, and all of international significance.

Nick's earlier Suffolk project overlapped with a longer and more extensive dig in West Sussex, at Boxgrove near the south coast. The site became famous around the world thanks to the discovery of a leg bone and a couple of teeth – still, as I write, the oldest human remains yet known from Britain. Both John McNabb and Simon Parfitt dug there, and it was Boxgrove that first brought Simon to Suffolk. The hominin remains – launched on the front page of *The Times* in 1994, the year the earlier Barnham dig ended – were important. But Boxgrove was also distinguished by its wonderful preservation and huge quantities of animal remains and fine flint artefacts. Simon recognized that understanding Barnham would help him solve the controversial challenges posed by Boxgrove.

Along the coastal plain that runs between Sussex and Hampshire are the eroded remnants of cliffs and beaches formed by the sea at various times when its level was higher than today's. Where the plain meets the edge of the hills to the north, there had once been a towering chalk cliff rising as much as 100 metres (330 feet) above the shore. For generations, quarries have reached down in search of the ancient sands and gravels.

As in Suffolk, these quarries attracted archaeologists, who found flint handaxes. But it wasn't until the 1970s that scientists began to understand the complex geology, and the significance of the artefacts became apparent. In 1982 Mark Roberts, the son of a local plumber, dug a small trench in one of the gravel pits for his student dissertation. He continued to dig for the following fourteen years, battling for permissions, grants and academic approval, and attracting a large group of volunteers, fellow students and early career specialists. They brought Boxgrove fame. And more importantly, they convinced a sceptical archaeological world that their radical ideas were correct.[6]

When Mark started out at Boxgrove, it was widely believed that there had been four major ice ages. The Boxgrove flints were Hoxnian (then determined as the middle of three interglacials), like those at Barnham, and were made around 200,000 years ago. As they were digging in Sussex, however, an array of new sciences identified a much longer and more complex pattern of glacials and interglacials, now labelled Marine Isotope Stages (MIS). As many as a dozen major interglacials were recognized over the past million years. It became clear that one of the best ways of telling one from another now lay with the fauna. Simon Parfitt, fresh from his degree when he joined the team, had the exciting task of analysing the animal remains from Boxgrove.[7]

Simon identified a range of creatures that included nearly a dozen he would not have expected to find together in a Hoxnian fauna. He was able to confirm this by studying the remains from Nick's dig at Barnham. While concluding that the latter was indeed Hoxnian, by then dated to 400,000 years ago (MIS 11), he found that Boxgrove was older and came in the warm period before the great Anglian glaciation – MIS 13, around 500,000 years ago. Boxgrove was an astonishing 100,000 years older than Barnham.

Simon's claims were controversial partly because not everyone agreed on what should replace the old four-stage Ice Age scheme. But what really threw the lion among the eagle owls were the artefacts. Suspicion of Boxgrove's greater antiquity had been growing for some time among geologists, but many archaeologists had refused to accept that there had been any humans in Britain before the Hoxnian

Clactonian. And to compound the problem, the Boxgrove flints were not Clactonian. They were Acheulean handaxes – among the finest ever seen. And that wasn't the end of it.

Boxgrove's exceptional preservation – owing to a lagoon that covered remains in fine silt, after which cliff falls had safely buried everything at great depth – allowed Mark and his colleagues to see something extremely unusual. They could identify individually butchered animals, and the flints used with considerable skill to cut them up. They could see exactly how the beautiful handaxes had been made using specialized tools that had never been seen before of that age anywhere in the world. The remains showed clearly that, notwithstanding wolves, bears, hyenas, lions and rhinos, these early people were the top beast, in command of their landscape and very far from unsophisticated.

For Nick and Mac, the Boxgrove handaxes confirmed their Barnham thesis: in the bigger picture, it didn't matter much whether a collection was Acheulean or Clactonian, as early humans in northern Europe were clearly perfectly capable of making handaxes if they wanted to. A surprise discovery in 2003, however, presented a greater challenge.

During works associated with High Speed 1, the train line linking London with the Channel Tunnel, the bones of an elephant carcass were uncovered near the Ebbsfleet International station in north Kent. It was the same extinct species seen at Barnham, the straight-tusked elephant, and the same age, around 400,000 years old. Rather than scattered fragments, however, this was a complete animal, and it was covered in Clactonian flint tools. The man tasked with directing the excavation and analysis was another Boxgrove veteran, Francis Wenban-Smith. Francis is a skilled flint-knapper and an expert in ancient stone technology. He didn't believe a word of Mac and Nick's case for dismissing the Clactonian, and was one of the few academics to have said so. High Speed 1 had handed him what seemed to be the perfect opportunity to prove his point. Here, he wrote in the report published in 2013, was the chance to address, and perhaps finally to resolve, 'the so-called "Clactonian question"'.[8]

Francis and his team from Oxford Archaeology spent the best part of a year excavating at Ebbsfleet and exploring the complex geology. They determined that the elephant died beside an alder swamp near a densely wooded tributary of the Thames. There were some eighty flints around the body, and nearly two thousand nearby on drier land. All of these were flakes or simple cores, the best Clactonian collection of this age. There was not a hint of handaxe manufacture. At a higher stratigraphic level, however (so not quite as old, though still within the Hoxnian), were many handaxes in a variety of shapes and sizes.

Simon Parfitt, who studied the animal bones, was impressed by the elephant's exceptional size, half as big again as a modern African savannah elephant. It was about forty-five years old, of prime age, almost certainly male, approaching 4 metres (13 feet) high at the shoulder and weighing 9 tonnes: that's similar to the weight of a London bus, and it would have been able to wrap its trunk over the roof. Can we imagine Palaeolithic people bringing down such a monster with sticks and stones?

The surprising answer, given by Simon, Francis and colleagues, is that that is probably what happened. Because of their size, even modern elephants have no natural predators, and prime-age bulls rarely die in the wild. Though close to a swamp, the Ebbsfleet elephant was not in it and would not have been trapped. Which leaves humans as the most likely cause of death, perhaps armed with spears: Hazzledine Warren found a wooden spear tip of this age at Clacton – the oldest spear known – and there is a suggestion of spear use, in a damaged horse bone, at Boxgrove.

The simple sharp flints had been knapped on the spot from nodules collected nearby, and surely were used to cut up the meat. Despite the vast amount of flesh, on the evidence of the flints, Francis thinks no more than a dozen people were there, probably fewer. He goes on to argue that not only was this particular elephant killed, but also hunting these enormous creatures was what early humans at this time did, and may have been the key to their ability to move successfully into Europe out of Africa.

What of the handaxes? The contrast between the two Ebbsfleet collections is striking – one of pure Clactonian style, the other Acheulean, with none of the mixing that Nick found at Barnham. For Francis, an archaeologist with an unusual appreciation of the skills and experience required to actually make these tools, the distinction speaks of different people. Did handaxe makers arrive in a second migration, he wondered, possibly even of another human species? On balance he thought not, and opted for a single population in southeast England that during the course of the interglacial added handaxes to their repertoire.

Mac remained unconvinced: the flints with the elephant were too few to unseat his case. For the non-believers, then, this could be fitted into a broad technological pattern in which people sometimes made handaxes and sometimes didn't, starting with Boxgrove and continuing for many millennia. But what if flint use were to be found very much older than Boxgrove, with no handaxes at all? Arguably that could take the debate back to its origins, with a simpler technology persisting through several interglacials before a more sophisticated, take-it-or-leave-it handaxe-making type of human arrived. The last site we will visit seems to suggest just that. It is time to return to East Anglia.

When Mark and Simon were out there convincing the world that there were humans in Britain as long as half a million years ago, it seemed at the time that there had been none before Boxgrove. That soon changed. Inspired by his study of cutmarked bones from Sussex, Simon decided to search the Natural History Museum for more butchered remains.

The museum has many fossils collected in the 19th and early 20th centuries from Norfolk and Suffolk beaches. Most came from what's known as the Cromer Forest-bed Formation, muds and sands laid down by rivers often long before Boxgrove and now washing out from the bottom of sea cliffs ('forest' in the name refers to preserved plant remains that include tree stumps). In 1998 Simon found what he was looking for: clear cutmarks from an ancient flint knife, on a bison bone from Happisburgh – pronounced 'Hazebru' – in Norfolk, unnoticed since it had been picked up almost exactly a century before.

This was the start of a new journey into the past. The first artefacts were found in 2000, a handaxe at Happisburgh (the same age as Boxgrove) and a small flint flake in the cliff at Pakefield, further down the coast in Suffolk. The museum already had a major project going called the Ancient Human Occupation of Britain, under Chris Stringer's direction, so it was a relatively simple matter to mount excavations, first at Happisburgh and then at Pakefield. The latter was immediately successful. Dodging waves and falling rocks and sand, Simon, Nick and their colleagues found more flint flakes and a rich collection of small animal bones. Among these were remains of a vole known to have died out before MIS 16: the artefacts were 700,000 years old. The discovery made the front cover of *Nature,* proof of northern Europe's oldest known humans. But that wasn't the end of it.

The really spectacular finds came from Happisburgh. Neither place was easy to work at, on the foreshore on the edge of the North Sea against tall and unstable cliffs. But Pakefield was dangerous, and every high tide flooded the archaeologists' trenches. There was a wider beach at Happisburgh, and in the search for evidence of early humans Nick, Simon Parfitt and Simon Lewis cored down from the top of the cliff, excavated at its foot and searched out to sea. By 2010 Happisburgh too was in *Nature.* Northern Europe's oldest humans were older still.

Various lines of evidence showed that people had been there at least 850,000 and perhaps 950,000 years ago – it is not yet possible to say to which of two interglacial periods the finds date. An unidentified early human species had been using flint tools beside a large, slow-flowing river (an earlier and larger manifestation of the Thames) fringed by reed-swamp, alder carr, marsh and pools, and backed by forest, demonstrated not just by pollen but also by such remains as pine cones and leaves. As at Barnham, some four or five hundred thousand years later, their world was rich with fish and large mammals.

This was a difficult site for the archaeologists to excavate. Not only did they have to haul all their stuff – from sandwiches to wheelbarrows – down a steep cliff and back every day, but also they had to deal with tides and sometimes appalling weather. Nick likes to tell how on occasions they had water coming at them from four sides – flowing out of the cliff, rising up from the ground, falling out of the sky and crashing in from the sea. Work became almost impossible after 2011, when what little protection the beach offered washed away. But the erosion gave them an unexpected bonus.

In May 2013 Nick, Simon Parfitt, Simon Lewis and brothers Martin and Richard Bates were on the beach 150 metres (500 feet) south of the site. Storms had removed the sand, revealing hardened grey muds. They were, in effect, walking on a landscape nearly a million years old. But they were not the first to do so.

Martin, who had been studying Bronze Age footprints preserved on a Welsh beach, now thought he could see bare human prints that would have to be much older. The others were sceptical, but a few

Excavation in 2010 at Happisburgh, Norfolk, at the bottom of a coastal cliff. The black colour in the trenches reflects the unusually high organic content of the deposits, which are around 900,000 years old.

A mass of human footprints at Happisburgh made 900,000 years ago, preserved
in hardened ancient estuary muds.

days later they returned with Sarah Duffy from York University, to record the surface with intensive photography. It was smothered in sand. They'd brought a hose so they could wash it down with clean fresh water, but a cliff fall the day before had taken out the supply to a nearby standpipe. So instead they went to work with buckets of seawater. The Natural History Museum had sent someone with a camera, and in the video you can see Sarah trying to work under an umbrella in fading light, and Nick and Simon Parfitt talking excitedly with rain streaming down their faces while a muddy sea roils close behind them. Darkness forced them to leave. They returned a week later with a laser scanner. The marks had all but gone.

Nonetheless, thanks to the fortuitous timing, Sarah was able to create 3D images that made it quite clear they really had found human footprints – the oldest in the world outside Africa. There were forty-nine, made by adults and juveniles walking south together, perhaps in a group of five.

The ephemeral prints and the few, small flints at Happisburgh add up to proof that humans were present significantly further north than they have been seen anywhere else in the world at this distant time. This is interesting for a reason that is not immediately obvious. Archaeologists tend to think of early Europeans as Africans learning to cope with new environments. They do well, but when it gets cold, when the glaciers start to grow, they seek warmth and move south. By around 300,000 years ago, Neanderthals evolve their stocky bodies partly as a way of coping with a colder climate – but eventually they become extinct, ceding to new waves of emigrating Africans: modern humans.

Whether it is 850,000 or 950,000 years ago, the climate at what is now Happisburgh is not as warm as it will be later at Barnham, or is today. The more southerly humans of this time live in tropical forest, steppe and Mediterranean habitats, but at Happisburgh (as indicated by remains of beetles) people experience summers similar to those in southern Britain today and winters 3 to 6°C (5 to 10°F) colder. Conifers and grassland are replacing oak and elm, heralding the onset of cooling before the start of a major glacial stage. But for the herds of horse and mammoth, this would be like southern Sweden and Norway today.

The implication is that people are adapting to the world around them as it changes. How do they do this? They would have to be eating different foods. Perhaps they wear clothes (the prints show no footwear). Perhaps they build shelters and they know how to use and control fire, for which, like clothing, there is no evidence to say. And we should not forget the likelihood that they are themselves having an effect on the world around them. But however they do it, they are using their intelligence and skills to cope with an environment to which they are not naturally a perfect fit. And they are doing this with the simplest, most basic flint tools. Hazzledine Warren would have called them Clactonians.[9]

*

I have said only that Acheulean is a more sophisticated technology than Clactonian. I should explain how.

Since the 19th century archaeologists have sought to copy Palaeolithic implements by experiment, teaching themselves to make flakes and handaxes. This work revealed that to create even the simplest useful flake – a piece of flint with a sharp edge knocked off a larger core – requires strength, co-ordination and skill. Random bashing does not do the trick.

For a successful flake to be removed from a piece of flint held in one hand, a pebble used as a hammer in the other needs to be brought down at a particular angle and with precise force, close to an edge that itself offers the right angle. The shape of the flake will be partly determined by the conformation of the core; force waves will follow ridges left when earlier flakes were struck off. Thus flakes of a desired shape can be obtained by creating ridges on a core in a succession of removals.

The front of a flake, where it snaps away from the core, is smooth and more or less flat. But near the point where the hammer hits there is a rounded swelling, known as a bulb; the core has a corresponding hollow. Hard stone hammers produce prominent bulbs, giving cores quite a sculptural effect with large ridges and hollows, and flakes a chunky look.

Finer working is possible, however, with a hammer of softer material such as bone, antler or wood. With a soft hammer, shaped into a rod that is held at one end, it is possible to remove flakes that have little or no bulb, and that are thinner, longer and flatter. Early in the Boxgrove excavations, Francis Wenban-Smith suspected that the handaxes they were finding had been made with soft hammers. He and John McNabb collected the same flint from the quarry that would have been used half a million years before, and made new handaxes. They roughed them out with hard hammers, and finished them with soft. Comparing their waste with that from the excavations, Francis showed that the fine Boxgrove handaxes had indeed been made with soft hammers. This was the first demonstration of such a technology at so remote a time. Later actual hammers were excavated, made with bones from bison, bear and elephant, or antler from giant deer, heavily battered and studded with tiny slivers of flint.

Francis demonstrated the making of a handaxe for me. It took him about fifteen minutes, starting with a stone hammer, moving to an antler hammer (he used two) and occasionally reverting to the stone. Typically, as well as thousands of small flakes and chips, around a hundred larger flakes will be generated in such a task, each of which will have been carefully planned and executed: the ridges and hollows on an emerging handaxe can determine what is possible several further removals down the line. It is like playing 3D chess.[10]

So Clactonian flakes and Acheulean handaxes don't just look different: hard-hammer Clactonian and soft-hammer Acheulean technologies demand different ways of thinking. It takes skill to make Clactonian flakes. But a fine handaxe requires a greater intellectual commitment from the maker, as well as – it seems impossible to avoid this conclusion – a sense of style, design and symmetry.

As I stand with Nick in the clay pit at Barnham, I remember watching Francis make a handaxe. In front of us is where in the 1990s they found hard-hammer flakes and cores, as well as two handaxes and soft-hammer flakes, in the same deposit. This was the place where the Clactonian–Acheulean distinction died. But now, Nick is telling me, they have realized they were wrong.

They have more than doubled the size of the original trench by extending its length. Importantly, the excavations are set back against the quarry edge, where they have cleaned a long vertical section to show the layers of silt and gravel. At the west end, Nick explains, closer to Area I, they have found more of the same, with Clactonian flakes and cores at a low level. At the east end are more soft- and hard-hammer flakes, and this is where earlier they found the handaxes (or, to be strictly correct, where they found one: the second, remarkably, appeared in a tiny excavation in 1999, when Channel 4's *Time Team* visited the site).[11]

The gravel surface on which the flints lie extends across the excavation, and was also found in Area I. But now, with their larger trench, Nick and his team can see that the higher layer of black clay containing the soft-hammer flakes in Area I enters at a lower level and soon peters out. At one time there was a gravel bank close to the water where people knapped Clactonian flakes. Part of that became covered in silt, but not all. Then later, when other people came with a different, soft-hammer technology, to the west they sat on a soil that had buried the earlier flints. But further east, where there was no soil, their flint debris fell onto the gravel and became mixed up with older flakes already there. It couldn't have been more perfectly designed if, 400,000 years ago, early humans had decided to confuse future archaeologists. Confirming this analysis, the older Clactonian flints are more weathered than the soft-hammer flints.[12]

Now there is a consistent pattern across southeast England. There are discrete non-handaxe collections at Barnham, Clacton, Ebbsfleet and Swanscombe (another important Hoxnian site, near Ebbsfleet). Handaxes appear at a later date at both Barnham and Swanscombe. At Beeches Pit, yet another important Hoxnian site, not far from Barnham but not quite so old, there are just handaxes. It happens so suddenly, says Nick, that it has to mark the arrival of new groups of people.

The diggers are tidying up their work for a break. Nick and I make our way out of the quarry, where we find Simon Parfitt looking at newly washed bones. Over mugs of tea, we talk about what this means for early Britain.

'The Clactonian question,' says Nick, 'has been very insular – about what's going on in Britain. But to answer it you've got to look to Europe.'

A whistling kettle breaks through the noise of voices, as people walk in and out of the metal hut. There is a range of accents – diggers come from up the road and from across Europe – but all speak English.

'The two-fold divide,' says Nick, 'is over-simplifying what's going on. There are small groups moving about. That accelerates if you've got climate or environment change. Suddenly one group happens to drift into Britain. They might come from Brittany, where it's very

**xii** A few of the artefacts from the grave of the Amesbury Archer, who died around 2335 BC. Born in central Europe, he may have brought the antler pin with him. Other items include boar tusks, gold hair tresses, copper knives, sandstone wristguards and one of five Beaker pots.

**xiii** The Heelstone, the only large undressed megalith at Stonehenge, may have been on the site naturally long before Stonehenge was built.

**xiv** Neolithic houses imagined at the Stonehenge visitor centre, based on evidence from Durrington Walls.

**xv** RIGHT A red deer frontlet from the new excavations at Star Carr. More such frontlets have been found at the site than in the rest of Europe.

**xvi** BELOW The western platform at Star Carr, with small houses near the lake edge, as imagined by Marcus Abbott.

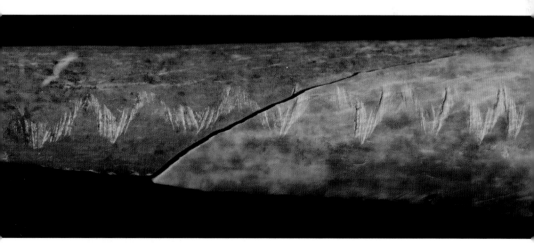

**xvii, xviii** A shaped human skull-cup (TOP) and human radius (BOTTOM) from Gough's Cave. The marks on the radius (from a right arm) have been interpreted as having had some ritual or ceremonial meaning.

**xix** TOP Excavating on the southern edge of the clay quarry at Barnham in 2017, where archaeologists have been able to separate two distinct episodes of early human activity.

**xx** BOTTOM Excavation in 2010 at Happisburgh, at the bottom of a coastal cliff.

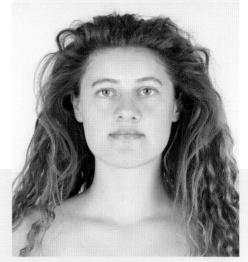

xxi Facial reconstructions by Hew Morrison of a woman buried c. 2100 BC with a Beaker pot near Achavanich, northeast Scotland, done before aDNA study (RIGHT) and after (BELOW).

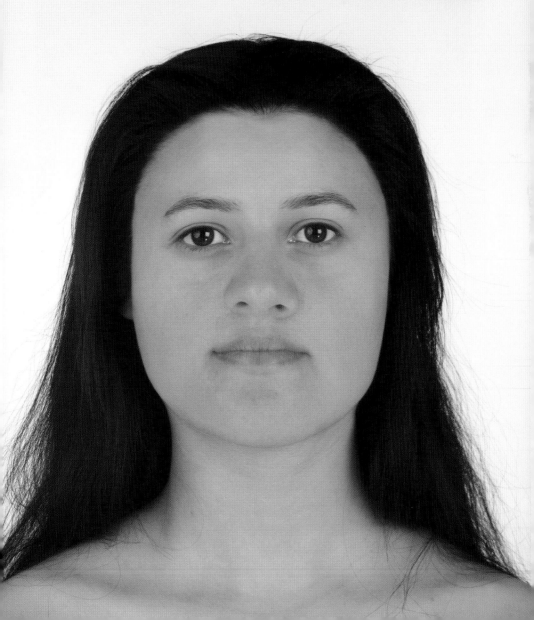

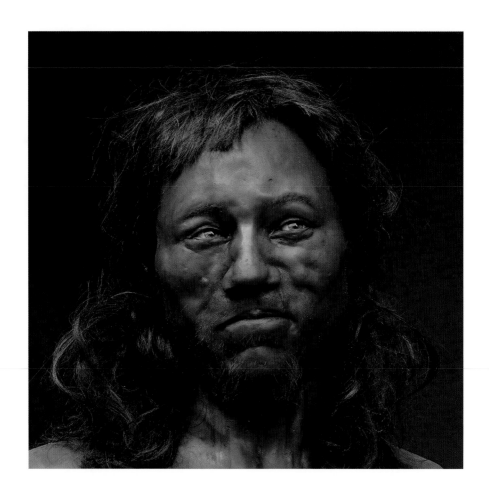

**xxii** Reconstruction by Adrie and Alfons Kennis of the head of Cheddar Man, who died early in the Mesolithic, c. 8250 BC, with skin, hair and eye colour as suggested by aDNA study.

difficult to make handaxes out of the sort of stone they have to use, or from the Somme valley where you get classic Acheulean handaxe-making populations. Or from central Europe where handaxes are simply not part of their repertoire. There's huge variety, a mosaic of different things. And the hominin evidence,' he adds, 'is changing fast. New fossil finds have a mix of features; it was more complex than the two separate species we used to believe in – Neanderthals and before them *Homo heidelbergensis*.'

'If the industries are distinct,' asks Simon, 'they're entities, yeah?'

Like Nick, Simon has glasses and a trimmed salt-and-pepper beard. He wears a green cardigan over a blue cotton shirt, its muddy sleeves pulled up to his elbows.

'For long periods there is limited interaction between those groups,' answers Nick. 'They're retaining an identity, and that must be reflected in some way in their genetics – probably at a sub-species level.'

In a finds tray I see a small handaxe, from the area where animal bones are preserved. Does it matter, I ask, whether groups are making handaxes or not?

'Yes, it's really important,' replies Nick. 'You've made something yourself, it's yours. It's almost the beginning of what you could call craftsmanship, pride in what you are doing. But,' he adds, 'there is no technological advantage to having a handaxe. You could carry a handful of flakes.'

Simon's research confirms this. He recently looked at animal bones from Swanscombe, dividing them into two parts, depending on whether they had been found with Clactonian flints or handaxes. Both collections are dominated by prime-age game, animals least likely to die naturally. 'To me that means the humans are hunting,' says Simon, 'and that hunting behaviour is very similar, although the stone technology is different.'

'We've got burnt flint at Barnham,' says Nick, 'associated with the handaxe makers. Perhaps fire was something else that the Clactonians didn't have.'

They have found a lot of flint crazed and discoloured by fire, but they are still unsure what it means. Were the fires natural? The excavator of nearby Beeches Pit believes there were hearths there – and Simon, at least, agrees. Other debatable evidence for fire appears consistently elsewhere in Europe at around this time. But some archaeologists are now questioning whether even Neanderthals, present until 40,000 years ago and always assumed to be effective fire-users, had such full control. This is not just about heat, light and cooking. Fire acts as a group focus, says Nick. It conjures a domestic situation, with people sitting together to discuss things, forging identities.

Fire had been offered as one explanation, along with a major volcanic eruption or even a meteorite, for something curious seen across northern Europe in the middle of the Hoxnian period, when the forest was at its peak. Pollen shows that trees, especially hazel, took a sudden hit, and that for about three centuries, around 415,000 years ago, there was an unusually high amount of grassland, with ferns, heathers and mosses: it's known as the non-arboreal phase, or NAP. A recent study has shown there was a significant, temporary climatic cooling at this time.[13]

The changes in temperature and vegetation must have affected people in Europe, and the foods they relied on. If the Clactonians were the first to reach Britain after the previous glaciation, arriving perhaps from the east, then maybe the non-arboreal event was what pushed handaxe makers across the land bridge in a second colonization.

The Barnham diggers are moving back to the trenches. Under the trees on the outside edge of the quarry, heaps of excavated silt lie on plastic sheets, drying out and waiting to be hosed through very fine sieves. And so it goes on. You never know which small creature will turn up next.

For the past three decades understanding of these very early times has leaped ahead, through a succession of international research projects. There have been many significant discoveries, but advances have also come from the communal and competitive environment in which scientists have developed new ideas and new techniques of analysis. Not long ago – when the current senior researchers were starting their careers – the early peopling of Britain was seen as a simple thing. It began 200,000 years ago, and there was a quick succession of a few human species, who got steadily better at what they were doing. But the more we learn, the more complex it becomes.

There were people in Britain nearly a million years ago. They faced environments every bit as challenging as those faced by humans hundreds of thousands of years later, but they weren't doing the same things and they may have been evolving locally. Across Europe, even within Britain, there were distinctive groups, making different types of stone tools. At present we can only guess, but perhaps they were also doing other things differently – preparing food in different ways, using or not using fire, wearing different clothes and behaving differently towards one another. Out of this mix appeared the first Neanderthals. Surely, we may now imagine, they would have displayed considerable variety of appearance and actions across Europe, as well as, in their range from Wales to Asia and Siberia, genetic diversity.

When *Homo sapiens* arrived from the south 45,000 years ago (an event itself likely to have been an extended series of colonizations by different groups), they discovered a Europe rich in nature and humanity. It was a further five millennia before Neanderthals finally died out, but by then, through interbreeding, some of their genes were embedded in their competitors; a small amount survives in us. The earliest origins of modern Europe lie in one of the most concentrated and diverse pools of humanity ever seen on Earth.

Chapter 10

# Journeys

*A million years of history*

While researching this book, I went to East Anglia to visit a dig where creative work on an industrial scale is writing a local version of the national story. Archaeologists had been working for eighteen months at one of Highways England's largest schemes, the enlargement of the A14 west of Cambridge. It is probably the busiest single excavation project the country has yet seen, though work on the route of the High Speed 2 railway promises to break all records. The prior evaluation trenches alone, laid end to end, reached over 17 miles (28 kilometres). With a combination of selective excavation after stripping off surface soil, and full excavation at thirty sites, a total of 360 hectares has been investigated. Complete ancient villages, industrial zones and religious monuments have been recorded; 15 tonnes of bones and artefacts and 150 tonnes of soil have been removed for scientific analysis. As many as 250 archaeologists were on site to keep things on schedule, for which a consortium of British consultancies was formed, contracting another from Rome, and employing staff nearly three quarters of whom were originally from outside the UK.[1]

Discoveries range from a Victorian blacksmiths' shop and brick kilns, part of an abandoned medieval village and three Anglo-Saxon villages to a Roman military supply base, farms and forty pottery kilns. There are many prehistoric settlements and field layouts, hundreds of burials (at one site, the remains of sixty-five Bronze Age cremations had been deposited around a large mound) and three henges. Thus far, the finds tell a story parallel to that featured episodically in the first six chapters of this book; word may have reached the Brampton villagers of the Weymouth massacre, and it seems unlikely that none of those who built the henges had ever heard of Stonehenge. As I write, nothing of Mesolithic or Palaeolithic age has been identified, though many such finds have been made elsewhere in this part of England.

This is a journey we have taken in previous chapters through ten other sites. The selection could have been different. Work on some of those described here, such as Black Loch and Must Farm, continues, but at many potential candidates excavation is at too early a stage for me to present a meaningful story. Substantial eras have been skipped because there are no relevant standout digs, and it would anyway have been impossible to cover everything in a single book. We have missed, for example, Yorkshire's distinctive Iron Age chariot burials, which had undoubted continental connections that are yet hard to pin down. We have seen none of the spectacular wealth of Early Bronze Age élites who succeeded the Beaker settlers (here the immediate contacts were with northwest France). The formative time of the first Neolithic farmers, with their imported crops and animals, technologies and beliefs, has had only a mention. There are no Neanderthals.

This is *a* history of Britain, not *the* history, and I need hardly add there will be further discoveries that will bring new insights and surprises. Nonetheless, a different set of stories would have given a similar picture: of an astonishing variety of practices, of sophisticated achievements, of coherent economies and belief systems, of individuals seeking to live and to make their mark, and of societies adapting to changes in climate, technologies and people. Importantly, what we do not see is an unfathomable, mysterious past reaching back from the Roman Conquest with no shape. Instead, we can describe a succession of worlds, with characteristic peoples and cultures, each, in our long history, at least as significant as the Middle Ages or the Victorian era – and many of considerably greater duration. Never has our government sold the nation so short on the international stage, as when it presents would-be new British citizens with our story before Rome in three paragraphs.[2]

It is, perhaps, a surprise to find such a rich past, especially when we bear in mind how much of the story is missing, and how fast it is changing. For many of us the biggest challenge, to our ideas of the past as well as ourselves, is the emerging picture of people on the move: of trade and social exchange, of journeys around Britain and across the Channel and North Sea, and of significant migrations, including the arrival of entirely new populations on such a scale that native, indigenous people became a small minority, never to recover. If we go back as far as the first sign of people, at Happisburgh nearly a million years ago, between then and now there may have been as many as twenty occasions in Britain when the existing human population entirely or substantially disappeared, and was replaced.

The most dramatic of these events saw the arrival of new species. We can't even be sure of how many, but at a minimum *Homo antecessor* was replaced by *Homo heidelbergensis* around 500,000 years ago, who had ceded to or evolved into Neanderthals by 300,000 years ago, who were replaced by *H. sapiens* some 40,000 years ago. We saw how at Barnham, around 400,000 years ago, there may have been a further, unidentified species change. This basic evolutionary tale conceals a greater number of population replacements, since on perhaps a dozen further occasions severe cold drove people out, as happened to the descendants of the modern humans at Gough's Cave some 14,000 years ago. And when the climate warmed enough to allow other people back, sufficient time had passed that they could have had no memory of the landscapes, the hills, rivers and coastlines, and the soils and rocks that supplied some of their most precious materials.

With the arrival of hunter-gatherers at Star Carr 11,300 years ago began the unbroken era of humans in these islands. New research tools help us to explore migration during this time. Isotope analysis came first, revealing individual journeys of often surprising distance, such as those of the Amesbury Archer, or people buried at Cliffs End, in London and near Weymouth. Information from aDNA, first becoming available for Britain only as I was writing this book, brings another, powerful dimension, with the ability to frame entire populations and their relationships and movements.[3]

We have too few fossils for these sciences to help us much with the most ancient people of these islands. Once we reach the Mesolithic, however, the possibilities for dramatic new insights are legion. That starts with a bang, with the Somerset skeleton known as Cheddar Man. He died around 10,250 years ago, just a few centuries after people left the lake edge at Star Carr. His genome is among the oldest British ones we yet have. The man who came to represent ancient Britons for generations of tourists, who was once said to have living descendants in the village down the road, was black.

Cheddar Man's aDNA tells us he probably had blue/green eyes, dark brown or possibly black hair, and dark or black skin. When I heard this news early in 2018, my immediate reaction – perhaps as a magazine editor – was to think, there go all the reconstruction illustrations. Not a single black person had been drawn in representations of prehistoric Britain. Now we had every reason to think that the people at Star Carr had dark skin and hair, as their descendants would have done for thousands of years until the first farmers arrived. Or to put it another way, and to echo a statement I made early in Chapter 7, Britain after the Ice Age has essentially belonged to red deer, wolves, and black hunter-gatherers.[4]

It's too early to say what this means. However, we can note in passing that it doesn't prove that pre-Mesolithic humans in Britain had skin as dark. If pigmentation is linked to the strength of the sun, and if evolution lightens skin at more northern latitudes, one factor affecting colour would be the length of time people had been in the north. On current understanding, for example, Neanderthals had been living at high latitudes for considerably longer than modern humans have yet been present in Europe. They may, by the time hypothetically dark *sapiens* arrived – possibly helping to push them to extinction – have had paler skin.

Up to the Mesolithic era, everyone living in Britain arrived, or had immediate ancestors who arrived, on foot. People walked across landscapes that reached without interruption from the north of Scotland, across northern Europe down to the tip of Italy, and eastwards out to Asia. If the sea level was high and Britain was isolated from the continent, nobody came. From around 8,000 years ago, relatively late in the Mesolithic and after the tsunami had swept across what remained of Doggerland, the North Sea and the English Channel finally took their modern shape, and walking ceased to be an option. From that moment, everyone coming to Britain did so in a boat. This is the meaning of island Britain: surrounded by sea, the British Isles were a beacon to those who sailed. Facing a long and varied continental coast from Norway to Spain and Portugal, Britain was directly accessible to a wider range of people and cultures than would ever have been possible were it landlocked.

The first sailors that we can yet recognize were the first farmers, making the narrowest Channel crossing into southeast England around 6,000 years ago. Their boats must have been capacious enough to bring livestock – domesticated sheep or goats, cattle and pigs – at least in the form of trussed lambs, calves and piglets. New houses, technologies and ways of earning a living (farmed meat and crops instead of game, fish and seafood) betray the arrival of substantial numbers of people from outside Britain, and the complete disappearance of a way of life reaching back over 5,000 years.

Dairy foods, entirely new, may have been of particular significance. Ancient DNA evidence shows that lactase persistence – when an enzyme that enables infants to digest milk continues to be produced throughout adulthood – was largely absent among European people until long after the arrival of cows and ewes. Why breed dairy animals if you can't consume one of their key products? The answer seems to lie in fermentation – making cheese, yogurt and other dairy foods – which removes most of the lactose from milk. What looks like Neolithic cheese-making equipment has been found on the continent, and chemical traces of 5,200-year-old cheese have been identified in Neolithic Croatia. Protein from cattle, sheep and goat milk has been found on the teeth of lactose-intolerant Bronze Age pastoralists in Mongolia.[5]

Archaeology and aDNA suggest that the new lifeways were carried westwards by people from the Near East via two routes: to the south along the Mediterranean and up through Spain, and through central Europe following the Danube River valley. As the archaeology would predict, Neolithic aDNA in Britain shows both of these streams, especially the former. There is a small and constant amount of older hunter-gatherer DNA in the Neolithic genome, but it's the same, and no more, as seen in continental populations, and it's quite possible that it was brought by the new immigrants – who did not mix with the last hunter-gatherers at all. It should come as no surprise, with their long ancestry across Europe back into Asia, that the migrant farmers had lighter skin – but they may not have been what we would call white, with intermediate to dark skin, brown eyes and black or possibly dark brown hair.

With the new scientific trio of isotopes, aDNA and increasingly precise radiocarbon dating, we can now write histories of people's lives, as well as painting their worlds. In time, this is going to offer entirely new ways of understanding the past, of how and why things changed. We can get a taste of that from an old excavation in Dorset. A brilliant new study reminds us that people moved locally as well as across continents.

Hambledon Hill is a National Trust property with distant views across beautiful countryside and villages, reaching to the sea 20 miles (30 kilometres) to the south and further to the north and west. Its northern spur is sculpted by the grassy banks and ditches of a great rambling Iron Age fort. There are other, less obvious earthworks on the hill that reach out along spurs to the south and east, and over a larger area than the fort. These were the subject of a major excavation project between 1974 and 1986, after it was realized that ploughing was destroying the remains. It turned out that they were all Neolithic.

It began about 3650 BC with a causewayed enclosure around the highest point of the hill, similar to the two near Stonehenge, and a long barrow. Over the following three centuries a succession of out-works took in all three of the spurs with a separate enclosure at the south, to surround an area unmatched at this time anywhere else in Britain. There was copious evidence for conflict. Massive timber gateways and palisades were burnt to the ground. Banks were pushed over into ditches, burying bodies of apparent victims (all men), two of whom had flint arrowheads among their bones.

On the basis of the views out and the types of pottery and stone tools brought to the site, some of which came from as far away as Cornwall, 150 miles (250 kilometres) distant, the excavator suggested that people had reached the hill from the south and west. The remains of over seventy-five of them had been recovered in the digs, and Sam Neil wondered if isotope analysis might show where they had really come from.[6]

She and her colleagues analysed teeth from twenty-two people. Strontium isotopes for most of them, including all the children, are consistent with their having lived locally. The isotopes do allow for the possibility that some could have come from further afield – eastern

England, northeastern France or the Netherlands, for example, but not Somerset, Devon or Cornwall – but most of the artefacts could have been made within 20 miles (30 kilometres) of the site, supporting a relatively local origin for the majority of people there. Five adults, however, were not locals.

A young woman and four men had isotope signatures suggesting their most likely home area was in the far southwest of England, where some of the rarer and finer artefacts at the site had been made. They may not all have been there to trade. Three of them, all adult men, had suffered violent deaths: one was buried under the burnt rubble of a collapsed rampart, and another had an arrowhead among his ribs. A second young man with an arrowhead in his chest may have been a local victim of another attack. All these bodies were buried on the east side of the hill. To emphasize the point, most of the twenty-two people studied could have grown up locally. Of the five who certainly did not, three demonstrably died when the hill was assaulted (and it's not impossible that the other two did too).

We can drive from Cornwall to Dorset in a couple of hours with no great fuss. In the Neolithic, the journey would have taken longer – a week, perhaps, by foot, if done directly – but it's likely Hambledon was a destination among many, and arrival the end of a succession of treks each with their own reasons. In addition, archaeology suggests we would have moved from one culture area to another. The few artefacts that survive show different styles; enclosure and funerary-monument architecture differ; and more than we can see may also have distinguished the regions, perhaps even dialect. Wessex seems to have lain between two culture zones, and may have been the area where descendants of immigrant farmers who crossed the sea in the east, and ultimately came up the Danube, met those from the west and the Mediterranean.

In later centuries this border zone featured four of the country's largest henges, ranging from near the coast of Dorset to north Wiltshire, each surrounded by monumental baubles of which Stonehenge is the greatest; as we saw, isotopic research suggests a significant number of those buried there in its early history were not local, with possible origins across southern England and Wales at the nearest. Those great earthworks may have had their roots in warring and trading between different groups. The identification of conflict between strangers on Hambledon Hill is currently unique, but as research continues will surely not remain so.

Even as I write, a new study has been published that throws unexpected light on journeying pigs: they seem to have travelled to the Wessex henges from all over Britain. Pigs would not, of course, have embarked on such astonishing expeditions on their own, and the animals were analysed to see what they might reveal about people mobility, in the absence of suitable Late Neolithic human remains. Domestic pig bones, on the other hand, are so common that archaeologists think that pork was consumed in huge quantities at communal feasts. From finds of tusks in graves, we know that boars were well-regarded creatures in the Neolithic and Chalcolithic (the Amesbury Archer had an exceptional four tusks around his head). Richard Madgwick, an archaeological scientist at Cardiff University, wondered if the pigs had a story to tell.[7]

In a large and pioneering study, in which isotope statistics for five different elements were measured, Richard looked at pigs from the four henge complexes. Most of the bones came from Durrington Walls, but all the sites showed the same pattern: many of the animals had grown up in different regions, some coastal and some inland, perhaps including Ireland. In eight cases, highly radiogenic strontium values point to a number of possible distant locations, five of them probably in Scotland.

Richard's study raises many questions, some of them about the science – the principal issue being that we don't currently have the data to determine where most of the pigs actually came from. But the basic conclusion remains. We can now add to the story of ancient Britain the extraordinary image of pigs being herded – or even carried – across Britain for very large distances, and in large numbers, over 4,500 years ago. And if the pigs and their carers were moving, we might imagine that other things and other people were too.

Does this mean that Wessex, and Stonehenge in particular, was a draw from across the British Isles and even beyond? Perhaps, but until similar studies are done outside Wessex, we have no wider context. Henges like the three at Thornborough in North Yorkshire, recognized as being at the centre of natural routeways, might have been way stations for great pilgrimages – or attractions in their own right. We cannot yet say that no pigs travelled from Wiltshire to Orkney.

What we can say is that there seems to have been a remarkable amount of movement within the British Isles. Whether that makes Britain a 'nation', as the press suggested when the science was released, is another question – to which the answer is surely no. There are remarkable affinities between things being made across Britain at this time, notably pottery, and the monumental variations on themes of henges and timber architecture imply shared visions. But we could make a similar point, for example, of Europe at any time in history, with its distinct polities, languages and cultures. Late Neolithic Britain would have been a place of many peoples, with local traditions and understandings. That is not incompatible with the simultaneous habit of long-distance journeying. And the latter is quite different from something that brought it all to an end: a major population change across the UK.

Around 2450 BC (4,500 years ago), new technologies and styles (Beaker pottery, a new prominence of archery, metallurgy, new religions and so on) appeared at the same time as a dramatic change in aDNA that is directly traceable to the continent, from where the cultural changes also came. We are far from understanding what happened either then or at the start of the Neolithic, and for this in future we will rely on both archaeology and genetics. However, relative population sizes will very likely have been important, with migrants often settling on unused land and perhaps coming to dominate simply through sheer numbers (when famers first arrived with a growing population, they may rarely have seen any hunter-gatherers, in relative equilibrium after millennia of occupation).

As 1,500 years before, the new people had significantly lighter skin and paler eyes than those already living in Britain. Typically, it seems, they would have looked different (and I have noted that they had different head shapes) even without the effects of their dress, behaviour and speech. There is regional variety – Beaker people in Scotland were doing some things differently from Beaker people in Wessex – but overall it's quite possible that many natives and immigrants kept themselves apart, and that the apparent continuation of rituals at old monuments may have a more complex explanation.

The answer to the question posed earlier – was Stonehenge built by immigrants? – is 'Yes', however you look at it. The site's sanctity was founded by early immigrant farmers, and its later history manipulated by further immigrant farmers. Whether the great stones themselves were raised by people who made Grooved Ware (more likely) or Beaker pottery (less so, though that may change as research continues), set against millennia of Mesolithic hunter-gatherers, both these peoples and their different cultures were intrusive. Logically, of course, that is the lot of island nations: if no one arrived in boats, there would be no one there.[8]

After the Beaker immigration, there is no indication of another change so dramatic, and it may be that the total population reached a level where it would have been unthinkable. There is, however, much evidence of relatively minor movements linking Britain with the rest of Europe. The amount of journeying to (and presumably from) Cliffs End may have been exceptional, but the idea of travel was certainly not unique. Throughout the Bronze and Iron ages there are strong archaeological suggestions not only of trade and contact, but also of physical movement of people across the North Sea and the Channel. By the time classical observers came to write about the people of Britain, from their perspective we were yet more northern European folk, with our own talents and oddities to be sure, but not some isolated race from another world.

This is a new area, with much research in progress and emerging stories, and doubtless some big surprises to come. Until very recently many archaeologists downplayed or entirely rejected migration as having had any great role in British prehistory. Yet the idea that we are a nation of migrants is not new: it was once a dominant theme. It's interesting to look briefly at why such a change in thinking occurred. It tells us as much about ourselves as about our past.

Every society has its story of where its people came from – its origin myth. Often, these are wonderful, imaginative tales, created and shaped by powerful narrators. In Korea, Hwanung, son of the Lord of Heaven, gave a bear and a tiger garlic and mugwort, saying he would make them human if they ate nothing else and stayed in a cave for a hundred days; the bear became a woman, and in the absence of the tiger, who gave up waiting, she had a child with Hwanung. In British Columbia a curious raven prised open a large clam and men crawled out; he found women in another mollusc, and sat back and watched them play. The Ik in Kenya believed in a god who was half male and half female, who gave birth to their region's different peoples.

Prehistoric stories are of course lost to us, but surviving British myths are based on migration, not creation. Many think of the

English as Anglo-Saxons, the outcome of close contact with the European continent, and of settlement by Germanic peoples after Rome left Britain. *Our Island Story*, a children's book published in 1905 and still popular,[9] features a string of transformative arrivals: Romans (twice), St Alban, Hengist and Horsa, St Augustine, Sweyn Forkbeard, Canute and William the Conqueror. Before them came primeval native Britons, descended from what we would today call a Mediterranean refugee.

In *Our Island Story*, Leeby Marshall says that 'some people think' the story of Brutus 'is only a fairy tale'. It survives today in a retelling by Geoffrey of Monmouth, a medieval bishop, and, with less elaboration, in older texts said to have been compiled around AD 800 by a Welsh monk called Nennius – and perhaps he didn't make it up, as loosely similar stories describing continental Celts appear in the older classical literature. Brutus, reports Nennius, was descended from Aeneas, a Trojan hero in the east Mediterranean. Having accidently killed his father, Brutus fled Italy with his supporters, was chased into France by the Greeks, and eventually settled in a previously uninhabited Britain, which is named after him.[10]

The notion of 'a distinctively British character' melded from 'successive groups of invaders' was the triumphant principle of a pavilion at the 1951 Festival of Britain.[11] Originally called 'Origin of the British People' and opened as 'The People of Britain', it used artefacts ('the relics of our ancestors'), graphics and reconstructions to showcase 'addition[s] to our racial stock' at the start of the Mesolithic, Neolithic, Bronze Age and Iron Age (welcome to the Celts), and Roman, Anglo-Saxon and Viking eras. Jacquetta Hawkes, a prominent archaeologist of the time, was the pavilion's expert adviser. (This was, incidentally, the last comprehensive national exhibition of British prehistory to be held in the UK.)

Antiquaries had long looked overseas for the ancient past's inspirations. Inigo Jones, a 17th-century architect, thought Stonehenge 'a work, built by the Romans, and they the sole Founders thereof'. Walter Charleton, a philosopher, retorted that it had been made by Danes. Geoffrey of Monmouth claimed the stones themselves had come from Ireland.[12] By 1940, when Gordon Childe published *Prehistoric Communities of the British Isles*, pan-European connections were woven into the fabric of our remote past. They explained why things changed, and they also helped to say when. Early writing in the east Mediterranean offered chronologies that could be extended into pre-literate northern Europe with the imported artefacts and technologies found by archaeologists.

The first powerful voice against what he called the 'invasion neurosis' – Hawkes's 1951 displays had actually simplified the number of imagined immigrant takeovers – was Grahame Clark, the excavator of Star Carr. In an influential article published in 1966, he noted that British archaeologists had begun 'once again to appreciate the achievements of their prehistoric forbears', linking this to the 'waning [of British] imperial power'. Only the first farmers and Beaker people survived his withering analysis as 'intrusive'.[13]

By then, archaeologists had something that Childe and his predecessors did not: radiocarbon dating. Now everything could be aged independently of supposed connections elsewhere, and as Colin Renfrew (like Grahame Clark, a Disney Professor of Archaeology at the University of Cambridge) was quick to recognize, the result was that these fell apart.[14] Innovations across prehistoric Europe often turned out to be older than their supposed sources in Egypt, the Aegean or the Middle East. Science and a change in attitude allowed British archaeologists to look inward, to focus on indigenous development and initiative. They turned away from explanations that involved outside interference, some even rejecting migration as a factor in the introduction of farming, or in the adoption of everything that came with Beaker pottery. At the extreme, four centuries of Roman occupation were said to have done little to interfere with the long march of indigenous prehistoric culture, and Anglo-Saxon migration was dismissed altogether.

Childe, Clark and Renfrew (now a peer in the House of Lords) are among the greatest archaeologists of the past century, gifted with eloquence and mastery of their material. Nonetheless, neither Childe's conviction that movement was fundamental to the progress of European civilization, nor its almost trivial role granted by some followers of Clark and Renfrew, were backed by science. Both were hunches that suited their times: Childe's in a Britain withdrawing from a world stage but pivotal in Europe riven by conflict, succeeded by a vision of ancient self-sufficiency suited to a nation focusing on local identity and suspicious of globalization.

It is no exaggeration to say that early aDNA results have shaken the world of British archaeology. Some of the reasons are practical.

Archaeologists who have been used to working at a measured pace in relatively small teams can feel overtaken by enormous groups of research scientists, most of whom they have never heard of, churning out new data on a vast scale by the week. There are concerns that scientists talk about migration, invasions and population wipe-outs without knowing much at all about the underlying archaeology, and some are worried about the ethics of uncontrolled sampling of human remains. The real challenges, however, are to accepted ideas about population movements and how these affected early societies. It's an area that had become academically unfashionable. Put simply, archaeologists don't have the stories of ancient peoples or the ways of thinking about the past into which they can slip the new data. And they know that a torrent of information has barely begun.

British origin myths, however, are framed not as a muddle of individual journeys, small groups moving back and forth or even substantial population replacements, but quite specifically as invasions. Invaders are enemies, arriving in boats brandishing swords and spears while British women and children look down in fear from coastal cliffs. This was how the Festival of Britain told it seventy years ago, by extending Leeby Marshall's story of Dark Age heroics back into prehistory. It was how a BBC TV series in 2017, grasping the new aDNA data, led its presenter to say, 'There have been battles for Britain for millennia.'[15] It's the most fundamental myth, imagining an isolated and unified island people, both indifferent to and ignorant of what happens beyond the seas, until every so often they are buffeted by foreigners whom they absorb, and move on as renewed Britons. And it's fundamentally wrong.

To be sure, Roman armies came to southeast England in ships – Caesar claimed more than eight hundred of them, and Claudius may have had more – and at least some of them probably landed between the cliffs of Dover and Pegwell Bay. The successful assault in AD 43 ushered in dramatic and long-lasting changes that affected everybody. But there is a bigger picture.

For generations, people in that part of Britain had been in close contact with the continent. The North Sea and the Channel joined lands distant only as measured on a map. Classical writers described a tribe in north France called the Parisii, and another in east Yorkshire called the Parisi (Hull could truly call itself the Paris of the north); in both regions archaeologists have identified unusual practices, centuries before the Roman empire, of burying people with horses and two-wheeled carts or chariots.

By the time Claudius arrived, tribes in southern England were allying not only with the continent but also with Rome. Strabo, a Greek geographer, described seeing Britons in the city, tall and bandy-legged. Immediately before the Roman Conquest, a man was buried down the road from Camulodunum, which in less than twenty years became a Roman city burnt to the ground by Boudica. Dubbed the warrior because of his spear and shield, he took with him a wealth of Roman treasures, including a tall wine jar, fine glass vessels and a bronze jug, all from Italy, and a whole cupboard-full of fine continental pottery. Decades earlier, a similar grave in Hertfordshire was packed with imports, including an Italian silver jug. On the south coast, Fishbourne Roman palace, its opulence unmatched north of the Alps, may have been built for a local client king whose predecessor had sought safety in Rome and, say some, provided Claudius with a political excuse to invade.

London was an exception, a civic version of a Roman fort populated by people from overseas and serviced by locals, a Wild West of entrepreneurs, soldiers and lawyers in the midst of what today we would have made a national park, with water birds, verdant hills and a timeless river. Hadrian's Wall must have severely disrupted local communities, marching across tracks and fields and displacing villages, and the new roads similarly ignored the existing landscape. But elsewhere what we almost always see is accelerated evolution.

Iron Age roads and fields are refurbished or adjusted, and farmsteads step up with rectangular buildings in the new Roman style, sometimes with bricks, glass and mosaic floors, instead of round houses of timber and reed. Vineyards are set out, new drains installed and tribal capitals become formal cities. Before Claudius, Strabo had written, Britain was known for exporting slaves. Now an enforced peace and a Europe-wide market brought new opportunities for many people. But, as usually happens with rapid social change, others benefited less, especially in the countryside. And lives had been disrupted over a century before the Conquest, not least with the abandonment of many of the hillforts that had dominated the landscape for generations in favour of lower-lying towns. Many of those went on to become the walled towns of Roman Britain.

When it comes to Anglo-Saxons, the difference between a large-scale invasion by Germanic people, as described by early historians, and the evidence of archaeology is greater yet. There is no doubting strong continental connections, and aDNA confirms the implications of new house and artefact styles and new burial practices: there were immigrants, and they settled. But claims by the first genetic studies using modern DNA, of an overwhelming Anglo-Saxon migration (with as much as 95 per cent of the native population said to have been replaced), now seem to be exaggerated.

In one Anglo-Saxon cemetery in East Sussex, isotopes separated natives from migrants. There were ten of the former and nine of the latter, who might have come from elsewhere in southern England or the continent, but only one of whom could be said not to have been born in Britain. The migrants had less valuable items in their graves.[16]

A separate aDNA study looked at the remains of people in Cambridgeshire, seven from two Anglo-Saxon cemeteries (one of them in a village whose name means Hengist's farm), and three from Iron Age burials. How did the alleged invaders compare to the pre-Roman natives? Put simply, one of the 'Anglo-Saxons' was 'Iron Age', five were 'Anglo-Saxon' (comparable to modern Dutch people) and one was mixed. Next, the same team looked at thirty modern people from England, Scotland and Wales. They were more Iron Age than Anglo-Saxon. Finally, with a larger sample still, the scientists found that between 25 and 40 per cent of modern British ancestry was contributed by Anglo-Saxon immigrants, with the higher numbers, as you would expect, in eastern England. Interestingly, similar to the picture in Sussex, the 'Iron Age' burial in the 'Anglo-Saxon' cemetery, a woman, was in the wealthiest grave.[17]

On the one hand, then, we can see a significant continental contribution to the people of Britain between AD 400 and 900. There is likely to have been 'Viking' blood there too, but it is early days. The difficulty with genetics on its own is that by now, with the UK involved in three millennia of mix and migration around northwest Europe, different 'peoples' are becoming defined less by their genes and more by their myths and cultures. This can work both ways. Some of the 'Anglo-Saxon' aDNA could have arrived during the centuries of Roman occupation or perhaps even before; and people crossing the North Sea into Britain in AD 500 could have looked genetically 'Iron Age'. Further studies will throw much light on this.

On the other hand, there is little scientific support for anyone in modern Britain to think of themselves as Anglo-Saxon. At most, Anglo-Saxon or Germanic genetic traits constitute less than half the British genome. A recent overview of archaeological evidence in the West Midlands, for example, found great social and cultural change in the centuries immediately following the Roman era (formally taken to have ended in AD 410, when Britannia was told by Rome to look after itself). That change does not seem to have been caused directly by migration, however; in that region, there are none of the new, distinctive cemeteries found in the east, where buildings have more in common with the Low Countries and Scandinavia than anything elsewhere in England.

It would make more sense for the nation, if we wanted to claim some kind of genetic ancestral origin, to look to our remoter past... but only so far back. In 1994, announcing its scoop of the news that archaeologists had found a 500,000-year-old human fossil at Boxgrove, *The Times* was unable to hide its pride. 'Here was not the short and stumbling figure of Neanderthal Man', wrote its leader writer about a bone that indicated a statuesque, muscular male. 'Every Englishman may walk a little taller in the recognition that he is descended from such a striking creature.'[18] The trouble with this (leaving aside the question of what Englishwomen were to think) is that the striking creature was *Homo heidelbergensis*, from whom the deficient Neanderthals were later descended. To call Boxgrove Man English is, frankly, a bit of a stretch.

Clearly we cannot seek genetic ancestry in the Ice Age, during which different species and different modern human cultures came and entirely disappeared. Nor among the last hunter-gatherers, as they all but vanished when farmers arrived. Nor the people who built Stonehenge (probably), as their genes too barely exist, thanks to a second wave of migration that changed the British genome far more than any Anglo-Saxon or Viking settlers were able to do.

Are we, then, Beaker people? There might be something in this. There's a firm baseline – the arrival into these islands of a new culture and a transformative technology, metallurgy – that we can date quite precisely to around 4,500 years ago. We might have to say goodbye to Stonehenge, but we get to claim some of Europe's best Bronze Age gold, the oldest plank boats, round houses and the most accomplished Iron Age art, to say nothing of Romans fussing about

IOUs, the Staffordshire Hoard and, ahem, a robust defence against Viking invaders. And here's the best bit. No one's quite sure what the fine Beaker pots, proudly buried with the dead and so distinctive in their shapes, tartan-like decorations and reddish clays, were for. But one popular theory is that they held an alcoholic drink made with malted barley. What could be better for Britain than ditching an origin myth about Brutus in favour of one about beer?

Of course, as with all good myths, there is a twist. Beaker people, in one form or another, were to be found scattered across the continent, from Ireland to Poland and down to the Mediterranean coast, Sardinia and north Africa: they were not unique to the UK.[19] Perhaps our real ancestry is to be found in that wider Europe, a cultural pool that drew people from far beyond, back to the very origins of humanity millions of years ago. If anything makes us different, here in Britain, it is the place where we live, its climate, landscapes and resources, its views out on the world, its history and its particular stories buried beneath our feet. Stonehenge, Star Carr and Gough's Cave, the flints at Barnham and the footprints at Happisburgh – these are places and things that matter to me as much as Roman London, the Staffordshire Hoard or a medieval cathedral.

We may carry little of the hunter-gatherers' genomes, but this is not the only way to look at biological ancestry. Working back from the present, our family trees expand exponentially, as another generation brings in two people for every one that followed. It doesn't take long on that journey before every living person in the world today shares a common ancestor: that person was alive, it has been calculated, more than a millennium *after* Beaker people first crossed the Channel into Britain. Continuing backwards, the tree embraces more common ancestors, until the point comes when everyone then alive, and whose line of descent is unbroken, was an ancestor of everyone alive now. And when was that? About a millennium before the first farmers came to Britain. All of us, even those who have just flown in from halfway round the world, can trace roots back to dark-skinned hunter-gatherers stalking deer in the mist with flint-tipped spears and arrows, watching the wind, feeling the ground under their feet, and wondering what's to become of them.

# NOTES

**Preface**

1   *The National Curriculum in England* (London: Department for Education, 2013), 169.

2   *The Songlines*, by B. Chatwin (London: Vintage, 1998), 228.

**Chapter 1: A Viking Massacre**

1   The burial pit, 'one of the most exciting and unexpected archaeological discoveries to have been made in Britain in recent years', as Louise Loe, Angela Boyle, Helen Webb and David Score open their text, is described in Loe *et al.* 2014. The book also contains contributions from nineteen others, and the specialists thanked for further help are almost uncountable.

2   *The English Heritage Book of Maiden Castle*, by Niall M. Sharples (London: Batsford, 1991).

3   While I was writing this book, a Roman-age human skull was stolen overnight from an excavation in Yorkshire. 'People often complain that digs aren't publicized until after they've finished', tweeted an archaeologist. 'This is why.'

4   Her full title is Head of Heritage Burial Services.

5   *'Remember Me to All': The Archaeological Recovery and Identification of Soldiers who Fought and Died in the Battle of Fromelles 1916*, by L. Loe *et al.* (Oxford: Oxford Archaeology, 2014).

6   Appendix 3 in Loe *et al.* 2014.

7   'Lead isotope analysis of tooth enamel from a Viking age mass grave in southern Britain and the constraints it places on the origin of the individuals', by J. Evans *et al.*, *Archaeometry* 60 (2018), 859–69.

8   The six skeletons in this group are 3687, 3764, 3786, 3791, 3804 and 3806.

9   *The Oxford Henge and Late Saxon Massacre with Medieval and Later Occupation at St John's College, Oxford* (Reading: Thames Valley Archaeological Services, 2014). '"Sprouting like cockle amongst the wheat": the St Brice's Day Massacre and the isotopic analysis of human bones from St John's College, Oxford', by A. Pollard *et al.*, *Oxford Journal of Archaeology* 31 (2012), 83–102.

10  *The Anglo-Saxon Chronicle*,
    translated by J. Ingram and J. Giles
    (London: Everyman Press, 1847),
    at http://www.gutenberg.org/
    ebooks/657. For Viking ships (and
    much else) see Williams *et al.* 2014.

11  *King Alfred the Great (A
    Ladybird Book)*, by L. Peach
    (Loughborough: Wills and
    Hepworth, 1957).

## Chapter 2: The Staffordshire Hoard

1   What is now Historic England
    was called English Heritage
    in 2009. It was divided into
    two in 2015: Historic England,
    which continues the statutory
    work, struggling with shrinking
    government grants; and a new
    English Heritage, a charity
    managing sites open to the
    public. For simplicity, I will call
    the organization that deals with
    archaeology Historic England,
    regardless of date.

2   Treasure is essentially old items
    of gold or silver, or collections of
    old coins or prehistoric metal: see
    https://finds.org.uk. If you find
    it, you have to inform the coroner,
    and if a museum wants it they
    have to pay you an independently
    assessed reward.

3   In the five days after the press
    conference, the Hoard website
    received half a million views.
    People queued outside for hours
    in an unusually cold Birmingham
    to see the first objects, and
    the museum had to extend its
    opening hours.

4   *Beowulf: A New Translation*, by S.
    Heaney (London: Faber & Faber,
    1999).

5   'Any seasoned digger', T. Tatton-
    Brown, *Current Archaeology*
    (January 2011), 4; Carver,
    *Antiquity* 85 (2011), 230. The early
    thrill, shock and puzzlement
    among academics at news of the
    find could be sensed at a 2010
    British Museum symposium of
    leading Anglo-Saxon specialists
    and all those involved with the
    Hoard (see https://finds.org.uk/
    staffshoardsymposium). *British
    Archaeology* featured the discovery
    in 2009 (109), conservation and
    research progress in 2013 (131),
    and the helmet in 2018 (164),
    reporting other developments as
    they happened.

6   The Hoard was acquired on 9
    June 2010 jointly by Birmingham
    Museum and Art Gallery and the
    Potteries Museum and Art Gallery,
    Stoke-on-Trent. 'It caused quite
    a stir in staff hearts', wrote Deb
    Klemperer, Principal Collections
    Officer at Stoke, 'when a bill for
    £3,285,000 arrived on our desks.'
    Terry and Fred, the landowner,
    shared the reward.

7   The lab in Birmingham became a
    community for some of the best
    scientists and specialists in their
    fields from across Europe, as
    well as for many volunteers and
    apprentices – as must have the
    workshops where the treasures
    had been created over a thousand
    years before.

8   Excavation of the treasure at
    Sutton Hoo began on 13 July, the
    same day and month on which
    Terry's nephew rang Duncan
    about his discovery.

9   Archaeologists use 'copper
    alloy' as a catch-all for impure

coppers, bronze (copper with tin, manganese, silicon or other additives) and brass (copper with zinc or other metals). Only scientific analysis can determine an exact alloy.

10  Leahy: *Independent* 25 September 2009; Geake: *Daily Mail* 25 September 2009; Carver 2017, 194–95; Brooks: *Sunday Times* 22 November 2009; Preston: *Daily Telegraph* 25 September 2009. Many theories about the Hoard fall at the lowest hurdles, misdating it, for example, or ignoring key features of its contents.

11  'Secrets of the Anglo-Saxon goldsmiths: analysis of gold objects from the Staffordshire Hoard', by E. Blakelock *et al.*, *Journal of Archaeological Science* 72 (2016), 44–56; 'Ion beam analysis of glass inlays from the Staffordshire Anglo-Saxon Hoard', by A. Meek, *Journal of Archaeological Science: Reports* 7 (2016), 324–29.

12  For Mercia see *Warriors, Warlords and Saints: The Anglo-Saxon Kingdom of Mercia*, by J. Hunt (Alcester: West Midlands History, 2016).

13  I find Chris Fern's reading more convincing, but it has to be said that George Speake, who worked closely with Chris on the restoration of the helmet, thinks it likely the Hoard came together after a single battle. 'Swords and even the helmet,' he tells me, 'could be seen as heirlooms.'

14  The battle's location is not known. Suggestions include three sites to the north of the Hoard, between 65 and 95 miles (100 and 150 kilometres) away, and another to the west at 55 miles (90 kilometres) – allowing time enough for a determined rider to reach the area ahead of an exhausted army. Neither is the site of Penda's imaginary power base known, one possibility being Tamworth, 10 miles (15 kilometres) to the east, a town known to tourists as 'the ancient capital of Mercia'.

15  The definitive record of the Hoard, and more online, is Fern *et al.* 2019, published after this book went to press.

16  Prittlewell was published as this book went to press. See Blackmore *et al.* 2019.

**Chapter 3: Roman Occupation**

1  Shepherd 1998. In the title poem of *Queuing for the Sun* (Calstock: Peterlee Poets, 2003), U. A. Fanthorpe identified the Bucklersbury queue as London's first great example (not trivial, like those at Harrods sales), precursor to Tutankhamun (1972) and Monet (1999).

2  *Building the Future, Transforming our Past: Celebrating Development-Led Archaeology in England, 1990–2015*, by M. Pitts and R. Thomas (London: Historic England, 2015). The front cover image shows display hoarding around the Bloomberg dig.

3  For Roman Britain see *The Oxford Handbook of Roman Britain*, ed. M. Millett, L. Revell and A. Moore (Oxford: Oxford University Press,

2016), and *Roman Britain: A New History*, by G. de la Bédoyère (London: Thames & Hudson, revised edn 2013).

4   In the fifty years before the Roman invasion, among other Mediterranean products olives, coriander and celery were being used in Silchester, Hampshire. London's historic centrality was cemented by paved roads, still visible in the modern network, that crossed Britain to the Roman provincial and financial capital on the Thames.

5   A larger Watling Street crossed England from northwest to southeast and passed London.

6   London mythology imagines the Walbrook as a river harbouring Roman ships. On the evidence of MOLA's excavations, it was a group of small streams with a natural bank blocking its mouth.

7   Amminus, Antedi, Tincommius, Verica or Verlamio; there are many others. *Coins and Power in Late Iron Age Britain*, by J. Creighton (Cambridge: Cambridge University Press, 2000).

8   Tomlin (2016); *The Story of the Bloomberg Writing Tablets* (Bloomberg 2017, www.youtube. com/watch?v=lhm-no9PGEI).

9   Actually, we read AD 61, but the Bloomberg tablets confirm previous archaeological susp- icions that Tacitus (see below in main text) was a year out.

10  They may be telling us something we can't interpret: though written in different hands, all three tablets spell London with a double 'L'.

11  One tablet opens with the name of the sender, Taurus, written over Taurinus (or vice versa, Tomlin couldn't tell which), perhaps indicating a dictated letter corrected after a read-through, a writer being unlikely to misspell his own name. Styluses had a little flat wedge at the top for minor changes, like a rubber eraser on the end of a pencil.

12  *An Early Roman Fort and Urban Development on Londinium's Eastern Hill*, by L. Dunwoodie, C. Harward and K. Pitt (London: Museum of London Archaeology, 2015).

13  'The complex origins of Lant Street's Roman citizens', by V. Ridgeway, *British Archaeology* 153 (2017), 40–45.

14  '"Written in Bone": new discoveries about the lives and burials of four Roman Londoners', by R. Redfern, M. Marshall, K. Eaton and H. Poinar, *Britannia* 48 (2017), 253–77.

15  Designed by John Hutton, the glass panels are to be rehung in the new Bank Underground station entrance. See 'Mithras reborn: London Mithraeum', by L. Fowler, *British Archaeology* 158 (2018), 30–37.

16  The whole series, a TV classic, can be watched online at https://archive.org/details/ QuatermassAndThePit- EpisodeOne.

# Notes

## Chapter 4: Living in Round Houses

1  *Said and Done: The Autobiography of an Archaeologist*, by O. G. S. Crawford (London: Weidenfeld & Nicolson, 1955); 'Archaeology and modern times: Bersu's Woodbury 1938 & 1939', by C. Evans, *Antiquity* 63 (1989), 436–50.

2  'Outside in: the structure of an Early Iron Age house at Dunston Park, Thatcham, Berkshire', by A. Fitzpatrick, in *The Iron Age in Wessex: Recent Work*, ed. A. Fitzpatrick and E. Morris (Salisbury: Trust for Wessex Archaeology, 1994), 68–73. 'Food, sex and death: cosmologies in the British Iron Age with particular reference to East Yorkshire', by M. Parker Pearson, *Cambridge Archaeological Journal* 9 (1999), 43–69.

3  'Cultural grouping within the British pre-Roman Iron Age', by F. R. Hodson, *Proceedings of the Prehistoric Society* 30 (1964), 99–110. *Prehistoric Dwelling: Circular Structures in North and Central Britain c. 2500 bc–500 ad*, by R. Pope (PhD thesis, University of Durham 2003). *The Iron Age Round-House: Later Prehistoric Building in Britain and Beyond*, by D. Harding (Oxford: Oxford University Press, 2009). Elsewhere in Europe round houses were commonly found only in Ireland, along the Channel coast in France and, in a very different context, in northwest Spain and Portugal.

4  'The Scientific basis for the reconstruction of prehistoric and protohistoric houses', by P. Reynolds, *euroREA: Journal for (Re)construction and Experiment in Archaeology* 3 (2006), 58–68.

5  Crone and Cavers 2016.

6  At another round house experiment, where several buildings were reconstructed in the 1980s at a hillfort in Wales called Castell Henllys, local reed also had to be supplemented by imports from Hungary, reminding us not to take such resources for granted in Iron Age Britain: see H. Mytum and J. Meek, *British Archaeology 165 (2019)*, 36–41. Julia Muir Watt, development manager at the Whithorn Trust, oversaw the Black Loch round house project. In a post-construction analysis, it was noted that 'Craftsmen were a diverse group, not used to working together, nor working to budgets and timetables, and without a great understanding of Health and Safety legislation.' One wonders how different that might have been in the Iron Age.

7  Knight and Murrell 2012. See also news reports in *British Archaeology* – 116 and 120 (2011), 147, 148, 149 and 150 (2016) – with doubtless more to come.

8  The Flag Fen excavation followed a pioneering project, also led by Francis Pryor, in which much evidence for Bronze Age farming was recorded on the dry land. Parallel rows of posts picked up where a droveway between fields on the west side of the fen ended, and continued across the water to the east side. See Pryor 2001.

9  Trees were felled between 1283 and 1246 bc to make bridge posts

# Notes

at Must Farm, identical to the first row of posts at Flag Fen, cut down between 1287 and 1242 BC: www.mustfarm.com, Dig Diary 43. These dates were obtained by dendrochronology. As I write, the village's age has been determined by the less precise process of radiocarbon dating.

10  In graves, there is a strong correlation between men and women identified by their bones and particular types of weapon and ornament.

11  The oldest incomplete wheel found in the UK, made around 1300 bc, is from Flag Fen.

12  Isotope analysis can demonstrate that someone had grown up, or spent part of their life, somewhere other than where they were buried. It can also show that an individual could have spent their life in the local area. But a 'local' signature can also be generated by similar conditions far from a site: it is easier to prove distant origins than it is to prove local. On its own, isotope analysis is prone to underestimate movement.

## Chapter 5: Paths of the Dead

1  For the comprehensive report on Cliffs End Farm see McKinley et al. 2014.

2  'And Isaac spake unto Abraham and said, "My father. Behold the fire and the wood: but where is the lamb for a burnt offering?"' (Genesis 22).

3  The report numbers of these burials are older woman 3675, girl

3674, young woman 3680, boy 3676, man 3673. I have simplified some of the descriptions, which are often qualified.

4  A twenty-year-old man or woman, also late Bronze Age, probably died from a dagger blow in the back. A rib with a sharp cut was found in the ditch around the northern enclosure.

5  'The mummies of Bronze Age Britain', by T. Booth et al., British Archaeology 145 (2015), 18–23. Further radiocarbon dating may also help untangle events at Cliffs End (at Cladh Hallan some body parts were of significantly different ages), though existing dates are compatible with everyone in the pit having died at more or less the same time.

6  Stuart Needham offers another possible explanation for the bone tube: a slide for a ligature that killed the man (McKinley et al. 2014, 226).

7  Varying object styles at Salcombe raise the possibility of two wrecks, one 1300–1150 bc, the other 1000–800 bc.

8  Clark 2004. See also The Dover Bronze Age Boat in Context: Society and Water Transport in Prehistoric Europe, ed. P. Clark (Oxford: Oxbow Books, 2004).

9  Claimed by the Sea: Salcombe, Langdon Bay, and Other Marine Finds of the Bronze Age, by S. Needham et al. (York: Council for British Archaeology, 2013).

10  The Prehistory of European Society, by V. G. Childe (Harmondsworth:

266

Penguin, 1958). His suicide was revealed only in 1980, when a letter he had requested be kept secret for a decade was finally released. 'Life ends best', Childe concluded, 'when one is happy and strong' (*Antiquity* 54, 1980, 1–3).

11 S. Timberlake and P. Marshall, in *Mining for Ancient Copper: Essays in Memory of Beno Rothenberg*, ed. E. Ben-Yosef (Pennsylvania: Eisenbrauns, 2018), 418–31.

12 'The long demise of the Wantsum Sea Channel: a recapitulation based on the data', by D. Perkins, *Archaeologia Cantiana* 127 (2007), 249–59.

13 There is also the peculiarly modern option of giving parts of our body to others or to scientific research. For most of us, I suspect, this is not a matter of our continuing existence, but of the lives of others, and we imagine that in due course those parts too would be buried or cremated.

14 '*Pegwell Bay, Kent – a Recollection of October 5th 1858* ?1858–60 by William Dyce', by C. Payne *et al.*, at tate.org.uk. When the Ordnance Survey first mapped the area in 1872, beside a benchmark they established at Ebbsfleet they noted the 'Supposed Site of the Landing of St. Augustine and Christian Missionaries A.D. 597 Also of The Saxons A.D. 449.'

### Chapter 6: Shaped by Beliefs

1 For fieldwork inside the World Heritage Site see *The Stonehenge Landscape*, by M. Bowden *et al.* (London: Historic England,

2015); *Stonehenge World Heritage Site Synthesis: Prehistoric Landscape, Environment and Economy*, by M. Canti *et al.* (London: English Heritage, 2013); *Research Activity in the Stonehenge Landscape 2005–2012*, ed. T. Darvill (London: Historic England, 2016); Parker Pearson 2012 and Parker Pearson *et al.* 2019 (Riverside Project). For commercial excavations in and outside the WHS see Pitts 2018, and earlier research *Hengeworld*, by M. Pitts (London: Arrow, 2001).

2 Beaker aDNA: 'The Beaker phenomenon and the genomic transformation of northwest Europe', by I. Olalde *et al.*, *Nature* 555 (2018), 190–96; '*Beakers: How ancient DNA is changing the way we think about prehistoric Britain*', by I. Armit and D. Reich, *British Archaeology* 160 (2018), 14–19. Mesolithic/Neolithic *aDNA*: 'Ancient genomes indicate population replacement in Early Neolithic Britain', by S. Brace *et al.*, *Nature Evolution and Ecology* (2019).

3 Often quoted, this idea seems to have been let loose by Alan Titchmarsh, a TV gardener ('Middle man', *Observer* 10 October 2004).

4 'Recent investigations at two long barrows and reflections on their context in the Stonehenge World Heritage Site and environs', by D. Roberts *et al.*, *Internet Archaeology* 47 (2018), 10.11141/ia.47.7.

5 For cattle in long barrows see *Earthen Long Barrows*, by D. Field (Stroud: Tempus, 2006), Ch. 7.

6 The key trend in pottery styles was for them to become more heavily decorated over time; round-based bowls were later replaced by flat-bottomed vessels that could be stood upright. There are further regional and temporary subdivisions, but the main types are known as Bowls (Early Neolithic), Peterborough Ware (Middle) and Grooved Ware (Late).

7 The Stonehenge Hidden Landscapes Project (2010–15) was led by the University of Birmingham with the Ludwig Boltzmann Institute for Archaeological Prospection and Virtual Archaeology, Vienna. The First Monuments Project, led by Bournemouth University and the German Archaeological Institute, Berlin (2011), had similar results. 'The Stonehenge Hidden Landscapes Project', by Chris Gaffney *et al.*, *Archaeological Prospection* 19 (2012), 147–55; 'Stonehenge, Wiltshire, UK: high resolution geophysical surveys in the surrounding landscape, 2011', by T. Darvill *et al.*, *European Journal of Archaeology* 16 (2013), 63–93.

8 'The dead of Stonehenge', by C. Willis *et al.*, *Antiquity* 90 (2016), 337–56.

9 The Stonehenge Riverside Project (2004–09) was run jointly by UCL and the universities of Sheffield, Bristol, Bournemouth and Manchester; post-excavation studies continued as the Feeding Stonehenge Project. The sarsens were excavated by Colin Richards.

10 'Strontium isotope analysis on cremated human remains from Stonehenge support[s] links with west Wales', by C. Snoeck *et al.*, *Nature Scientific Reports* 8 (2018). As noted in the text, the analysis supports (but cannot prove) links with many other places too.

11 *The Amesbury Archer and the Boscombe Bowmen: Bell Beaker Burials at Boscombe Down, Amesbury, Wiltshire*, by A. Fitzpatrick (Salisbury: Wessex Archaeology, 2011).

12 'Excavating the living dead', by A. Barclay, *British Archaeology* 115 (2010), 36–41.

13 'Stonehenge's Avenue and "Bluestonehenge"', by M. J. Allen *et al.*, *Antiquity* 90 (2016), 991–1008.

**Chapter 7: Deer Hunters**

1 Britain and the continent were first separated around 450,000 and 160,000 years ago, when water plunged over high chalk cliffs into what is now the English Channel. When climate cooled and sea levels fell, Britain became a European peninsula again, until warming recreated the channel. The last time this happened was in the centuries leading up to 8,000 years ago. See 'The catastrophic final flooding of Doggerland by the Storegga Slide tsunami', by B. Weninger *et al.*, *Documenta Praehistorica* 35 (2008), 1–24; Gaffney *et al.* 2009.

2 An old tradition gave excavation finds to universities so students could learn from them.

3 For the main project see Milner *et al.* 2018 and Milner *et al.* 2013

# Notes

(short overview). B. Taylor (*'The occupation of wetland landscapes during the British Mesolithic'*, unpublished PhD thesis, University of Manchester 2012) reviews the wider landscape, including his own excavation. For a history of work see 'Star Carr in a Postglacial lakescape: 60 years of research', by N. Milner *et al.*, *Journal of Wetland Archaeology* 11 (2011), 1–19.

4 Chemistry also explained Star Carr's disgusting smell. 'We're all used to it,' said Nicky, 'If you blindfolded me, I could tell which site I was at!' Grahame Clark thought the rigour good for students. 'The physical remoteness of the site,' he wrote, 'and its extreme unattractiveness, compounded by mud, ooze, rising water, and all too attentive clegs (small [blood-feeding] horseflies), only served to enhance the morale of the party': *Star Carr: A Case Study in Bioarchaeology*, by J. G. D. Clark (Reading, Mass.: Addison-Wesley Publishing, 1972), 8.

5 We recognize these people, even if nothing else survives (usually the case), from their stone tools, whose changing technologies and styles divide time into successive periods, much as historians use terms like 'Norman' or 'Tudor' as signposts.

6 'The resilience of Postglacial hunter-gatherers to abrupt climate change', by S. Blockley *et al.*, *Nature Ecology & Evolution* 2 (2018), 810–18.

7 Microlith manufacture is one of the defining technologies of the Mesolithic.

8 Idly Googling as I write, I find this in a recent British newspaper: 'The human brain got so big because life was tough on the African savannah around two million years ago, according to new research.'

9 'The timing and causes of a unique chimpanzee community fission preceding Gombe's "Four-Year War"', by J. T. Feldblum *et al.*, *American Journal of Physical Anthropology* 166 (2018), 730–44.

10 The long Mesolithic era has its own history: see 'Making and breaking microliths: a Middle Mesolithic site at Asfordby, Leicestershire', by L. Cooper *et al.*, *Proceedings of the Prehistoric Society* 83 (2017), 43–96.

11 M. C. Langley *et al.*, in *Osseous Projectile Weaponry*, ed. M. C. Langley (Dordrecht: Springer, 2016), 143–59.

12 This was the subject of one of my first peer-reviewed publications, in *World Archaeology* 11 (1979), 32–42; earlier consideration tended to see Star Carr as a dry-land site that happened to have been preserved.

13 *Antlerworking Practices in Mesolithic Britain*, by B. Elliott (PhD thesis, University of York 2012).

14 *Memorable Meetings in the Mesolithic*, by N. Overton (PhD thesis, University of Manchester 2014). Neil also describes a roe cranial fragment with a possible perforation from Thatcham. I see a good case for these roe 'frontlets', though not everyone

agrees. If roe skulls had been worn, their different shape and smaller size would have made them quite unlike red deer masks.

15  The art is dated only by its style, which suggests a Magdalenian context (see next chapter) around 14,000 years ago.

## Chapter 8: Cannibals

1  I have edited the quoted passages from several imaginative pages in *Man: The Primeval Savage. His Haunts and Relics from the Hill-tops of Bedfordshire to Blackwall*, by W. G. Smith (London: Edward Stanford, 1894).

2  *The Man-Eating Myth*, by W. Arens (Oxford: Oxford University Press, 1979), and 'Eating people is wrong', by P. Bahn, *Nature* 348 (1990), 395 ('much evidence for prehistoric cannibalism is...the result of wishful thinking imposed on bone assemblages'). More generally see *The Archaeology of Death and Burial*, by M. Parker Pearson (Stroud: Sutton, 1999), and *The Palaeolithic Origins of Human Burial*, by P. Pettitt (Abingdon: Routledge, 2011).

3  *Neanderthals Among Mammoths: Excavations at Lynford Quarry, Norfolk*, ed. W. Boismier *et al.* (Swindon: English Heritage, 2012).

4  Cook 2013.

5  This warmer period is known in Europe as the Bølling Interstadial, and in Britain as the earlier part of the Windermere Interstadial. It lasted from 14,700 to 14,100 years ago. Ashton 2017, 241–44.

6  The Ancient Human Occupation of Britain (AHOB) project has a website at www.ahobproject.org, and features in the next chapter.

7  'The exploration of Gough's Cave and its development as a show cave', by D. Irwin, *Proceedings of the University of Bristol Spelaeological Society* 17 (1985), 95–101; 'Gough's Old Cave – its history', by D. Irwin, *PUBSS* 17 (1986), 250–66.

8  Jacobi 2004. Tooth growth stages indicate occupation in summer (horse and red deer) and winter (red deer).

9  The recent excavations at Gough's Cave are well described in Stringer 2006, Ch. 6, and Ashton 2017, 248–54.

10  'Cannibalism in Britain: taphonomy of the Creswellian (Pleistocene) faunal and human remains from Gough's Cave (Somerset, England)', by P. Andrews and Y. Fernández-Jalvo, *Bulletin of the Natural History Museum (Geology)* 58 (2003), 59–81.

11  'The edible dead', by T. Taylor, *British Archaeology* 59 (2001), 8–12.

12  'When humans chew bones', by Y. Fernández-Jalvo and P. Andrews, *Journal of Human Evolution* 60 (2011), 117–23.

13  'Earliest directly-dated human skull-cups', by S. Bello, S. Parfitt and C. Stringer, *PLoS One* 6 (2011), https://doi.org/10.1371/journal.pone.0017026.

14 'Upper Palaeolithic ritualistic cannibalism at Gough's Cave (Somerset, UK): the human remains from head to toe', by S. Bello *et al.*, *Journal of Human Evolution* 82 (2015), 170–89.

15 'The early Lateglacial re-colonization of Britain: new radiocarbon evidence from Gough's Cave, southwest England', by R. Jacobi and T. Higham, *Quaternary Science Reviews* 28 (2009), 1895–1913.

16 'An Upper Palaeolithic engraved human bone associated with ritualistic cannibalism', by S. Bello *et al.*, *PLoS ONE* 12 (2017), https://doi.org/10.1371/journal.pone.0182127.

17 'Strange medicines', by C. F. Gordon Cumming, *The Popular Science Monthly* (1887), 750–67.

## Chapter 9: Elephant Hunters

1 The excavations described here at East Farm, Barnham, were co-directed by Chris Stringer and Nick Ashton; see Ashton 2017, Ch. 7. For earlier work at Barnham see Ashton *et al.* 1998. The results of a previous project directed by Stringer, the Ancient Human Occupation of Britain, whose large team included Ashton, Lewis and Parfitt, are described in Stringer 2006.

2 'New faunal analyses and amino acid dating of the Lower Palaeolithic site at East Farm, Barnham, Suffolk', by R. Preece and K. Penkman, *Proceedings of the Geologists' Association* 116 (2005), 363–77.

3 'The human occupation of Britain during the Hoxnian Interglacial', by N. Ashton, *Quaternary International* 409 (2016), 41–53.

4 Roman rabbits: *British Archaeology* 86 (2006), 7.

5 *The British Lower Palaeolithic: Stones in Contention*, by J. McNabb (London: Routledge, 2007).

6 *Fairweather Eden: Life Half a Million Years Ago as Revealed by the Excavations at Boxgrove* (2nd edn), by M. Pitts and M. Roberts (London: Arrow Books, 1998); *Boxgrove: A Middle Pleistocene Hominid Site at Eartham Quarry, Boxgrove, West Sussex*, by M. Roberts and S. Parfitt (London: English Heritage, 1999).

7 Earlier in the last century, the Hoxnian was equated with a Europe-wide Mindel-Riss Interglacial, also known as the Great Interglacial. The Hoxnian is currently seen as the main warm era within that longer interglacial period (Marine Isotope Stage 11, starting 424,000 years ago), which saw temperatures drop significantly before a new glacial era finally set in 360,000 years ago (MIS 10). See Ashton 2017, Ch. 3.

8 *The Ebbsfleet Elephant: Excavations at Southfleet Road, Swanscombe in Advance of High Speed 1, 2003–4*, ed. F. Wenban-Smith (Oxford: Oxford Archaeology, 2013). Like the Boxgrove monograph (above), this can be found online for free by searching for the book title prefaced by 'PDF'.

9 For Pakefield and Happisburgh, see Ashton 2017, Ch. 4, Stringer

2006, Ch. 1, and features in *British Archaeology*: 86 (2006, Pakefield), 114 (2010, Happisburgh excavations) and 135 (2014, Happisburgh footprints).

10 Pitts and Roberts 1998 (above, note 6), Ch. 40.

11 *Elveden and Barnham, Suffolk, Time Team* Series 7, Episode 6, broadcast 2000, http://www.channel4.com/programmes/time-team/on-demand/27818-006.

12 'Handaxe and non-handaxe assemblages during Marine Isotope Stage 11 in northern Europe: recent investigations at Barnham, Suffolk, UK', by N. Ashton *et al.*, *Journal of Quaternary Science* 31 (2016), 837–43.

13 'The δ18O stratigraphy of the Hoxnian lacustrine sequence at Marks Tey, Essex, UK: implications for the climatic structure of MIS 11 in Britain', by G. Tye *et al.*, *Journal of Quaternary Science* 31 (2016), 75–92.

**Chapter 10: Journeys**

1 'Big archaeology: the A14 Cambridge to Huntingdon road scheme', by S. Sherlock, *British Archaeology* 162 (2018), 16–25.

2 'Early Britain', in *Life in the United Kingdom: A Guide for New Residents* (Norwich: TSO/Home Office, 2017, 15–16), contains nothing – apart from three dates owed to radiocarbon chronologies – that was not known in the 1930s.

3 My favourite recent books on human genetics are *A Brief History of Everyone who Ever Lived*, by Adam Rutherford (London: Weidenfeld & Nicolson, 2016), which is mostly about modern DNA, and *Who We Are and How We Got Here*, by David Reich (Oxford: Oxford University Press, 2018), about aDNA.

4 While this was the UK's first Mesolithic genome, it had been established in 2014 that contemporary continental Europeans had dark skin and blueish eyes. 'Ancient genomes indicate population replacement in Early Neolithic Britain', by S. Brace *et al.*, *Nature Evolution and Ecology* (2019).

5 'Fatty acid specific δ13C values reveal earliest Mediterranean cheese production 7,200 years ago', by S. McClure *et al.*, *PLOS One* (2018), 10.1371/journal.pone.0202807. 'Bronze Age population dynamics and the rise of dairy pastoralism on the eastern Eurasian steppe', by C. Jeong *et al.*, *Proceedings of the National Academy of Sciences* (2018), https://doi.org/10.1073/pnas.1813608115.

6 'Isotopic evidence for landscape use and the role of causewayed enclosures during the Earlier Neolithic in southern Britain', by S. Neil *et al.*, *Proceedings of the Prehistoric Society* 84 (2018), 185–205.

7 'Multi-isotope analysis reveals that feasts in the Stonehenge environs and across Wessex drew people and animals from throughout Britain,' by R. Madgwick *et al.*, *Science Advances* (2019).

8 Britain was not an island when people reached Star Carr, but as the archaeology and aDNA paint it, the first people to arrive in boats in significant numbers, the earliest Neolithic farmers, were effectively able to treat it as ownerless, or *terra nullius* – a practice sometimes indulged in by early modern Europeans seeking land to settle around the world that had in fact been inhabited for millennia by other people.

9 *Our Island Story: A Child's History of England*, by H. E. Marshall (London: T. C. & E. C. Jack, 1905). This comprehensive history, an enjoyable fantasy that should have gone the way of Bakelite electric plugs and the penny post, was praised by David Cameron when he was prime minister, and by Michael Gove, his education secretary; copies were given to schools by the *Daily Telegraph*. 'Spoilheap', *British Archaeology* 128 (2012), 66.

10 *Arthur and the Kings of Britain: The Historical Truths behind the Myths*, by M. Russell (Stroud: Amberley Publishing, 2017) – entertaining, if not without its own little myth-making.

11 'The Origin of the British People: archaeology and the Festival of Britain', by J. Hawkes, *Antiquity* 25 (1951), 4–8; *The South Bank Exhibition: A Guide to the Story it Tells*, by I. Cox (London: H. M. Stationery Office, 1951).

12 *Stonehenge*, by R. Hill (London: Profile Books, 2008).

13 'The invasion hypothesis in British Archaeology', by G. Clark, *Antiquity* 40 (1966), 172–89.

14 *Before Civilization: The Radiocarbon Revolution and Prehistoric Europe*, by C. Renfrew (London: Jonathan Cape, 1973).

15 *Invasion!*, presented by Sam Willis (BBC Four, December 2017).

16 'Isotopic analysis of burials from the early Anglo-Saxon cemetery at Eastbourne, Sussex, U.K.', by S. Hughes *et al.*, *Journal of Archaeological Science: Reports* 19 (2018), 512–25.

17 'Iron Age and Anglo-Saxon genomes from east England reveal British migration history', by S. Schiffels *et al.*, *Nature Communications* (2016), 10.1038/ncomms10408.

18 *The Times*, 17 May 1994.

19 Archaeology and genetics both show regional variations that belie the notion of any identifiable or self-conscious Beaker 'folk' (as Childe described them) or 'race'.

# FURTHER READING AND PLACES TO SEE

### Weymouth

Loe, L., A. Boyle, H. Webb and D. Score, 2014. *'Given to the Ground': A Viking Age Mass Grave on Ridgeway Hill, Weymouth*. Dorchester: Dorset Natural History and Archaeological Society.

Williams, G., P. Pentz and M. Wemhoff (eds), 2014. *Vikings: Life and Legend*. London: British Museum Press.

Where the South Dorset Ridgeway footpath crosses the A354 over a green bridge (views of Maiden Castle from nearby), there are information panels about the Viking massacre on the east side of the road cutting. The pit itself was close to the edge of the cutting on the opposite side. Dorset County Museum, Dorchester, has a display about the site, as well as Maiden Castle.

### Staffordshire Hoard

Fern, C., T. Dickinson and L. Webster (eds), 2019. *The Staffordshire Hoard: An Anglo-Saxon Treasure*. London: Society of Antiquaries.

Blackmore, L., I. Blair, S. Hirst and C. Scull, 2019. *The Prittlewell Princely Burial: Excavations at Priory Crescent, Southend-on-Sea, Essex, 2003*. London: MOLA.

Carver, M., 2017. *The Sutton Hoo Story: Encounters with Early England*. Woodbridge: Boydell.

Webster, L., 2012. *Anglo-Saxon Art*. London: British Museum Press.

See http://www.staffordshirehoard.org.uk. Selected items from the Hoard can be seen at the Birmingham Museum and Art Gallery; the Potteries Museum and Art Gallery, Stoke-on-Trent; Tamworth Castle; and Lichfield Cathedral. There is a National Trust visitor centre at the Sutton Hoo burial ground, and finds from the digs are on display at the British Museum. The Portable Antiquities Scheme website (https://finds.org.uk) has much useful information, as well as its finds catalogues, including ways you can get involved, advice about Treasure, how to treat your finds and how to contact your Finds Liaison Officer.

# Further Reading and Places to See

## London

Tomlin, R., 2016. *Roman London's First Voices: Writing Tablets from the Bloomberg Excavations, 2010–14*. London: Museum of London Archaeology.

Shepherd, J., 1998. *The Temple of Mithras, London: Excavations by W. F. Grimes and A. Williams at the Walbrook*. London: English Heritage.

Hingley, R., 2018. *Londinium: A Biography*. London: Bloomsbury Academic.

Bloomberg London contains an exhibition gallery and free museum called London Mithraeum Bloomberg SPACE. Visits to the reconstructed temple must be booked in advance; see https://www.londonmithraeum.com. The mosaic and statues mentioned in the text, along with much else from Roman London, can be seen in the Museum of London. The British Museum has a gallery devoted to Roman Britain.

## Black Loch and Must Farm

Crone, A. and G. Cavers, 2016. 'The Black Loch of Myrton: an iron age village', *British Archaeology* 151, 36–41.

Crone, A. *et al.*, 2019. 'Nasty, brutish and short? The life cycle of an Iron Age roundhouse at Black Loch of Myrton, SW Scotland', *Journal of Wetland Archaeology*.

Knight, M. and K. Murrell, 2012. 'Must Farm and Bradley Fen', *British Archaeology* 123, 15–21.

Pryor, F., 2001. *The Flag Fen Basin: Archaeology and Environment of a Fenland Landscape*. Swindon: English Heritage.

Cunliffe, B., 2018. *The Ancient Celts* (second edn). Oxford: Oxford University Press.

The Black Loch house reconstruction can be seen at the Whithorn Trust Visitor Centre. Must Farm archaeologists wrote a weekly excavation diary (mustfarm. com) and posted frequently on Facebook (facebook.com/MustFarmArchaeology) and Twitter (twitter.com/MustFarm), continuing with both during post-excavation. Some of the wood is being treated at the Flag Fen archaeological park, where attractions include reconstructed round houses and a large section of the wooden platform.

## Cliffs End

McKinley, J., M. Leivers, J. Schuster, P. Marshall, A. Barclay and N. Stoodley, 2014. *Cliffs End Farm, Isle of Thanet, Kent: A Mortuary and Ritual Site of the Bronze Age, Iron Age and Anglo-Saxon Period*. Salisbury: Wessex Archaeology.

Clark, P. (ed.), 2004. *The Dover Bronze Age Boat*. Swindon: English Heritage.

The Cliffs End excavation site is on a private housing estate, but the area has much to see. As well as the bay and cliffs, this includes the replica Viking ship (the *Hugin*), St Augustine's Victorian cross, and the Roman forts at Richborough and Reculver, both in the care of English Heritage. The Bronze Age boat has its own gallery in Dover Museum, which also features the Langdon Bay bronzes.

# Further Reading and Places to See

## Stonehenge

Parker Pearson, M., J. Pollard, C. Richards, J. Thomas, C. Tilley and K. Welham, 2019. *Stonehenge for the Ancestors. Part 1: Landscape and Monuments*. Leiden: Sidestone Press.

Parker Pearson, M., 2012. *Stonehenge: Exploring the Greatest Stone Age Mystery*. London: Simon & Schuster.

Pitts, M., 2018. 'Stonehenge without borders', *British Archaeology* 160, 20–35.

Stonehenge, with a visitor centre and museum, is in the care of English Heritage. Direct access to the stones is restricted, but can be gained early in the morning by booking well ahead for one of the world's great heritage experiences: search online for 'Stone Circle Access Visit'. Much of the landscape close to Stonehenge is owned by the National Trust, and is open for walking. There are Stonehenge displays at the Salisbury Museum and the Wiltshire Museum, Devizes.

## Star Carr

Milner, N., C. Conneller and B. Taylor, 2018. *Star Carr, Volume 1 and 2*. York: White Rose University Press.

Milner, N., B. Taylor, C. Conneller and T. Schadla-Hall, 2013. *Star Carr: Life in Britain after the Ice Age*. York: Council for British Archaeology.

Gaffney, V., S. Fitch and D. Smith, 2009. *Europe's Lost World: The Rediscovery of Doggerland*. York: Council for British Archaeology.

There is a Star Carr website at www.starcarr.com; the site is on private land. The 2018 monographs can be downloaded for free by searching for the titles online. Displays about the site can be seen at the Yorkshire Museum, York, the Rotunda Museum, Scarborough, the Museum of Archaeology and Anthropology, Cambridge, and the British Museum.

## Gough's Cave

Ashton, N., 2017. *Early Humans*. London: William Collins.

Cook, J., 2013. *Ice Age Art*. London: British Museum.

Jacobi, R., 2004. 'The Late Upper Palaeolithic lithic collection from Gough's Cave, Cheddar, Somerset, and human use of the cave', *Proceedings of the Prehistoric Society* 70, 1–92.

Stringer, S. 2006. *Homo Britannicus: The Incredible Story of Human Life in Britain*. London: Allen Lane.

Gough's Cave is a highlight of Cheddar Gorge & Caves in Somerset, which also includes a museum of prehistory and a clifftop walk. The Cheddar Man skeleton is on loan from the Longleat Estate to the Natural History Museum, London, where it can be seen in the Human Evolution gallery, along with a shaped skull-cup from the cave.

# Further Reading and Places to See

## Barnham

Ashton, N., 2017. *Early Humans*. London: William Collins.

Ashton, N., S. Lewis and S. Parfitt (eds), 1998. *Excavations at Barnham 1989–94*. London: British Museum.

Stringer, S. 2006. *Homo Britannicus: The Incredible Story of Human Life in Britain*. London: Allen Lane.

Stringer, S. 2011. *The Origin of Our Species*. London: Allen Lane.

The Barnham excavation is on private land. There is free access to the Norfolk beaches where the Happisburgh footprints (now gone) and other finds have been made, with the possibility of further significant discoveries.

# ACKNOWLEDGMENTS

*Digging up Britain* is about new excavations, but it has been long in the making. The book itself began as a different idea, commissioned by Colin Ridler. Shelved while I wrote about Richard III, it became what you now read with Colin's encouragement and gentle hectoring, which have been enormously valuable. My family have lived through three titles to see but two in print, and deserve huge thanks for their patience with something they never signed up to.

The understanding I brought to the project goes back further. I have been editing *British Archaeology* magazine for over fifteen years. I was studying for my PhD when I first excavated at Stonehenge. Star Carr, the subject of another chapter, featured in one of my first peer-reviewed articles, and I was a schoolboy when I found my first prehistoric site fifty years ago.

Such long familiarity with Britain's archaeology allows me to see how extraordinary is the current outpouring of new information. For every discovery reported by the media, there are hundreds more that never make the news. Research continues, and I have had to simplify complex material. It would have been quite impossible for me to have made sense of it all without help from the archaeologists doing the work, and I thank them all, especially for the efforts they have put into analysis and publication (only some of their names appear here). I must also thank excavation sponsors, here about half of them construction businesses, and half public institutions.

Much of the work I describe was in progress as I was writing, and I'm particularly grateful to those who shared their personal insights: Jane Evans and Louise Loe (Weymouth); Roger Bland, Jenni Butterworth, Deb Klemperer, Kevin Leahy, Duncan Slarke, George Speake and Leslie Webster, and especially Chris Fern (Staffordshire Hoard); Louise Fowler, Sophie Jackson, Nicola Kalimeris and Sadie Watson (London); Graeme Cavers, Anne Crone and Julia Muir Watt (Black Loch); Debbie Hickman, Mark Knight and Dave Webb (Must Farm); Dave Godden, Jacqui McKinley and Jörn Schuster (Cliffs End); Alistair Barclay, Tom Booth, Bob Clarke, Si Cleggett, Phil Harding, Matt Leivers, Mike Parker Pearson, Josh Pollard, Colin Richards and Christophe Snoeck (Stonehenge and Beakers); Chantal Conneller, Ben Elliott, Nicky Milner and Barry Taylor (Star Carr); Silvia Bello, Jill Cook and Chris Stringer (Gough's Cave); and Nick Ashton, Simon Lewis and Simon Parfitt (Barnham and Happisburgh).

# Acknowledgments

At Thames & Hudson, as well as Colin Ridler I'd like to thank Ben Hayes, Jen Moore and Sarah Vernon-Hunt (editing), Mark Ralph (proofreading), Celia Falconer (production), Adam Hay (design), Isabella Luta (picture permissions) and Victoria Brown (publicity).

# SOURCES OF ILLUSTRATIONS

2 Oxford Archaeology; 6 Mike Pitts; 13 Oxford Archaeology; 17, 21, 27 Mike Pitts, after Loe, Boyle et al., 2014; 32 Oxford Archaeology; 41 Portable Antiquities Scheme/ Photo Duncan Slarke; 42 Image Birmingham Museums Trust, courtesy National Museums Liverpool; 45 Photo Birmingham Museums Trust; 56 Image courtesy C. Fern; 71, 76, 77 Mike Pitts, after Museum of London Archaeology; 74, 84 Museum of London Archaeology; 90 Mike Pitts, after Gerhard Bersu; 96 Mike Pitts, after AOC Archaeology; 97, 99, 100 AOC Archaeology Group/Historic Environment Scotland; 106 Photo Mike Pitts; 107, 108 Mike Pitts, after Cambridge Archaeological Unit; 109, 111 Photos Mike Pitts; 118, 123, 127, 131 Wessex Archaeology; 136, 137 Mike Pitts; 139 Wessex Archaeology; 152 Mike Pitts; 155 Adam Stanford/Aerial Cam; 158 Photo Mike Pitts; 162 Adam Stanford/Aerial Cam; 165 Wessex Archaeology; 171 Mike Pitts; 174 The Trustees of the British Museum, London; 178 Scarborough Archaeological and Historical Society; 179 Photo Sue Storey; 180 Star Carr Project; 188 Mike Pitts, after Milner, Conneller and Taylor; 189 University of York/Photo Peter Shields; 192 Star Carr Project; 201 The Trustees of the Natural History Museum, London/ NHM Images; 211, 213 Dr Silvia M. Bello; 217 Mike Pitts, after Bello et al., 2017; 223 Photo Mike Pitts; 235 Dr Peter G. Hoare; 236 Dr Martin Bates, University of Wales; i, ii Oxford Archaeology; iii Barbican Research Associates/Photo Guy Evans; iv Staffordshire County Council; v Birmingham Museums Trust; vi, vii, viii Museum of London Archaeology; ix, x Wessex Archaeology; xi Whithorn Trust; xii Wessex Archaeology; xiii, xiv Photos Mike Pitts; xv Neil Gevaux; xvi Marcus Abbott; xvii, xviii The Trustees of the Natural History Museum, London/NHM Images; xix Jordan Mansfield/jordanmansfield.com; xx Photo Mike Pitts; xxi courtesy Hew Morrison and Maya Hoole; xxii Kennis & Kennis, Arnhem, the Netherlands

# INDEX

# Index

## Index